Minnesota History

A GUIDE TO READING AND STUDY

Minnesota History

A GUIDE TO READING AND STUDY

BY

Theodore C. Blegen

AND

Theodore L. Nydahl

UNIVERSITY OF MINNESOTA PRESS, Minneapolis

PRINTED IN THE UNITED STATES OF AMERICA AT
THE LUND PRESS, INC., MINNEAPOLIS

Library of Congress Catalog Card Number: 60-14287

Appreciation is expressed to the Minnesota Historical Society for permission to reproduce the maps in this volume from the following publications of the Society: William Watts Folwell, *A History of Minnesota*, volume 1 (1921 and a revised edition of 1956), volume 2 (1924), and volume 4 (1930); *Minnesota History* (September, 1925; December, 1930; Spring, 1954; and March, 1958).

PUBLISHED IN GREAT BRITAIN, INDIA, AND PAKISTAN BY THE OXFORD UNIVERSITY PRESS
LONDON, BOMBAY, AND KARACHI, AND IN CANADA BY THOMAS ALLEN, LTD., TORONTO

Preface

This Guide to the study of Minnesota history is to a large extent a new piece of work, though its foundation is the volume issued by the University of Minnesota Press in 1937 under the title *Minnesota, Its History and Its People: A Study Outline with Topics and References.* That outline has long been out of print, and it seemed highly desirable to bring it up to date and revise it thoroughly, taking into account not only events of the past two decades but also the extensive research and writing on Minnesota and its past that have marked the years since publication of the earlier edition.

It is our hope that this new Guide will be helpful to teachers, students, study clubs, and the wider public in their search for understanding of Minnesota's past. The centennials of the births of both territory and state have been observed since the earlier edition appeared, and these events, together with a deepening and widening of interest in the long sweep of our state history, have spurred a wealth of new contributions to enrich the literature of Minnesota history.

The Guide here presented — with its topical analyses, suggestions, questions, and citations of both secondary and primary sources — does not claim to be in any sense a complete outline and bibliography. Even for research students, however, such a systematic guide, with its selective listing of available published materials, should prove a useful tool.

The earlier edition included a sketch of the history of the state, and this, with other prefatory material intended primarily for teachers, we have not thought it necessary to reproduce in the present volume. Copies of the earlier edition are widely distributed in libraries and schools throughout the state, and teachers may find it desirable to consult that volume for such materials as are here omitted.

The history of Minnesota outlined in these pages is as rich in documentation as it is fascinating in scope and flavor. The documentation is evidence of the earnestness and zeal with which scholars and writers through the years have recorded the state's history and the painstaking care with which the Minnesota Historical Society and other libraries and historical organizations throughout the state have gathered up such records. The fascination of the story arises from its intrinsic interest, its sequence across more than three centuries, and the many-faceted aspects of life and development reflected in this region as a part of the larger history of America. We trust that this publication will contribute to a more general understanding of the importance and interest of Minnesota history from the days of native redmen and early explorers in the seventeenth and eighteenth centuries to the vigorous modern commonwealth of the second half of the twentieth century.

T. C. B. AND T. L. N.

May, 1960

Contents

LIST OF MAPS

Minnesota History

A GUIDE TO READING AND STUDY

A few suggestions to users of this book

READING references marked with an (*) are considered by the compilers to be of special importance or interest for the topic under consideration. Few users of this syllabus will be able to consult all the references given, and the asterisks are intended to furnish a little guidance in the matter of selection. A liberal number of brief comments on readings cited have also been included with a view to helping users select with some discrimination items for special study.

Since the Guide is intended to be helpful both to adults and to younger readers, the symbol † has been used to call special attention to materials particularly adaptable to study by younger readers.

Audio-visual aids of much interest are available through both the Minnesota Historical Society and the University of Minnesota, and teachers are advised to secure lists of such materials from these institutions.

Readers will quickly discover that the compilers have drawn heavily on articles and documents in *Minnesota History* and the *Gopher Historian*, both published by the Minnesota Historical Society. *Minnesota History* has appeared regularly since 1915 and is a mine of valuable reading materials relating to all periods and virtually all subjects in the field of our state history. The *Gopher Historian*, a newer publication, is designed for school use and particularly for younger readers. It is to be hoped that school libraries throughout the state will attempt to build up their files of these two publications.

I. THE LAND AWAITS THE WHITE MAN

1. *The Physical Basis of Minnesota Life*

A. Minnesota's Place in the Large Geographic Areas of the United States

Central position on the continent. Water highways into Minnesota. Minnesota as the gateway to the upper West.

B. Geologic History of the State

The basic granite formations. Later sedimentary and other formations. The iron deposits. The several ice sheets of the glacial age and their effects: leveling influence; gouging to form lakes; deposit of soil-making material; formation of Lake Agassiz and River Warren. The driftless area. Interglacial river systems.

C. Main Surface Features of the State and Their Effect upon Its History

Forests and prairie areas. Rivers and lakes. Water transportation as a factor in Minnesota history. Relation of forests, prairies, waters, and climate to settlement.

D. Important Basic Natural Resources

Soil: its variety; distribution of gray drift, red drift, and loess; humus. *Climate:* extremes of winter and summer; variations in temperature and precipitation; meteorological basis for weather (interplay of cold, dry Canadian air masses with warm, moist Gulf air masses); variations in rainfall and length of growing season in different parts of the state. *Forests:* deciduous and coniferous areas. *Minerals and subsoil treasures:* iron, stone, clay, sand, and gravel. *Water:* surface and ground; facility of transportation; water power. *Plant and animal life:* food and furs. *Attractiveness of physical environment.*

E. Human Adjustment to the Physical Environment

Adjustments made by Indians, by fur traders, by settlers. Effect of climate on life in Minnesota. The several occupational frontiers: fur trade, lumbering, agriculture, industry (small and large), mining, tourism.

F. How Minnesota Impressed Early Travelers

G. Meaning of "Minnesota"

QUESTIONS AND SUGGESTIONS

1. Just as one may ask how the geography of Minnesota has affected her his-

tory, one may also ask how her history has affected her geography. Has this been good or bad or both?

2. List changes which were effected in Minnesota by glacial action.

3. Minnesota is often called the "headwater state." Why? Glanville Smith answered this in his article (cited below) with the statement "Minnesota is the mother of three seas."

4. Locate the continental divides that account for the drainage system referred to in No. 3 above.

5. To describe the "driftless area" of Minnesota is in a sense to picture Minnesota as it would have appeared if glaciers had touched no part of it. Give such a description and explain why, without the glaciers, Minnesota would have taken on this appearance.

6. How did the term "big woods" originate? Where were the "big woods" located?

7. Minnesota is said to have a "continental" climate. What does this mean?

8. Map exercises: (a) On an outline map of Minnesota, show the main water highways and some of the portages used in early times. (b) Again using an outline map, show the forest coverage of Minnesota at the time of the coming of the white man. Designate the areas dominated by coniferous trees and those by deciduous trees. For an excellent map of Minnesota's pristine forest endowment consult a pamphlet publication of the state Department of Conservation entitled *Trees of Minnesota*, p. 3.

9. An interesting Sunday excursion may be had by studying the geological history of some locality near your home. Schwartz and Thiel's *Minnesota's Rocks and Waters* is full of suggestions for such studies. Part II of this volume is on "geological excursions through Minnesota" and has seven chapters on as many sections of the state. The Minnesota and St. Croix river valleys abound in rich examples. For the Mankato area there is the story of how the Blue Earth River stole the water of the Le Sueur River. St. Paul residents will be interested in the article by H. E. Wright, Jr., in the *Gopher Historian* (cited below).

10. Do you know of any considerable falls or rapids in Minnesota at which there is not a town or village? Towns or villages which owe their development in part at least to water power are these: St. Anthony, Preston, Zumbro Falls, Thief River Falls, International Falls, Fergus Falls, Park Rapids, Pelican Rapids, Terrace, Red Lake Falls, Taylors Falls, Grand Rapids, Little Falls, Sauk Rapids, Cannon Falls, Redwood Falls, Granite Falls, Northfield.

11. Name the towns in Minnesota whose development was influenced by being at or near the head of navigation of some river or lake. What towns owe their existence to the iron deposits?

12. Point out some relations between climate and economic life in Minnesota.

4

13. Historically, what natural resources have been of most importance in Minnesota? In what order have they been exploited?

14. The basic survey of the state's geology is to be found in the Annual Reports of the Geological and Natural History Survey of Minnesota (1873–98) and *The Geology of Minnesota*, 6 vols. (1884–1901). In the first volume of the latter is a good description of "The General Physical Features of the State" by N. H. Winchell, Minnesota's pioneer geologist.

15. On the map on the next page note the following: the shore line of Lake Agassiz at its greatest extent, the River Warren, the points of lowest and highest altitude, the figures which seem to represent the most common altitudes for the state, the Big Woods, the dividing line between the coniferous and deciduous forest areas, the western border of the driftless area, and the height of land known as the Coteau des Prairies. (The map is from William Watts Folwell, *A History of Minnesota*, 1:10.)

16. Maps showing the relation of Minnesota to the rest of the United States with respect to soil, vegetation, growing season, climate, temperature, rainfall, and other physical factors are found in Charles O. Paullin, *Atlas of Historical Geography of the United States*, Plates 2–5.

REFERENCES

BAKER, DONALD G., "Sources of Our Water Resources," *Conservation Volunteer*, 22:8–12 (Sept.–Oct., 1959).

*† BLEGEN, THEODORE C., *Building Minnesota*, pp. 3–11 (1938). Frequent reference will be made to this volume. While written primarily for the young student, it will be helpful to the mature reader.

† BORCHERT, JOHN R., *Minnesota's Changing Geography* (1959). Intended for use in the elementary grades. Exceptionally well done maps.

✓* BRINGS, LAWRENCE M., ed., *Minnesota Heritage* (1960). A collection of articles on many aspects of the state's development. J. Merle Harris, "Minnesota Heritage in the Making," pp. 10–39. The geology and geography of Minnesota.

† BURNS, BERT E., "The Lay of the Land in Southwestern Minnesota," *Gopher Historian*, 14:3–6 (Winter, 1959–60).

✓* FOLWELL, WILLIAM W., *A History of Minnesota*, 1:455–57 (1921 and a revised edition of 1956). On the meaning of "Minnesota."

† HAGG, HAROLD T., *Exploring Minnesota*, pp. 6–27 (1958). A textbook which follows the state guide for the teaching of the social studies in the sixth grade. Its language is suitable for the fourth- to sixth-grade level. There are numerous illustrations and helpful maps. The pages cited deal with Minnesota's geography and natural resources.

HART, IRVING H., "The Geologic Origin of the Savanna and Prairie River Portages," *Minnesota History*, 13:403–7 (Dec., 1932).

5

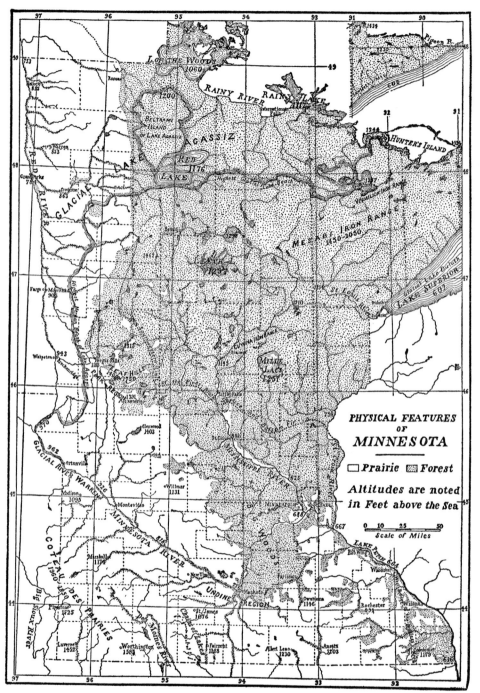

PHYSICAL FEATURES
OF
MINNESOTA

☐ Prairie ▨ Forest

Altitudes are noted
in Feet above the Sea

0 10 25   50
Scale of Miles

————"The Old Savanna Portage," *Minnesota History*, 8:117–39 (June, 1927). A very interesting account, with a map, of one Minnesota portage and how it was rediscovered.

*† HOLMQUIST, JUNE D., "Minnesota's Waterways," *Gopher Historian*, 10:1–2 (Spring, 1956). Also found in Poatgieter and Dunn, *Gopher Reader*, pp. 191–92.

† "How Glaciers Shaped the Land in East Central Minnesota," *Gopher Historian*, 13:3–5 (Spring, 1959). On the St. Croix River region. Excellent illustrations.

✓* JARCHOW, MERRILL E., *The Earth Brought Forth: A History of Minnesota Agriculture to 1885*, pp. 27–40 (1949). An excellent treatment of Minnesota's geography especially as it relates to agricultural assets.

† JENSON, PETER, "How the Red River Valley Was Formed," *Gopher Historian*, 14:3–5 (Fall, 1959).

† JOHNSON, H. NAT, *Minnesota Panorama, Saga of the North Star Empire*, pp. 1–5 (1957). Intended for the elementary student, particularly at the sixth-grade level. A fine survey treatment. Maps and illustrations by Oz Black are valuable. The mature reader who is looking for a brief overview of the state's early history will find this volume helpful.

† LINDQUIST, MAUDE L., and JAMES W. CLARK, *Minnesota: The Story of a Great State* (1950). A textbook for the sixth grade. It has units on resources, exploration, the state's growing up, conservation, public welfare, government, and citizenship.

NUTE, GRACE LEE, *The Voyageur's Highway: Minnesota's Border Lake Land*, pp. 71–78 (1941). Geology and geography of the north country.

PAULLIN, CHARLES O., *Atlas of the Historical Geography of the United States* (1932). An invaluable collection of maps. Most of them are rare items.

*† POATGIETER, A. H., and J. T. DUNN, *Gopher Reader*, pp. 191–210 (1958). The *Gopher Reader* should be in every library and school of the state. It is a collection of the best articles from the *Gopher Historian* up to 1958. These articles are aimed at the young reader, but they will be enjoyed as well by the mature and discerning student. The pages cited deal with geological forces that shaped Minnesota's geography and the nature and importance of the state's waterways.

* POSEY, CHESSLEY J., "The Influence of Geographic Features in the Development of Minnesota," *Minnesota History Bulletin*, 2:443–53 (Aug., 1918).

*† POTTER, ALAN, "Buried Treasure," *Gopher Historian*, 9:1–4 (Winter, 1954–55). The state's underground wealth. Also found in Poatgieter and Dunn, *Gopher Reader*, pp. 211–14.

* Powell, Louis H., "Around a Geologic Clock in Minnesota," *Minnesota History*, 15:141–47 (June, 1934).

Robinson, Edward Van Dyke, *Early Economic Conditions and the Development of Agriculture in Minnesota*, pp. 3–26 (1915). A compact discussion of the physical features and climate of Minnesota. Contains valuable charts and maps.

Schwartz, George M., "The Topography and Geology of the Grand Portage," *Minnesota History*, 9:26–30 (March, 1928).

* Schwartz, George M., and George A. Thiel, *Minnesota's Rocks and Waters: A Geological Story* (1954). The finest treatment on the subject. Especially valuable are Chapters 1, 2, 3, 8, and 9 on pp. 3–92 and 150–88.

Smith, Glanville, "Minnesota, Mother of Lakes and Rivers," *National Geographic Magazine*, 67:263–318 (March, 1935).

† Thiel, George A., "Iron Ores — Our Minerals of Might," *Gopher Historian*, 6:7–8 (Sept. 1951). The three ranges and the character of their deposits.

——— *Minnesota's Mineral Heritage*, Conservation Bulletin No. 12, Minnesota Department of Conservation (1947).

Upham, Warren, *Minnesota Geographic Names: Their Origin and Historic Significance* (Minnesota Historical Collections, vol. 17, 1920). The explanations are arranged by counties. A very detailed index adds greatly to the usefulness of the volume.

*——— *Minnesota in Three Centuries, 1655–1908*, 1:33–78 (1908). A good general account of the geology, physical features, climate, and flora and fauna of the state.

Wright, Herbert E., Jr., "The Rocks and the Land: St. Paul's Geological Story," *Gopher Historian*, 14:5–7 (Spring, 1960).

Zumberge, James H., *The Lakes of Minnesota: Their Origin and Classification* (1952). Bulletin No. 35 of the Minnesota Geological Survey. Illustrated.

[I. THE LAND AWAITS THE WHITE MAN]

2. *The Indians of Minnesota*

A. Native Tribes

Prehistoric remains in Minnesota. The Dakota, or Sioux, and the Ojibway, or Chippewa — meanings of these terms. Early intertribal relations; origin of the bitter hostility of the two tribes. Some white misconceptions of the Indian: a child of nature; a noble savage; a worthless degenerate; a vanishing race; a red devil. The Indian as a human being; his moral code.

8

B. Aspects of Indian Life in Minnesota

Points of similarity between Sioux and Chippewa more numerous than differences. Dissimilarities of the two nations: physical stature, shelter, clothing, food, mode of travel, care of the dead. Characteristics common to both nations: tribal organization, play of democracy in the council meeting, respect for family relationship, marriage, religion, dances, warfare, occupations, village life.

C. Effects of Civilization upon Minnesota Indian Life

Three difficult readjustments forced upon the Indian by the white man's coming: (1) from stone age civilization to fur trade economy with its metals and explosives civilization, (2) from fur trade economy to reservation life, (3) from reservation life to absorption by the American community.

D. Contributions of the American Indians to Civilization

Foods, plants, medicines. Food methods. Transportation methods. Warfare. Hunting. Games. Place names and other words. The role of the Indian in white settlement. The Indian in literature. Indian legends and songs as literature.

QUESTIONS AND SUGGESTIONS

1. Note the respective regions occupied by the Sioux and the Chippewa in Minnesota after 1825. See the map in Folwell, *History*, 1:80, reproduced on p. 10. Note also the location of the several divisions of the Sioux, Indian agencies, and the more important Indian villages.

2. The treaty line of 1825 was, in a sense, a part of the "permanent Indian frontier policy" of the United States. (a) What was the nature of this policy? (b) How was the treaty of 1825 different from those of 1837, 1851, 1854, 1855, 1863? (In your answer think of these latter as a group.)

3. Before 1871, whenever the United States dealt with Indians it did so by means of treaties. In what sense was this unfair to the Indian? What Indian concepts or practices led to frequent misunderstandings when the treaty method of negotiation was used?

4. Discuss differences between the Sioux and the Chippewa.

5. How did Indian warfare differ from the white man's mode of fighting?

6. Describe the game of *la crosse*.

7. Compare the dwellings of the Chippewa and the Sioux.

8. Describe the agriculture of the Minnesota Indians.

9. What was a *travois*?

10. Suggest some inventions or customs of the white man that altered the habits of life of the Minnesota Indians.

11. Dr. Charles A. Eastman, a Sioux born near Redwood Falls, and a graduate of Dartmouth and of the School of Medicine of Boston University,

INDIANS
IN
MINNESOTA

◎ Villages ▣ Agencies
▢ Trading Posts
⊕ Missions ⊟ Trails
⊠ Battle Grounds
⊠ Forts ⊞ Waterfalls

0 10   25   50
Scale of Miles

has written numerous books about the history and life of his people. Among these are *Indian Boyhood* (1903), *Old Indian Days* (1907), and *From the Deep Woods to Civilization* (1916).

12. Are there Indian legends relating to the region in which you live? material evidences of Indian origin? place names of Indian origin?

13. On the whole did the Indians of North America help or make more difficult the white man's conquest of the continent?

14. George Catlin painted the portraits of a number of Minnesota Indians in 1835 and 1836. The pictorial record of his trips through Minnesota may be studied in his *Letters and Notes*, vol. 2, plates 128–252, 264–79 (1841). His paintings are reproduced in color in a modern edition of his book: *North American Indians*, vol. 2, plates 232–45, 266–78 (1926).

15. It is worth noting the many place names of Minnesota that are of Indian origin — lakes, rivers, counties, towns, parks. Also, the many words or phrases now a part of our everyday speech that can be traced to Indian practice or speech.

16. Map exercise: On an outline map of Minnesota draw the boundaries of the land areas purchased from the Indians in the treaties of 1837, 1851, 1854, 1855, and 1863. See Folwell, *History*, 1:324.

17. Map exercise: Locate the Indian reservations of Minnesota today. Indicate the dates of their establishment. See the official state highway map.

REFERENCES

* † BLEGEN, THEODORE C., *Building Minnesota*, pp. 12–27.

BLEGEN, THEODORE C., and SARAH A. DAVIDSON, eds., *Iron Face: The Adventures of Jack Frazer, Frontier Warrior, Scout, and Hunter* (1950). A Narrative Recorded by "Walker-in-the-Pines" (Henry Hastings Sibley). Essentially a biography of a half-breed Sioux, well known to Sibley, whose life epitomizes the transformation from fur trader–Indian frontier to farm-town commonwealth.

* CAMPBELL, WALTER S. (Stanley Vestal), "The Plains Indians in Literature — and in Life," *Trans-Mississippi West*, edited by James F. Willard and Colin B. Goodykoontz, pp. 175–94 (1930). Develops the five misconceptions mentioned in section A of the outline above.

DENSMORE, FRANCES, *Chippewa Customs* (1929).

* EDWARDS, EVERETT E., "American Indian Contributions to Civilization," *Minnesota History*, 15:255–72 (Sept., 1934). An impressive summary.

* FOLWELL, WILLIAM W., *History*, 1:79–88. Some effects of white contact with the Sioux and the Chippewa. See also 1:159–60, 288, 305–7, 310, 320–21, 470–78.

* GILFILLAN, JOSEPH A., "The Ojibways in Minnesota," Minnesota Histor-

ical Collections, 9:55–128 (1901). The distribution of the Chippewa, their appearance, home life, food, and occupations. Written by a missionary to the Chippewa of northern Minnesota, 1873–98.

† HAGG, HAROLD T., *Exploring Minnesota*, pp. 29–34.

* HAWKINSON, ELLA, "The Old Crossing Chippewa Treaty and Its Sequel," *Minnesota History*, 15:282–300 (Sept., 1934).

*† HEILBRON, BERTHA L., *The Thirty-Second State: A Pictorial History of Minnesota*, pp. 26–36 (1958). The 477 pictorial representations in this volume are grouped into chapters. Each chapter begins with a brief analysis or outline of the subject or movement treated. Each illustration has its own annotation. Because of the exceptional worth of both the visual record and the accompanying text, frequent reference will be made to this book.

HOLCOMBE, RETURN I., *Minnesota in Three Centuries*, 2:278–81, 325–26 (1900). Chippewa cessions of 1837 and 1854.

* *The Indian in Minnesota*, a report to Governor Luther W. Youngdahl of Minnesota by the Governor's Interracial Commission (1947). This pamphlet of 80 pages gives an excellent historical summary as well as a picture of current problems.

JAMES, EDWIN, *Narrative of the Captivity and Adventures of John Tanner* (1956). A reprint of a volume first published in 1830. Captured when a boy by the Chippewa, Tanner lived as one of them for thirty years. His account of life with the Indians is a revealing one.

* LEVI, SISTER M. CAROLISSA, *Chippewa Indians of Yesterday and Today* (1956). Pp. 3–62, tribal history, religious background, early relations with whites — fur traders, missionaries, United States government officials. Pp. 131–278, Chippewa customs — social, ceremonial, economic — before and after white contact.

LONG, STEPHEN H., "Voyage in a Six-Oared Skiff to the Falls of Saint Anthony in 1817," edited by Edward D. Neill, Minnesota Historical Collections, 2:22–26, 37–40 (1889 reprint). Early versions of the legends of Winona and of the Falls of St. Anthony.

LYND, JAMES W., "History of the Dakotas," edited by Stephen R. Riggs, Minnesota Historical Collections, 2:143–74 (1889 reprint). Lynd lived among the Sioux to learn their language, habits, and characteristics. Most of his manuscript was destroyed in the Sioux Outbreak.

NEILL, EDWARD D., "Dakota Land and Dakota Life," Minnesota Historical Collections, 1:205–40 (1902 ed.). An excellent description of the Sioux.

NUTE, GRACE LEE, *The Voyageur's Highway*, pp. 59–70. The Chippewa Indians briefly described.

NYDAHL, THEODORE L., "The Pipestone Quarry and the Indians," *Minnesota History*, 31:193–208 (Dec., 1950). The role of the calumet in Indian af-

12

fairs and the quarries where the "catlinite" was obtained to be shaped into calumets.

†——"Peace * Pipe * Stone * Quarry," *Gopher Historian*, 14:7–10 (Winter, 1959–60). A condensation of the above article.

*† POATGIETER, A. H., and J. T. DUNN, *Gopher Reader*. Pp. 1–22, how the Sioux and the Chippewa lived when the whites made first contact with them. Pp. 36–38, 284–85, Indian contributions to American life and the Minnesota Indian in the mid-twentieth century. These same articles may be found in *Gopher Historian* (Oct., 1951, and Fall, 1955).

POND, GIDEON H., "Dakota Superstitions," Minnesota Historical Collections, 2:215–55 (1889 reprint).

* POND, SAMUEL W., "The Dakotas or Sioux in Minnesota as They Were in 1834," Minnesota Historical Collections, 12:319–501 (1908). Probably the best general account of the Sioux by a writer who knew them at first hand. Pond arrived in the Sioux country in 1834 as a missionary and devoted his life to the study of the Indian.

RIGGS, STEPHEN R., "The Dakota Language," Minnesota Historical Collections, 1:67–82 (1902 ed.). Riggs translated the Bible into the Dakota language.

ROBINSON, DOANE, *A History of the Dakota or Sioux Indians*, pp. 15–29 (1904 and a reprint of 1956).

RODDIS, LOUIS H., "The Last Indian Uprising in the United States," *Minnesota History Bulletin*, 3:273–90 (Feb., 1920). The Leech Lake uprising.

ROYCE, CHARLES C., comp., *Indian Land Cessions in the United States* (1899). Plates 33–35 show the Chippewa land cessions in Minnesota.

SCHMECKEBIER, LAURENCE F., *The Office of Indian Affairs*, pp. 1–90 (1927). The Indian policy of the United States to 1924.

SNELLING, WILLIAM JOSEPH, *Tales of the Northwest* (1936). These stories are faithful portrayals of Indian life as seen by one who observed the Indians at first hand in the early nineteenth century. Note especially pp. 50–61, 170–82, and 224–36.

UPHAM, WARREN, *Minnesota in Three Centuries*, 1:79–126. Origin and antiquity of the Indians of Minnesota, their tribes, and agriculture; Minnesota names of Indian origin.

WARREN, WILLIAM W., "History of the Ojibways Based upon Traditions and Oral Statements," Minnesota Historical Collections, 5:29–112, 125–36 (1885). Written by an educated half-breed Ojibway, this account reflects an intimate acquaintance with Chippewa traditions.

WINCHELL, NEWTON H., *The Aborigines of Minnesota* (1911). An account of the findings of the early archaeologists Brower, Hill, and Lewis. For an account of the Chippewa consult pp. 654–702.

II. THE GREAT POWERS STRUGGLE FOR CONTROL OF THE UPPER MISSISSIPPI REGION

3. *Military and Diplomatic Maneuvers*

A. Changing Flags in the Upper Northwest during the Seventeenth and Eighteenth Centuries

Loose claim to the interior of North America by three powers. Early penetration of the upper Northwest actually by but one flag — the French. Dominance of the French from 1660 to 1763. Colonial wars. Treaty of Utrecht (1713) and French loss of Hudson Bay country to the British. Importance of the year 1763 in diplomatic settlements. Minnesota East and Minnesota West. The American Revolution and Treaty of Paris (1783). Louisiana Purchase (1803) and the end of Minnesota East and West.

B. Factors in the Exploration of the Upper Northwest

The search for the road to Cathay. The fur trader–missionary combination. Lure of adventure. Qualities of the French which were advantageous in opening up the wilderness. The role of the Indian in French and British exploration. The Minnesota region in relation to French-British expansion and rivalry on the continent. Differentiation between the "on paper" and "actual" regimes of the French and the British.

C. Early Explorations: Upper St. Lawrence, Great Lakes, and Mississippi River (1608–70).

Champlain, Nicolet, Radisson, and Groseilliers — their relation to the British fur trade. Father Claude Allouez. St. Lusson. Jolliet and Marquette. Frontenac, governor-general. La Salle.

QUESTIONS AND SUGGESTIONS

1. For a discussion of the contest for control of the interior of the North American continent consult some standard text on the history of the United States. Bailey's *The American Pageant*, listed in the references, is a diplomatic history and treats this subject especially well.

2. Map exercise: The years of most important change in the control of the North American continent were 1713, 1763, and 1783. Using three outline maps of North America, show the essential changes effected by the treaties of these years.

3. What explorers of the Minnesota country were influenced by the idea of discovering a water route to the Pacific?

4. What routes were followed by the French on their journeys into the interior?

5. What two "gates" were discovered by the French for entry into the Minnesota country?

6. Suggest some doubtful points concerning the connection of Radisson and

14

Groseilliers with Minnesota history. Upon what sources is present knowledge of their "voyages" based? What difficulties in the establishment of the truth are illustrated by the history of these explorers? What is the primary importance of Radisson and Groseilliers in the history of the West? The best treatment of the work of these explorers is Grace Lee Nute, *Caesars of the Wilderness: Médard Chouart, Sieur des Groseilliers, and Pierre Esprit Radisson, 1618–1710.*

7. Reproductions of early French maps showing the increase of knowledge about the Great Lakes and Northwest region are to be found in Paullin, *Atlas*, Plates 19A, 20, 22A, 23, 24. The routes of French explorers in the West are shown on Plate 39A.

8. How do you explain France's almost complete loss of colonial empire to the British at the end of what is often called "the Second Hundred Years' War"?

REFERENCES

* BAILEY, THOMAS A., *The American Pageant: A History of the Republic*, pp. 44–63 (1956). The struggle of the European powers for control of the interior of the North American continent. Excellent maps.

* † BLEGEN, THEODORE C., *Building Minnesota*, pp. 31–48.

* ———— *The Land Lies Open*, pp. 3–73 (1949). A series of sketches of French explorers and fur traders whose work helped unroll the map of Minnesota.

BLEGEN, THEODORE C., and PHILIP D. JORDAN, *With Various Voices: Recordings of North Star Life*, pp. 3–9 (1949). Brief descriptions by Radisson and Hennepin of the Lake Superior region and St. Anthony Falls respectively.

* FOLWELL, WILLIAM W., *History*, 1:1–52. The French occupation of Minnesota.

MORISON, SAMUEL E., and HENRY STEELE COMMAGER, *The Growth of the American Republic*, 1:85–91, 119–31 (1950). Many another history of the United States will give a comparable treatment of the rivalry for empire of France, England, and Spain.

* NUTE, GRACE LEE, *Caesars of the Wilderness: Médard Chouart, Sieur des Groseilliers, and Pierre Esprit Radisson, 1618–1710* (1943). The finest biography of these two French explorers.

———— "Radisson and Groseilliers' Contribution to Geography," *Minnesota History*, 16:414–26 (Dec., 1935).

PAULLIN, CHARLES O., *Atlas of the Historical Geography of the United States*. Plates 19A, 20, 22A, 23, 24, 39A and accompanying text.

UPHAM, WARREN, "Groseilliers and Radisson, the First White Men in Minnesota," Minnesota Historical Collections, vol. 10, part 2, pp. 449–594 (1905).

———— *Minnesota in Three Centuries*, 1:127–278. An account of Groseilliers and Radisson.

[II. THE GREAT POWERS STRUGGLE FOR CONTROL OF THE UPPER MISSISSIPPI REGION]

4. *The French Regime (1660–1763): Exploration and Beginnings of the Fur Trade*

A. Explorations and Attempts at Occupation of the Upper Mississippi Country, 1670–1700

Accault, Augelle, and Hennepin. Discovery of the Falls of St. Anthony Hennepin's writings. Du Luth, statesman-explorer; Mille Lacs, 1679. Du Luth's meeting with Hennepin, 1680; importance for French control of the West. Perrot and Fort St. Antoine on Lake Pepin. Le Sueur and Fort L'Huillier on the Blue Earth River. Extent of French penetration in Minnesota.

B. Withdrawal from Minnesota Country, 1700–27

Factors explaining this temporary withdrawal.

C. Reoccupation and Promotion of Fur Trade, 1727–63

La Perrière and the Jesuits; Fort Beauharnois; the Mission of St. Michael the Archangel. Weakness of the upper Mississippi outpost. La Vérendrye and his sons: expedition of 1731; the building of a chain of northern posts, Fort St. Charles; the Mandan expedition. The fur trade.

D. Contributions of the French to Minnesota and the West

Made known the resources and possibilities of the Minnesota region. Opened the routes to the upper Northwest. Explored the region. Inaugurated the fur trade and proved its richness. Placed relations with the Indians upon a friendly basis. French place names. Lore and legend.

QUESTIONS AND SUGGESTIONS

1. There were perhaps three main motives that brought the French into the Northwest. What were these?

2. Describe a typical French fur trading post. Miss Nute does so in her article "Posts in the Minnesota Fur-Trading Area," cited below.

3. Describe the activities of the "wood rangers" or *coureurs de bois*; the *voyageurs.*

4. Study Father Hennepin's journey in Minnesota. What places in Minnesota can you identify on his map? (See the folded in map in the original edition of *A Description of Louisiana,* or the reproduction in the Cross translation cited below, p. 22.)

5. What facts are known concerning Du Luth's trips into Minnesota?

6. What was the purpose of La Perrière's expedition of 1727? its results? An

16

interesting account by Father Michel Guignas, one of the founders of the Mission of St. Michael the Archangel, may be found, in an English translation, in *Minnesota History*, 6:362–69 (Dec., 1925).

7. The story of Le Sueur and his mining operations in the blue, or green, earth of the Mankato region is one of extraordinary interest. What did the exploring party live on during the winter of 1700–1?

8. Topic: Agriculture at Fort St. Charles. See Lawrence J. Burpee's edition of the La Vérendrye journals and a review in *Minnesota History*, 9:147 (June, 1928). See also Blegen's article on Fort St. Charles, cited below.

9. How much actual governmental control did the French exercise in the Minnesota region? By what means did the French maintain their authority over this region?

10. What effects did the British victory in the French and Indian War have upon Minnesota history?

11. Map exercise: Locate on an outline map of North America Montreal, Quebec, Ottawa River, Georgian Bay, Sault Sainte Marie, Straits of Mackinac, Green Bay, Fox River, Wisconsin River, Chequamegon Bay, Bois Brule River, Fort St. Antoine, Fort Beauharnois, Fort L'Huillier, Fort St. Charles.

12. Draw up a list of French names for lakes, rivers, counties, and towns of Minnesota. Give the meanings of as many of these as you can.

13. Can you think of any effects which this French regime had on the later development of Minnesota?

REFERENCES

* † BLEGEN, THEODORE C., *Building Minnesota*, pp. 31–48.

* —— "Fort St. Charles and the Northwest Angle," *Minnesota History*, 18:231–48 (Sept., 1937). An informative account of La Vérendrye's explorations and fur trade activities. With slight modifications, this material is found also in Blegen's *The Land Lies Open*, pp. 61–73.

* BRINGS, LAWRENCE M., ed., *Minnesota Heritage:* Grace Lee Nute, "By Minnesota Waters," pp. 89–100. French explorations and the fur trade.

BURPEE, LAWRENCE J., ed., *Journals and Letters of Pierre Gaultier de Varennes de la Vérendrye and His Sons* (1927).

CROUSE, NELLIS M., *La Vérendrye, Fur Trader and Explorer* (1956). The first attempt in one volume to cover the entire career of this famous French explorer and fur trader.

* FOLWELL, WILLIAM W., *History*, 1:1–52. The French occupation of Minnesota.

GUIGNAS, MICHEL, "With La Perrière to Minnesota in 1727," *Minnesota History*, 6:364–69 (Dec., 1925).

* † HEILBRON, BERTHA L., *The Thirty-Second State*, pp. 3–10.

HENNEPIN, LOUIS, *A Description of Louisiana,* translated by J. D. G. Shea, pp. 188–258 (1880).

——— *Father Louis Hennepin's Description of Louisiana, Newly Discovered to the Southwest of New France by Order of the King,* translated by Marion E. Cross (1938). Note the introduction by Grace Lee Nute.

HOLAND, HJALMAR R., "Radisson's Two Western Journeys," *Minnesota History,* 15:157–80 (June, 1934).

* KELLOGG, LOUISE P., ed., *Early Narratives of the Northwest, 1634–1699,* pp. 29–65, 213–334 (1917). One of the best collections of documents for the French regime. Note especially the account of the pageant of 1671 at Sault Ste. Marie and Du Luth's narrative.

——— "Fort Beauharnois," *Minnesota History,* 8:232–46 (Sept., 1927).

*——— "The French Regime in the Great Lakes Country," *Minnesota History,* 12:347–58 (Dec., 1931). A suggestive and readable brief essay.

——— *The French Regime in Wisconsin and the Northwest* (1925). An interesting and ably written book by the leading authority on the subject.

"Le Sueur, the Explorer of the Minnesota River," Minnesota Historical Collections, 1:261–77 (1902 ed.).

LIGNE, PRINCE ALBERT DE, "Father Louis Hennepin, Belgian," *Minnesota History,* 11:343–51 (Dec., 1930).

"Louis Hennepin, the Franciscan," Minnesota Historical Collections, 1:247–56 (1902 ed.).

* McWILLIAMS, RICHEBOURG G., trans. and ed., *Fleur de Lys and Calumet, Being the Pénicaut Narrative of French Adventure in Louisiana,* pp. xx, 21–59 (1953). An eyewitness account of the Le Sueur expedition up the Mississippi and Minnesota rivers in 1700. Translated from the French.

NEILL, EDWARD D., *History of Minnesota,* pp. 99–200, 809–22, 832–40, 844–65 (1882). A narrative of the French regime in Minnesota written by a pioneer scholar.

† NUTE, GRACE LEE, "The Adventures of Two Great Explorers," *Gopher Historian,* 6:1–3 (Nov., 1951). Radisson and Groseilliers.

*†——— "The Life of the Voyageur," *Gopher Historian,* 11:10–13 (Winter, 1956–57). A portrayal of the life of these French fur traders by the outstanding authority on the subject. Brief.

——— "Marin versus La Vérendrye," *Minnesota History,* 32:226–38 (Dec., 1951). A newly discovered diary reveals the participation in the French fur trade of a second generation to carry these names. The time: the last decade before French loss of control to the British.

——— "Posts in the Minnesota Fur-Trading Area, 1660–1855," *Minnesota History,* 11:353–85 (Dec., 1930). A map showing the location of the posts accompanies the article; it is reproduced on p. 33 below.

18

*——— *The Voyageur* (1931 and reprint 1955). Delightful reading as well as excellent scholarly research. Note especially the chapters on "Furs and Fur Traders," "Voyaging," and "Voyageur Songs."

*——— *The Voyageur's Highway*, pp. 1–44. A brief but fascinating account of French and British fur activity on the northern border.

† OMACHI, TOMOKO, "The Captive Friar," *Gopher Historian*, 6:10–11, 19 (Nov., 1951). Father Hennepin.

PARKMAN, FRANCIS, *La Salle and the Discovery of the Great West*, pp. 48–82, 131–43, 242–82 (1907 and a reprint of 1955). A classic account of French explorations. Parkman's narrative of La Salle's story may also be found in *American Heritage*, 8:6–19 (April, 1957), where sixteen reprints of George Catlin's paintings of the expedition accompany the article.

PÉNICAUT, JEAN, "Annals of Louisiana," Historical Collections of Louisiana and Florida, by B. F. French, new series, pp. 60–74 (1869). Excerpts from Pénicaut's account, by a different translator, are to be found in Minnesota Historical Collections, 3:1–12 (1880). See also McWilliams above.

*† POATGIETER, A. H., and J. T. DUNN, *Gopher Reader*, pp. 40–50, 58–70. French explorers, character of the French fur trade, life of the voyageur, Grand Portage. Excellent illustrations. Note the maps and charts on pp. 40, 48, 50, 63, and 65. These same articles may be found in *Gopher Historian* (Fall, 1956).

"Sieur du Luth, the Explorer between Mille Lacs and Lake Superior," Minnesota Historical Collections, 1:257–60 (1902 ed.).

† "A True Account by an Explorer," *Gopher Historian*, 11:13, 16 (Fall, 1956). From the La Vérendrye journal. Note also the outline and time chart on pp. 14, 15.

UPHAM, WARREN, *Minnesota in Three Centuries*, 1:127–278. Includes accounts of Groseilliers and Radisson, Du Luth, Hennepin, Perrot, Le Sueur, and La Vérendrye and his sons.

† WILSON, CLIFFORD P., "La Vérendrye's Search for the Western Sea," *Gopher Historian*, 6:4–5 (Nov., 1951). Reprinted from the *Beaver* (Sept., 1938).

[II. THE GREAT POWERS STRUGGLE FOR CONTROL OF THE UPPER MISSISSIPPI REGION]

5. *The British Regime (1763–83): More Exploration and Full Flowering of the Fur Trade*

A. British Control and Occupation, 1763–83

The situation of the British in the West after the defeat of the French

19

in the French and Indian War, ending in 1763. Proclamation of 1763. British title to Minnesota East, but not Minnesota West.

B. Early Exploration: Robert Rogers and Jonathan Carver

The plans of Robert Rogers. The expedition of James Tute and the search for the Northwest Passage. The relation of Carver to Rogers and Tute. The extent of Carver's travels in Minnesota. Carver's book. His historical importance. The Carver claim.

C. Taking over the French Fur Fields, with Continuing Exploration a Counterpart of Fur Activity

Main areas of the fur trade. Early prominence of the independent trader; the rise of the large companies. The notable careers of Peter Pond and David Thompson. Traders and trading posts in Minnesota: Grand Portage and its importance; Fort Charlotte; Jean Baptiste Cadotte; Jean Baptiste Perrault and the post at Fond du Lac; Leach Lake; Sandy Lake; the situation in the Red River Valley; Alexander Henry the Younger.

D. Organization and Methods of the Fur Trade

Commercial hierarchy; classes of men. Continued use of the French *voyageur*. Decline of the independent trader. Rivalry of companies and expansion of operations. The Hudson's Bay Company. The Northwest Company. Kinds of furs. Trade goods. The credit system. Size of the trade. International aspect of the trade.

E. Continued British Occupation Despite American Title, 1783 to about 1819

The Quebec Act, 1774. The American Revolution and the Treaty of Paris, 1783; the title to Minnesota East; land cession by Virginia. The Ordinance of 1787; David Thompson and his map. Minnesota interests in the War of 1812; the Earl of Selkirk and settlements in the Red River Valley. Entrance of John Jacob Astor, American fur promoter. Bitter rivalry of the "Big Three" fur companies: Hudson's Bay, Northwest, and American. The "phony war." United States measures to exclude foreign traders from American soil, 1816. End of the British fur trade in Minnesota.

QUESTIONS AND SUGGESTIONS

1. How much of Minnesota came under British domination by the Treaty of Paris, 1763?
2. To what part of Minnesota did the term "Minnesota West" apply?
3. What was "the first written constitution nominally in effect in Minnesota"?
4. Who was Robert Rogers? Describe his plans with reference to the West.
5. What was the specific purpose of Carver's journey to Minnesota in 1766?

20

6. Indicate the importance of Detroit, Michilimackinac, Prairie du Chien, Grand Portage, and Montreal as centers of the fur trade.
7. What was the typical organization of the fur trade? Explain the status of the following classes: *bourgeois* or partners (in Montreal and in departments), clerks, interpreters, *voyageurs* or *engagés, mangeurs de lard* or pork eaters, *hivernantes* or winterers or Nor'westers.
8. Select one fur trader for special study. There are several good firsthand accounts of fur traders' experiences in Charles M. Gates, *Five Fur Traders*. Original accounts are available elsewhere for Alexander Henry the Elder and the Younger, Jean Baptiste Perrault, Gabriel Franchère, and others.
9. What routes into Minnesota country were most commonly used by the fur trader during the British regime? Which of these had the heaviest traffic?
10. Take note of the Northwest Company, especially the formation of the company, expansion of its activities, geographic areas in which it dominated, and the strategic trading posts in Minnesota country. Miss Nute's article on "Posts in the Minnesota Fur-Trading Area" will be helpful.
11. Explain from a geographic point of view the location of a trading post at Grand Portage. Of what importance was Grand Portage to the fur trade?
12. Describe life and activities at Grand Portage during a typical trading season about the year 1785.
13. Illustrate the world-wide scope of the fur trade.
14. How long did the British retain their northern Minnesota trading posts? How do you account for their retention after 1783? After 1794?
15. Why did Congress pass the act of 1816 relating to the fur trade? What was its nature?
16. Map exercise: On an outline map of Minnesota, locate the chief fur trading posts of the French and British periods.

REFERENCES

* ALVORD, CLARENCE W., "When Minnesota Was a Pawn in International Politics," *Minnesota History Bulletin*, 4:309–30 (Aug.–Nov., 1922).

BARDON, RICHARD, and GRACE LEE NUTE, "A Winter in the St. Croix Valley, 1802–3," *Minnesota History*, 28:1–14, 142–59, 225–40 (March, June, Sept., 1947). Reminiscences of a fur trader in the employ of the British XY Company. His movements: Montreal to Grand Portage to winter post on the St. Croix and back.

* † BLEGEN, THEODORE C., *Building Minnesota*, pp. 49–79.

*——— *The Land Lies Open*, pp. 74–84. Jonathan Carver and Peter Pond, colonials, reach Minnesota.

* Brings, Lawrence M., ed., *Minnesota Heritage*: Grace Lee Nute, "By Minnesota Waters," pp. 100–5. British explorations and the fur trade.

* Buck, Solon J., *The Story of the Grand Portage* (1931). A revision of his article in *Minnesota History Bulletin*, 5:14–27 (Feb., 1923). The best account of a single trading post in Minnesota.

Burpee, Lawrence J., "Grand Portage," *Minnesota History*, 12:359–77 (Dec., 1931).

Burt, Alfred L., *The Old Province of Quebec* (1933). Note especially the chapters on "Peace and War," "The Quebec Act," and "The Shadow of the Peace."

Carlstedt, Ellworth T., "When Fond du Lac Was British," *Minnesota History*, 20:7–18 (March, 1939). Role of Fort St. Louis and the Fond du Lac post in the fur trade of northern Minnesota. A good portrayal.

Carver, Jonathan, *Travels*, pp. 1–180 (1778). This is the first edition of Carver's *Travels*, published in London. There were many later editions, notably that of Boston, 1797. An edition of 1956 by the Minneapolis firm of Ross and Haines is a reprint of the third edition.

Cuneo, John R., *Robert Rogers of the Rangers* (1959).

* Folwell, William W., *History*, 1:53–79, 89–101, 492–502.

Fridley, Russell W., "The Writings of Jonathan Carver," *Minnesota History*, 34:154–59 (Winter, 1954). Considers the amazing popularity of Carver's travel book, its many editions. There is some discussion of the Carver claim to land.

Gates, Charles M., ed., *Five Fur Traders of the Northwest* (1933). Original narratives and diaries of Peter Pond, John Macdonell, Archibald N. McLeod, Hugh Faries, and Thomas Connor.

† Hagg, Harold T., *Exploring Minnesota*, pp. 45–50.

Hart, Irving H., "The Site of the Northwest Company Post on Sandy Lake," *Minnesota History*, 7:311–25 (Dec., 1926). Contains two maps and a diagram of the post.

* Heilbron, Bertha L., *The Thirty-Second State*, pp. 11–25.

*† Holmquist, June D., "The Great Carrying Place," *Gopher Historian*, 6:6–8 (Nov., 1951). One of the best brief accounts of Grand Portage. Note the map and two photographs; they are excellent. Also found in Poatgieter and Dunn, *Gopher Reader*, pp. 48–50.

Innis, Harold A., *Peter Pond, Fur Trader and Adventurer* (1930).

† Johnson, H. Nat, *Minnesota Panorama*, pp. 6–11.

Kellogg, Louise P., *The British Regime in Wisconsin and the Northwest* (1935). A companion volume to Dr. Kellogg's book on the French regime.

*——— "The Mission of Jonathan Carver," *Wisconsin Magazine of His-*

tory, 12:127–45 (Dec., 1928). An important article based mainly on Carver's diaries.

MONK, GEORGE H., "Description of Northern Minnesota by a Fur-Trader in 1807," *Minnesota History Bulletin*, 5:28–39 (Feb., 1923). Gives an unusually detailed picture of northern Minnesota fur trade and Indian life. Dr. Nute contributes an informing preface.

* NUTE, GRACE LEE, "The Fur Trade in the Northwest," in Gates, *Five Fur Traders*, pp. 3–8. An unexcelled brief account.

*——— "Posts in the Minnesota Fur-Trading Area, 1660–1885," *Minnesota History*, 11:353–85 (Dec., 1930).

*——— *The Voyageur*.

*——— *The Voyageur's Highway*, pp. 1–10, 19–47, 48–58.

† O'MEARA, WALTER, *The Grand Portage* (1951). A novel based upon the fur trade of the border country during the British period.

*† POATGIETER, A. H. and J. T. DUNN, *Gopher Reader*, pp. 48–50, 56–57, 62–70. Grand Portage, Peter Pond, and Jonathan Carver.

ROBERTS, KENNETH, *Northwest Passage* (1938). A historical novel of high quality. Key figures are Major Robert Rogers and Jonathan Carver in search of a "northwest passage."

ROSS, ALEXANDER, *The Red River Settlement: Its Rise, Progress, and Present State* (1957). The Selkirk settlement from its beginnings in 1812 to about 1855. A reprint of a volume first printed in London in 1856.

ROSS, FRANK E., "The Fur Trade of the Western Great Lakes Region," *Minnesota History*, 19:271–307 (Sept., 1938). Attempts an overall view of trade during the French, British, and American periods.

* SMITH, G. HUBERT, "Great Carrying Place," *Naturalist*, 9:6–8 (Fall, 1958). Grand Portage.

STEVENS, WAYNE E., "The Fur Trade in Minnesota during the British Régime," *Minnesota History Bulletin*, 5:3–13 (Feb., 1923). One of the best brief articles on this subject.

*——— *The Northwest Fur Trade, 1763–1800* (1928). A scholarly monograph on the British fur trade. Note the chapters on "Expansion and Monopoly," "Organization," and "Methods" of the fur trade.

TOHILL, LOUIS A., *Robert Dickson, British Fur Trader on the Upper Mississippi* (1927). A shorter account of Dickson by the same author may be found in *Minnesota History*, 6:330–42 (Dec., 1925).

[II. THE GREAT POWERS STRUGGLE FOR CONTROL OF THE UPPER MISSISSIPPI REGION]

6. *The United States and Its Growing Assertion of Authority in the Upper Midwest (1783–1842)*

A. Government-Sponsored Exploration — Westward and Northward
  Jefferson and the Louisiana Purchase. The Lewis and Clark expedition.
  Zebulon Pike and his expedition of 1805–6: instructions; Indian treaty;
  journey to northern Minnesota; Leech Lake; general results.
B. The American Left Flank in the War of 1812
  Importance of the fur country. The American policy of defense in the
  Northwest. Prairie du Chien. British fur interests and the war. Robert
  Dickson. Situation in the Northwest at the end of the war. The North-
  west in the Treaty of Ghent.
C. New Frontier Defense
  Situation in the Northwest after 1815: continuance of British occupa-
  tion of the Minnesota fur country; threat of conflict from the fur rivalry;
  the Indians. New plans for defense: treaties with the Indians; exclusion
  of foreign fur traders; building of forts. Calhoun's board of officers.
  Larger aspects of the Yellowstone expedition. Forts established in the
  Northwest, 1815–25: Howard, 1816; Crawford, 1816; Armstrong, 1817;
  Snelling, 1819.
D. The Establishment of Fort Snelling
  Major Long, 1817. Thomas Forsyth, 1819. Leavenworth and the establishment of Fort St. Anthony (Fort Snelling). Kearney, 1820. Early his-
  tory of Fort Snelling.
E. The Army and the Frontier
  Relation of the army and the westward movement. Functions of the
  army: defense and protection; enforcement of law and order; surveying,
  building roads and bridges. Industrial and cultural activities of the army
  post. Fort Snelling, spearhead of civilization, forerunner of Minnesota.
F. Diplomatic Negotiations between England and the United States: Northern Border Dispute
  Flaws in the Treaty of Paris, 1783; Mitchell's map. Jay's Treaty, 1794.
  The Convention of 1818 and the decision to accept the traders' "cus-
  tomary route"; extreme claims of both Canadians and Americans. The
  Webster-Ashburton Treaty, 1842, and agreement on the Pigeon River.
  The treaty of 1908 and actual placing of boundary markers. The treaty
  of 1909 and establishment of the International Boundary Commission.
  The Rush-Bagot Agreement, 1817; unique character of Canada–United
  States border.
G. Preservation of Canoe Country: Creation of Quetico-Superior Wilderness
  Area, 1950
  The lengthy campaign of both Canadians and Americans to make an air
  reserve. Cooperation of the two governments. President Truman's ex-
  ecutive order of December 17, 1949.

24

1. When did the area of Minnesota west of the Mississippi become American soil?
2. Relate Pike's exploration of 1805–6 to the Lewis and Clark expedition. The routes of Pike and other American explorations of Minnesota are shown on Plate 39B in Paullin, *Atlas.*
3. What were Pike's instructions? How well was he equipped to carry them out?
4. Examine the text of Pike's treaty of September 23, 1805, printed in Folwell, *History,* 1:93.
5. Did Pike's expedition bring the British period in Minnesota to an end?
6. What part did Robert Dickson play in the War of 1812? What was the attitude of the Indians of the Minnesota region during the war?
7. How did the United States secure its site for Fort Snelling?
8. With respect to Minnesota's northern border: (a) Explain why a diplomatic problem arose between England and the United States. (b) Trace negotiations and tell of settlements, making reference to "the Long Lake," the Kaministikwia River, the "customary route," Mitchell's map, the Northwest Angle, and the 49th parallel.
9. See p. 111 for a map of Northwest Angle. Note the "most northwest corner of Lake of the Woods" at the westernmost end of the Northwest Angle inlet.
10. When was the final location of the northern boundary of Minnesota effected? A map in Paullin, *Atlas,* Plate 28, shows the northern boundary of Minnesota as it was thought to be in 1804. Compare with Plates 29, 31B, and 32. The various proposed boundary lines from Isle Royale to Lake of the Woods are given on Plate 91B, and those southward and westward of Lake of the Woods on Plate 93B.
11. In what sense would the French or British fur trader of the eighteenth century feel at home in Quetico-Superior country in the twentieth century?
12. Map exercise: On an outline map of Minnesota, shade the section Canada would have won had her extreme claims following the 1818 convention been satisfied. Do the same for American extreme claims. (The Kaministikwia and St. Louis rivers come into play here.) On the same map, shade and locate the Northwest Angle.

REFERENCES

* ALVORD, CLARENCE W., "When Minnesota Was a Pawn in International Politics," *Minnesota History Bulletin,* 4:309–30 (Aug.–Nov., 1922).
* BABCOCK, WILLOUGHBY, "The Background of Fort Snelling," *Gopher Historian,* 11:17–19 (Fall, 1956). Steps leading to the establishment of the

fort; its significance. This article is also found in Poatgieter and Dunn, *Gopher Reader*, pp. 81–83.

BEMIS, SAMUEL F., "Jay's Treaty and the Northwest Boundary Gap," *American Historical Review*, 27:465–84 (April, 1922).

*† BLEGEN, THEODORE C., *Building Minnesota*, pp. 73–87.

"The Boundary at the Lake of the Woods," *Minnesota History Bulletin*, 5:46–47 (Feb., 1923).

* FOLWELL, WILLIAM W., *History*, 1:76–79, 88–100, 133–40. The Louisiana purchase, the Pike expedition, establishment of Fort Snelling.

* HANSEN, MARCUS L., *Old Fort Snelling, 1819–1858*, pp. 1–30 (1918 and reprint of 1958).

* HEILBRON, BERTHA L., *The Thirty-Second State*, pp. 37–57.

HILL, A. J., "How the Mississippi River and the Lake of the Woods Became Instrumental in the Establishment of the Northwestern Boundary of the United States," Minnesota Historical Collections, 7:302–52 (1893).

HOLLON, W. EUGENE, *The Lost Pathfinder, Zebulon Montgomery Pike*, pp. 54–89 (1949). An entertaining biography of the first government-sponsored explorer into Minnesota.

* HOLMQUIST, DONALD C., "Everlasting Wilderness," *Gopher Historian*, 6:14–16 (Sept., 1951). The Quetico-Superior area and the fight to keep it a canoeist's paradise.

KEYSOR, CHARLES W., "The 40 Years' War," *Kiwanis Magazine*, 35:19–21, 52, 54 (Jan., 1950). The story of the fight for Quetico-Superior as an air reserve wilderness area.

LOVELACE, MAUD HART, *Early Candlelight* (1949). A novel. The author has been careful about proper historical background and atmosphere. Its setting: the period immediately preceding territorial status.

NEILL, EDWARD D., *History of Minnesota*, pp. 240–99, 319–40. This account of Minnesota history from Pike's expedition to the first settlement is rich in descriptive material.

* NUTE, GRACE LEE, *The Voyageur's Highway*, pp. 11–18. Deals with the dispute over Minnesota's northern border.

PAULLIN, CHARLES O., *Atlas of the Historical Geography of the United States*. Plates 28, 29, 31B, 32, 91B, 93B, and accompanying text. For Mitchell's map see plate 89.

PIKE, ZEBULON M., *The Expeditions of Zebulon Montgomery Pike*, edited by Elliott Coues, vol. 1 (1895). Coues gives an authoritative sketch of the life of Pike on pp. xix–xxiii, 1–cxiii.

"Pike's Explorations in Minnesota, 1805–6," Minnesota Historical Collections, 1:302–42 (1902 ed.). A version of Pike's *Journal* prepared by Edward D. Neill and abridged and annotated by J. Fletcher Williams.

*† POATGIETER, A. H., and J. T. DUNN, *Gopher Reader*. Pp. 79–87, establish-

26

ment of Fort Snelling; its importance; other frontier forts. Pp. 289–90, the Northwest Angle.

PRATT, JULIUS W., "Fur Trade Strategy and the American Left Flank in the War of 1812," *American Historical Review*, 40:246–73 (Jan., 1935). An important study of the place of the Northwest in the War of 1812. The northern military frontier did not end at Detroit; the true American left flank extended to the Missouri.

PRUCHA, F. PAUL, "An Army Private at Old Fort Snelling in 1849," *Minnesota History*, 36:13–17 (March, 1958). Pictures the trials of a soldier at a frontier fort.

——— "Fort Ripley: The Post and the Military Reservation," *Minnesota History*, 28:205-24 (Sept., 1947). The second fort built in Minnesota (Snelling being the first). Its importance dropped with the establishment of Fort Ridgely in 1853.

——— "The Settler and the Army in Frontier Minnesota," *Minnesota History*, 29:231-46 (Sept., 1948). The need for Forts Snelling, Ripley, Ridgely, and Abercrombie admirably described — also, the frontier demand that these military reservations be opened to settlement.

* SCHOOLCRAFT, HENRY R., *Narrative Journal of Travels through the Northwestern Regions of the United States Extending from Detroit through the Great Chain of American Lakes to the Sources of the Mississippi River in the Year 1820*, edited by Mentor L. Williams (1953). Mr. Williams' introduction to this volume contains a brief but excellent treatment of the efforts of the United States to assert its authority in the Upper Midwest through exploration and establishment of forts. Calhoun's defense program is described. Note especially pp. 1–12.

UPHAM, WARREN, *Minnesota in Three Centuries*, 1:329–46, 357–59, 362–64. Pike and Long expeditions.

VAN CLEVE, CHARLOTTE O., *"Three Score Years and Ten": Life-Long Memories of Fort Snelling, Minnesota, and Other Parts of the West*, pp. 7–23 (1881). A story of singular charm. The author's parents accompanied the troops who came to establish the first military post in Minnesota, afterward named Fort Snelling. She was born at Prairie du Chien, on the way to Minnesota, and spent her childhood at Fort Snelling and other army posts.

WESLEY, EDGAR B., "The Army and the Westward Movement," *Minnesota History*, 15:375–81 (Dec., 1934). A masterly brief presentation of a large subject. The army posts were pioneers in industry and culture as well as first in occupation.

WOODALL, ALLEN E., "William Joseph Snelling and the Early Northwest," *Minnesota History*, 10:367–85 (Dec., 1929).

III. AMERICANS BEGIN TO PENETRATE THE UPPER MISSISSIPPI FRONTIER

7. *Occupying and Exploring the Frontier*

A. Life at Fort Snelling

Building the fort. Troops and officers. Personalities. Lumbering, agriculture, and flour milling at the fort. The *Virginia*, 1823. The mails. The liquor problem. Social life. Professional men at the fort.

B. Later American Exploration in Minnesota

Expedition of Governor Cass, 1820; Long expedition of 1823; exploration of the Red River Valley. Giacomo C. Beltrami and his book. Schoolcraft and the source of the Mississippi, 1832; Dr. Houghton's work; Allen; Boutwell, discovery of Lake Itasca. George W. Featherstonhaugh, 1835: a "geological reconnoissance." George Catlin, artist, and his visit to the Pipestone quarry. Albert M. Lea. Joseph N. Nicollet, scientific explorer. Expedition of Samuel Woods and John Pope to the Red River Valley, 1849.

C. Summary of American Exploration

Dual nature of the earlier expeditions: military and scientific. Their notable expansion of geographical knowledge. Emphasis on scientific knowledge and discovery in the expeditions after the founding of Fort Snelling. The search for the source of the Mississippi as an incentive for exploration. Numerous published records of the expeditions. Cartography.

D. Elements in Minnesota Life of the 1820's and 1830's

Indians. French-Canadians. Fur traders. Soldiers. Negroes. Missionaries. Explorers. Red River settlers. Steamboatmen. Lumbermen.

QUESTIONS AND SUGGESTIONS

1. Imagine yourself stationed at Fort Snelling during the 1820's and 1830's. What must life have been like? What kinds of food, shelter, recreation, relations with the Indians, work, contacts with the rest of the United States?

2. Be sure to catch the picture of Fort Snelling as the center of the budding Minnesota community. Note the close and frequent relations with traders, missionaries, Indians, settlers. Observe the welcome accorded to visitors.

3. Items to watch for in each of the exploring expeditions: Was it government sponsored or of a private (personal) character? Did it have a specific aim in view? What route did it follow? What were accomplishments? Was there a published report?

4. Note the many counties, lakes, towns, avenues, and parks that have been named after early explorers and traders.

28

5. What were the considerations that influenced the American government to dispatch the Long expedition of 1823?
6. What was the importance of Dr. Houghton? What light does his report in Schoolcraft, *Narrative of an Expedition*, pp. 250–57, throw on the prevalence of smallpox epidemics among the Chippewa?
7. Note the map accompanying Nicollet's *Report*. This map, according to Folwell, not only recorded Nicollet's observations but also summarized the work of previous explorers and was a contribution of the first importance to American geography.
8. One of the puzzling minor problems of Minnesota history concerns the origin of the name "Itasca." For a solution see W. J. Peterson, "Veritas Caput: Itasca," *Minnesota History*, 18:180–85 (June, 1937).

REFERENCES

ADAMS, ANN, "Early Days at Red River Settlement, and Fort Snelling," Minnesota Historical Collections, 6:75–115 (1894). Mrs. Adams came to Fort Snelling from the Selkirk settlement in 1823 and lived in the family of Colonel Josiah Snelling until 1827.

* BABCOCK, WILLOUGHBY M., ed., "A Dragoon on the March to Pembina in 1849," *Minnesota History*, 8:61–74 (March, 1927). A spirited narrative of Wood's expedition to the Red River Valley.

*†——— "Later Explorers of Minnesota," *Gopher Historian*, 11:24–26 (Fall, 1956).

* BLEGEN, THEODORE C., *Building Minnesota*, pp. 88–97.

*——— *The Land Lies Open*, pp. 85–91. Search for the source of the Mississippi — Pike, Cass, Beltrami, Schoolcraft.

BLEGEN, THEODORE C., and PHILIP D. JORDAN, *With Various Voices*, pp. 13–43. Excerpts from the writings of the explorers Schoolcraft, Keating, Pope, and Woods.

* BOUTWELL, W. T., "Schoolcraft's Exploring Tour of 1832," Minnesota Historical Collections, 1:121–40 (1902 ed.). Extracts from Boutwell's contemporary diary.

* BRINGS, LAWRENCE M., ed., *Minnesota Heritage:* Grace Lee Nute, "By Minnesota Waters," pp. 105–11. American explorers in Minnesota country.

BROWN, RALPH H., ed., "With Cass in the Northwest in 1820. The Journal of Charles C. Trowbridge, May 24–September 13, 1820," *Minnesota History*, 23:126–48, 233–52, 328–48 (June, 1942). Excellent for those seeking a firsthand description of an expedition such as Cass's.

CATLIN, GEORGE, *Letters and Notes on the Manners, Customs, and Condition of the North American Indians*, 2:129–46, 160–209 (1841). Catlin visited Minnesota in 1835 and 1836. This is his account of the two visits.

*——— *North American Indians*, 2:147–66, 182–238 (1926). A later edition of Catlin's *Letters and Notes*.

* "Early Days at Fort Snelling," Minnesota Historical Collections, 1:345–59 (1902 ed.).

FLANAGAN, JOHN T., Introduction to William Joseph Snelling's *Tales of the Northwest*, pp. vii–xxv. This account of William Joseph Snelling depicts life at Fort Snelling in the 1820's.

* FOLWELL, WILLIAM W., *History*, 1:100–30. The explorations of Cass, Long, Beltrami, Schoolcraft, Featherstonhaugh, Nicollet, and Pope in Minnesota.

*† HEILBRON, BERTHA L., "How the Source of the Mississippi Was Found," *Gopher Historian*, 11:20–23 (Fall, 1956).

*——— "Lewis Cass, Exploring Governor," *Minnesota History*, 31:93–97 (June, 1950). A splendid brief account.

† JOHNSON, H. NAT, *Minnesota Panorama*, pp. 12–17.

KEATING, WILLIAM H., *Narrative of an Expedition to the Source of the St. Peter's River* (1959). An account of the Long expedition, 1823, written by a mineralogist and geologist. This narrative is one of the most interesting contributions to the early history of Minnesota. The edition cited is a reprint of one published in Philadelphia in 1824. Another edition appeared in London in 1825.

NEILL, EDWARD D., "Occurrences in and around Fort Snelling, from 1819 to 1840," Minnesota Historical Collections, 2:102–42 (1889 reprint).

NICOLLET, JOSEPH N., *Report Intended to Illustrate a Map of the Hydrographical Basin of the Upper Mississippi River* (Senate Document No. 237, 26 Congress, 2 session, serial 380; or House Document No. 52, 28 Congress, 2 session, serial 464). Nicollet's narrative relating to Minnesota is found on pp. 53–74 of the Senate document.

NYDAHL, THEODORE L., "The Pipestone Quarry and the Indians," *Minnesota History*, 31:193–208 (Dec., 1950). George Catlin, Charles Fremont, and others on exploring trips to "pipestone country."

PETERSON, WILLIAM J., "Veritas Caput: Itasca," *Minnesota History*, 18: 180–85 (June, 1937).

*† POATGIETER, A. H. and J. T. DUNN, *Gopher Reader*, pp. 72–78. Two articles on early exploration of Minnesota by Americans. These articles may also be found in *Gopher Historian*, 11:20–26 (Fall, 1956).

POTTER, ALAN, "The Man Who Found the Source of the Mississippi," *Gopher Historian*, 8:11–13 (Fall, 1953). Schoolcraft's expedition of 1832.

SCHOOLCRAFT, HENRY R., *Narrative Journal of Travels*, edited by Mentor L. Williams. For those interested in reading Schoolcraft's original account. The introduction by the editor, pp. 1–32, gives both the setting and an overall view of the Cass expedition of 1820. This journal of the expedition appeared first in 1821.

———— *Schoolcraft's Expedition to Lake Itasca: The Discovery of the Source of the Mississippi,* edited by Philip P. Mason (1958). This deals with his 1832 journey into Minnesota and is a companion volume to the above book. Besides Schoolcraft's account, the volume contains journals of three other members of the party: Dr. Douglass Houghton, Reverend William T. Boutwell, and Lieutenant James Allen.

———— *Narrative of an Expedition through the Upper Mississippi to Itasca Lake* (1834). The journal of Schoolcraft's expedition in 1832.

———— *Summary Narrative of an Exploratory Expedition to the Sources of the Mississippi River* (1855). A combined narrative of Schoolcraft's first journey into Minnesota with Cass in 1820 and his second journey to Lake Itasca in 1832.

SIBLEY, HENRY H., "Memoir of Jean N. Nicollet," Minnesota Historical Collections, 1:146–56 (1902 ed.).

UPHAM, WARREN, *Minnesota in Three Centuries,* 1:347–56, 359–62, 364–90. Explorations from Cass to Nicollet.

VAN CLEVE, CHARLOTTE O., *"Three Score Years and Ten,"* pp. 24–67. A brief excerpt from this account may be found in Blegen and Jordan, *With Various Voices,* pp. 191–201.

WOODS, SAMUEL, *Report of Major Woods, Relative to His Expedition to Pembina Settlement* (House Executive Document No. 51, 31 Congress, 1 session, serial 577). The official report of the expedition to Pembina in 1849.

[III. AMERICANS BEGIN TO PENETRATE THE UPPER MISSISSIPPI FRONTIER]

8. *The American Fur Trade*

A. John Jacob Astor and the American Fur Company

Astor's background and early training. His objects and methods in the fur trade. Formation of the American Fur Company. Attempts at cooperation with the Canadians. The Americans monopolize the field in Minnesota after 1816. Reorganization of the company in 1834; Ramsay Crooks.

B. The American Fur Company as Big Business

Transcontinental scope of the company. Headquarters and posts. Organization. Aspects of its activities: fur trading, manufacturing, retailing, banking, transportation. Political activities of fur magnates. Methods of dealing with competitors. Trade agreements. The fur trade in Europe: rivalry with the Hudson's Bay Company; European markets;

European trade goods. Subsidiary interests of the American Fur Company: land speculation, fisheries, maple sugar, banking. The fur trade and the settler.

c. Henry Hastings Sibley

Origins and early life. Arrival in Minnesota. Sibley and the Minnesota fur trade. Other activities. Sibley as a pioneer of culture. Influence.

D. Minnesota Fur Trade and Traders

Fur stations in Minnesota. Mendota; the Sioux Outfit. La Pointe and Fond du Lac; the Northern Outfit. Value of the business. Kinds of furs. Trade goods imported. Marketing the fur. Prices. Methods of conducting the fur trade. Independent fur traders. The problem of liquor. Some fur traders: Faribault, Brown, Provençalle, Renville, Aitkin, Borup, Rolette, Dousman, Bailly. Life at a trading post.

E. Decline of the fur trade

Reasons: depletion of furs, beaver hat out of style, panic of 1837. Expanding activities of the American Fur Company: Lake Superior fishing, copper and lead trade, cranberry business, banking, sale of sand. Bankruptcy of the American Fur Company, 1842. Fur trade activities at Pembina. Later history of the trade.

QUESTIONS AND SUGGESTIONS

1. What evidences existed in Minnesota during the American period of earlier French fur trade activities in the region?

2. Identify in relation to the American fur trade the following men: John Jacob Astor, Ramsay Crooks, William Aitkin, Jean Baptiste Faribault, Alexander Faribault, Joseph Renville, Norman W. Kittson, Hercules L. Dousman, Martin McCleod, Joe Rolette, Sr., Joe Rolette, Jr., Joseph R. Brown, Louis Provençalle.

3. On an outline map of Minnesota show the locations of posts of the American period. See Dr. Nute's article in *Minnesota History*, 11:353–85 (Dec., 1930) and her map, reproduced on the opposite page.

4. What was the American Fur Company's "Sioux Outfit"? Its "Northern Outfit"?

5. Subject for a report: The story of a given trading post of the American period.

6. The American Fur Company has been called an early example of "big business." Why? Dr. Folwell asserts that the Minnesota fur trade was a small business. Do you agree with this assertion?

7. An interesting firsthand narrative is Sibley's *Unfinished Autobiography*. Worth noting are Sibley's Michigan background, his description of the arrival at Detroit of *voyageurs* from Montreal, his portrayal of the country between Prairie du Chien and Fort Snelling, his description of Fort

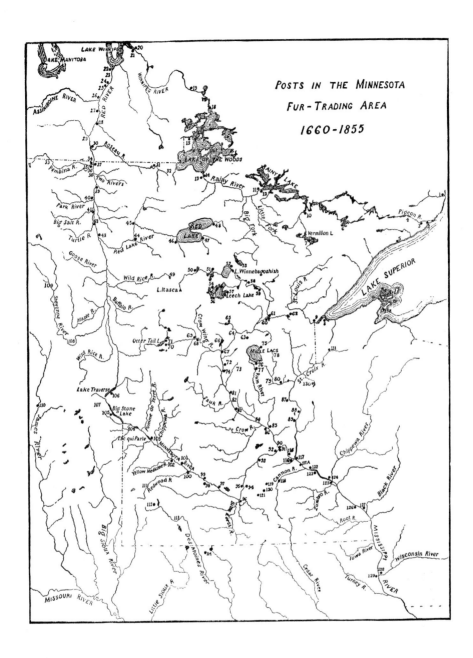

POSTS IN THE MINNESOTA
FUR-TRADING AREA
1660-1855

33

Snelling and Mendota, and his estimate of the *voyageurs* with whom he dealt at Mendota.

8. Subject for a report: Henry H. Sibley's career as a fur trader.

REFERENCES

* ACKERMANN, GERTRUDE W., "Joseph Renville of Lac qui Parle," *Minnesota History*, 12:231–46 (Sept., 1931).

BABCOCK, WILLOUGHBY M., "Louis Provençalle, Fur Trader," *Minnesota History*, 20:259–68 (Sept., 1939). An account of a fur trader who had charge of a post at Traverse des Sioux for twenty-five years.

*† BLEGEN, THEODORE C., *Building Minnesota*, pp. 111–18.

*——— *The Land Lies Open*, pp. 95–110. Henry H. Sibley, trader for the American Fur Company, a man of culture.

* FOLWELL, WILLIAM W., *History*, 1:131–33, 161–69. Astor and the American Fur Company, Sibley, the fur trade and the Indians.

HANSEN, MARCUS L., *Old Fort Snelling, 1819–1858*, pp. 135–45. The fur trade.

HART, IRVING H., "The Site of the Northwest Company Post on Sandy Lake," *Minnesota History*, 7:311–25 (Dec., 1926).

"Memoir of Joseph R. Brown," Minnesota Historical Collections, 3:201–12 (1880).

NUTE, GRACE LEE, "Alexander Faribault," *Minnesota History*, 8:177–80 (June, 1927).

——— "Beaver Money," *Minnesota History*, 9:287–88 (Sept., 1928).

*——— "The Papers of the American Fur Company," *American Historical Review*, 32:519–38 (April, 1927). Gives the best picture of the many-sided activities of the American Fur Company.

——— "Posts in the Minnesota Fur-Trading Area, 1660–1855," *Minnesota History*, 11:353–85 (Dec., 1930).

*——— *The Voyageur's Highway*, pp. 45–70. The American fur trade period.

† POATGIETER, A. H., and J. T. DUNN, *Gopher Reader*, pp. 51–55. A short play centering about the early fur trade activities of Henry H. Sibley at Mendota. There is an interesting map on p. 53.

* PRITCHETT, JOHN P., "Some Red River Fur-Trade Activities," *Minnesota History*, 5:401–23 (May, 1924).

RIFE, CLARENCE W., "Norman W. Kittson, a Fur-Trader at Pembina," *Minnesota History*, 6:225–52 (Sept., 1925).

SHORTRIDGE, WILSON P., "Henry Hastings Sibley and the Minnesota Frontier," *Minnesota History Bulletin*, 3:115–25 (Aug., 1919).

*——— *The Transition of a Typical Frontier*, pp. 1–26 (1922). An account of Sibley and the fur traders' frontier.

Sibley, Henry H., "Memoir of Hercules L. Dousman," Minnesota Historical Collections, 3:192–200 (1880).

———— "Memoir of Jean Baptiste Faribault," Minnesota Historical Collections, 3:168–79 (1880).

———— "Reminiscences; Historical and Personal," Minnesota Historical Collections, 1:374–96 (1902 ed.).

———— "Reminiscences of the Early Days of Minnesota," Minnesota Historical Collections, 3:242–77 (1880).

———— *The Unfinished Autobiography of Henry Hastings Sibley*, edited by Theodore C. Blegen (1932). The autobiography was first published in *Minnesota History*, 8:329–62 (Dec., 1927). This edition has also a selection of unpublished letters.

Upham, Warren, *Minnesota in Three Centuries*, 1:315–27. Sketches of ten fur traders whose names are borne by Minnesota counties.

Warren, William W., "History of the Ojibways," Minnesota Historical Collections, 5:378–86 (1885). The fur trade and fur traders among the Ojibways.

[III. AMERICANS BEGIN TO PENETRATE THE UPPER MISSISSIPPI FRONTIER]

9. *The Indian Agency System and Mission Activity*

A. The National Background: Indian Policy

The policy of dealing with the Indians by treaty, in force from 1781 to 1871, and attendant evils. Westward movement and pressure for land. Succession of treaties to buy Indian lands; hostilities with Indians. Indians left on reservations or pushed steadily westward. John C. Calhoun and the permanent Indian frontier policy (1825–40); the idea of a perpetual reserve west of the Mississippi in the "Great American Desert." Attempts to prohibit the liquor trade with the Indians. The Indian agent.

B. Lawrence Taliaferro and the Agency System in Minnesota

Main problems. Taliaferro's qualifications. His relations with Fort Snelling officers. Civilizing efforts. Taliaferro's attitude toward the work of the missionaries.

c. The Sioux-Chippewa Feud

Beginnings. Early episodes in the intertribal warfare. Nature of Indian warfare. Attempts at settlement based on a boundary line. The Fort Crawford conference; the line of 1825. Later clashes between the two traditional enemies. Example of primitive justice: the running of the gauntlet, 1827. Intertribal clashes in 1839 and 1842. The persistence of hostility.

36

J. Later Government Policy

Apportionment among the sects. Henry B. Whipple and his work among the Sioux and Chippewa.

QUESTIONS AND SUGGESTIONS

1. In government dealings with Indians, was the use of the treaty system wise? Was the role of the Indian agent important? How effective was liquor control? Explain the Indian's interest in the annuity system. Were annuities of benefit or harm to the Indian?

2. Which was harder to maintain, peace between the Sioux and the Chippewa, or between the Indians and the white men?

3. List the measures taken by the American government to protect the Indians in their contacts with the white men. How effective were they?

4. Did national policy toward the Indians of Minnesota differ from that toward the Indians of other regions?

5. How did Taliaferro himself summarize the results of his work as Indian agent? How did he regard the problem of Christianizing the natives? Why did he resign?

6. What was the "treaty line of 1825"? How did it come into being? Was the Indian boundary line of 1825 surveyed and marked? Consult the map showing this line in Blegen, *Building Minnesota*, p. 15, and in Folwell, *Minnesota*, 1:80.

7. What were the three main features of the permanent Indian frontier policy of the United States government? How permanent was it?

8. Eyewitness accounts of the running of the gauntlet in 1827 are given by Charlotte O. Van Cleve and William Joseph Snelling.

9. Interesting use of the Fort Snelling and Minnesota background for the period from 1834 to 1840 is made by Maud Hart Lovelace in her novel *Early Candlelight*.

10. What denominations and agencies were active in support of missionary work among Minnesota's Indians?

11. List outstanding missionaries among the Chippewa; among the Sioux.

12. Subject for a report: The work of any one of the missionaries — early contacts with the Indians, supporting denomination, methods, achievements, disappointments. Was this mission interest confined solely to the area of Minnesota?

13. As Folwell sees it, what difficulties beset missionaries in their work among the Chippewa and Sioux?

14. In connection with the basic problem of teaching Christian ideas to the Indians note that they had no words for sin, salvation, baptism, conversion, redemption, morality, and piety.

15. How did the missionaries feel about (a) their educational work among

the Indians? (b) their attempts at civilizing work? (c) the extent to which the core of the Christian faith was accepted by the Indian? (d) the effect upon their work of other Americans, especially the fur trader and the soldier?

REFERENCES

BABCOCK, WILLOUGHBY M., "Major Lawrence Taliaferro, Indian Agent," *Mississippi Valley Historical Review*, 11:358–75 (Dec., 1924).

*† ——— "Major Taliaferro," *Gopher Historian*, 5:8, 9, 20 (Nov., 1950). A good brief account of Minnesota's first Indian agent.

——— "Sioux versus Chippewa," *Minnesota History*, 6:41–45 (March, 1925).

*† BLEGEN, THEODORE C., *Building Minnesota*, pp. 98–110.

* ——— "The Pond Brothers," *Minnesota History*, 15:273–81 (Sept., 1934).

* ——— ed., "Armistice and War on the Minnesota Frontier" (including a sketch by Ezekiel G. Gear, "Sioux and Chippeways"), *Minnesota History*, 24:11–25 (March, 1943). A vivid contemporary account of two encounters in 1839 by one who was in Indian country when these "massacres" occurred.

* BRINGS, LAWRENCE M., ed., *Minnesota Heritage*: Grace Lee Nute, "By Minnesota Waters," pp. 111–19. Mission activity in Minnesota.

CARMAN, HARRY J., and HAROLD C. SYRETT, *A History of the American People*, 1:320–22 (1952). On the permanent Indian frontier policy.

FLANDRAU, CHARLES E., "Reminiscences of Minnesota during the Territorial Period," Minnesota Historical Collections, 9:204–9 (1901). Pioneer missionaries.

——— "The Work of Bishop Whipple in Missions for the Indians," Minnesota Historical Collections, vol. 10, part 2, pp. 691–96 (1905).

* FOLWELL, WILLIAM W., *History*. 1:79–88, 140–60, the Sioux-Chippewa feud, influence of the white man on the Indians, Taliaferro, land cessions; note the map opposite p. 81 showing the Indians in Minnesota. 1:170–212, 447–52, early Indian missions; the Dakota dictionary and grammar.

"Frederick Ayer, Teacher and Missionary," Minnesota Historical Collections, 6:429–37 (1894).

* GATES, CHARLES M., "The Lac qui Parle Indian Mission," *Minnesota History*, 16:133–51 (June, 1935).

HANSEN, MARCUS L., *Old Fort Snelling, 1819–1858*. Pp. 103–34, 176–86, the fort and Indian life, the Sioux-Chippewa feud, the Chippewa treaty of 1837. Pp. 146–58, the relations between the military and Taliaferro at Fort Snelling and the missionaries.

HOLCOMBE, RETURN I., *Minnesota in Three Centuries*. 2:153–200, 271–85, the Sioux-Chippewa feud; Indian treaties. 2:201–6, 219–70, the Dakota alphabet; Protestant missions.

LOVELACE, MAUD HART, *Early Candlelight*. The setting is Fort Snelling in the early days. Occasional mention is made of such men as Major Taliaferro, the Pond brothers, Father Galtier, Joseph Renville, and Pig's Eye Parrant.

* LYMAN, GEORGE D., *John Marsh, Pioneer*, pp. 49–180 (1930). A vivid account of life at Fort Snelling. Marsh was subagent to the Indians for some months and later became Indian agent at Prairie du Chien.

* MACLEOD, WILLIAM C., "Native Policy: North America," *Encyclopaedia of the Social Sciences*, 11:260–67 (1933). The best available account of the Indian policy of the United States.

*† MARTINSON, FLORA B., "The Pond Brothers — Missionaries," *Gopher Historian*, 12:29 (Winter, 1957–58). A brief outline biography.

NEILL, EDWARD D., ed., "Battle of Lake Pokegama, as Narrated by an Eye Witness," Minnesota Historical Collections, 1:140–45 (1902 ed.). One incident in the Sioux-Chippewa feud which occurred in 1841.

——— "History of the Ojibways," Minnesota Historical Collections, 5:457–510. The Chippewa under the United States government.

* NORTON, SISTER MARY AQUINAS, *Catholic Missionary Activities in the Northwest, 1818–1864* (1930). Describes Catholic missionary activities from 1818 to 1864 at Pembina, Lake Superior, and among the Sioux, Winnebago, and Chippewa.

NUTE, GRACE LEE, "The Edmund Franklin Ely Papers," *Minnesota History*, 6:343–54 (Dec., 1925).

PAXSON, FREDERIC L., *History of the American Frontier, 1763–1893*, pp. 275–85 (1924). On the permanent Indian frontier policy.

POND, SAMUEL W., "Indian Warfare in Minnesota," Minnesota Historical Collections, 3:129–38 (1880).

RHOADS, JAMES B., "The Fort Snelling Area in 1835, a Contemporary Map," *Minnesota History*, 35:23–29 (March, 1956). A map drawn by Lawrence Taliaferro is used as a point of departure to tell of the work of the Indian agent and to picture the Fort Snelling area.

RIGGS, STEPHEN R., "The Dakota Mission," Minnesota Historical Collections, 3:115–28 (1880).

——— "In Memory of Rev. Thos. S. Williamson, M.D.," Minnesota Historical Collections, 3:372–85 (1880).

——— *Mary and I*, pp. 16–137 (1880). Riggs's own story of his missionary experiences, 1837–57.

——— "Protestant Missions in the Northwest," Minnesota Historical Collections, 6:117–87 (1894).

ROBINSON, DOANE, *A History of the Dakota or Sioux Indians*, pp. 59–67, 143–71, 181–94. The Sioux-Chippewa feud, land cessions, and treaties.

SIBLEY, HENRY H., "Sketch of John Other Day," Minnesota Historical Collections, 3:99–102 (1880).

SNELLING, WILLIAM J., "Running the Gauntlet," Minnesota Historical Collections, 1:360–73 (1902 ed.).

TALIAFERRO, LAWRENCE, "Auto-biography of Maj. Lawrence Taliaferro. Written in 1864," Minnesota Historical Collections, 6:187–255 (1894).

TANNER, GEORGE C., "Early Episcopal Churches and Missions in Minnesota," Minnesota Historical Collections, vol. 10, part 1, pp. 203–31 (1905).

THOMAS, CYRUS, Introduction to *Indian Land Cessions in the United States*, compiled by Charles C. Royce, pp. 639–43. The Indian policy of the United States. Note Plates 33–34, which show the Indian land cessions in Minnesota.

VAN CLEVE, CHARLOTTE O., *"Three Score Years and Ten,"* pp. 74–79. Compare this account of running the gauntlet with that by William Joseph Snelling. Both are by eyewitnesses.

WHIPPLE, HENRY B., "Civilization and Christianization of the Ojibways in Minnesota," Minnesota Historical Collections, 9:129–42 (1901).

WILLIAMSON, T. S., "Earliest Schools in Minnesota Valley," Minnesota Historical Collections, 6:410–12 (1894). The school at Lac qui Parle.

WINCHELL, NEWTON H., *The Aborigines of Minnesota*, pp. 518–59, 616–54. A good discussion of the history, treaties, and reservations of the Sioux, of land cessions, and of the history of the Chippewa.

[III. AMERICANS BEGIN TO PENETRATE THE UPPER MISSISSIPPI FRONTIER]

10. *The Beginnings of Settlement*

A. The National Setting

Increase of population in the United States. The Erie Canal. The steamboat. The westward surge of population and advance of statehood. Jackson and frontier democracy.

B. The Selkirk Settlement and Minnesota

Origins of the Selkirk settlement. Swiss and other colonists; the halfbreeds. The feud between the Hudson's Bay Company and the Northwest Company. Union in 1821. The trek to the region about Fort Snelling. Later history of the Red River settlements.

c. Fort Snelling Squatters and St. Paul

Early nonmilitary visitors and residents at the Fort Snelling military reservation. Eviction of settlers on the reservation. The visit of Bishop Loras, 1839. Father Lucian Galtier. Early St. Paul history. The "Fashionable Tour" and its advertising value for Minnesota country.

D. The Lumber Settlements of the St. Croix Valley
Pine and the land cession of 1837. Marine. Stillwater and the lumber trade. Other St. Croix settlements.

E. Settlement at St. Anthony Falls
Natural advantages. Franklin Steele. Sawmilling. Town beginnings.

F. Other Early Minnesota Settlements

G. Character of the Early Settlements
Elements composing the population: French, Swiss, Yankees, others. The Maine lumbermen. Relative advantages of the early settlements: Stillwater, St. Paul, St. Anthony. Trade relations with the Red River settlements. Importance of the Mississippi. General settlement situation in 1849.

QUESTIONS AND SUGGESTIONS

1. With reference to Lord Selkirk's Red River colony: (a) Explain its origin. (b) Account for the discontent of so many of the settlers. (c) Explain the displeasure of the Northwest Company at its founding. (d) What part of the colony was made up of *bois brulés*, and who were they? (e) What became of the colony?

2. An interesting Minnesota story is that of Mrs. Ann Adams, who with her parents left Switzerland to join the Selkirk colony. In her narrative she tells of this migration, of the subsequent disappointments of the colonists, and of the trek to Fort Snelling in 1823.

3. Which was the more important in inducing the early settlers to come to Minnesota, lumbering or agriculture?

4. Apropos of the "Delta Country": (a) What treaty led to the first use of this label? (b) What forces led to the treaty? (c) Give the essence of terms granted to the Indians and tell why both the Sioux and the Chippewa were involved.

5. With the opening of the "Delta Country": (a) What type of settlement took place? (b) Would the term "land rush" apply to the movement of people into the region? (c) From whence did the people come who moved into "Delta Country"? (d) Did any towns appear here before the establishment of the Territory of Minnesota?

6. Note how extensive the original Fort Snelling Reservation was. What happened to it in 1852 and 1871? See the map and accompanying text in Folwell, *History*, 1:424 (1956 ed.). The map is reproduced on p. 42.

7. What connection did the Fort Snelling Reservation have with St. Paul's beginnings? "Pig's Eye" Parrant? Father Lucian Galtier?

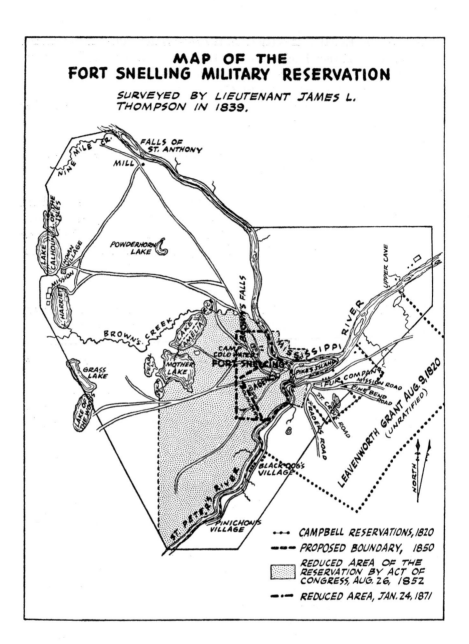

MAP OF THE
FORT SNELLING MILITARY RESERVATION

SURVEYED BY LIEUTENANT JAMES L.
THOMPSON IN 1839.

FALLS OF
ST. ANTHONY

NINE MILE CR.

MILL

LAKE OF THE ISLES

LAKE CALHOUN

TOWN VILLAGE

MISSION

LAKE HARRIET

POWDERHORN
LAKE

BROWN'S CREEK

LAKE AMELIA

MOTHER
LAKE

GRASS
LAKE

LAKE OF
THE WOODS

BROWN'S FALLS

MISSISSIPPI RIVER

UPPER CAVE

CAMP
COLD WATER

FORT SNELLING

PIKE'S ISLAND

FUR COMPANY

MISSION ROAD

PINE BEND

RABBIT

ST. CROIX ROAD

TRADERS ROAD

LEAVENWORTH GRANT AUG. 9, 1820
(UNRATIFIED)

BLACK DOG'S
VILLAGE

ST. PETER'S RIVER

PINICHON'S
VILLAGE

NORTH

— · · — CAMPBELL RESERVATIONS, 1820

— — — PROPOSED BOUNDARY, 1850

REDUCED AREA OF THE
RESERVATION BY ACT OF
CONGRESS, AUG. 26, 1852

— · — REDUCED AREA, JAN. 24, 1871

8. Of the early centers of population in Minnesota, which seemed to have the most natural advantages for becoming a great city?

REFERENCES

ADAMS, ANN, "Early Days at Red River and Fort Snelling," Minnesota Historical Collections, 6:75–115 (1894).

*† BLEGEN, THEODORE C., *Building Minnesota*, pp. 119–25.

—— "The 'Fashionable Tour' on the Upper Mississippi," *Minnesota History*, 20:377–96 (Dec., 1939). On the popularity of steamboat excursions to Minnesota country in the 1830's and 1840's.

CHRISTIANSON, THEODORE, *Minnesota: The Land of Sky-Tinted Water*, 1:147–70 (1935).

FOLSOM, WILLIAM H. C., "History of Lumbering in the St. Croix Valley," Minnesota Historical Collections, 9:293–305 (1901). Settlement in the St. Croix Valley.

* FOLWELL, WILLIAM W., *History*, 1:213–30, 422–34, 452–54. First settlements, the Fort Snelling Reservation, Steele's preemption at the Falls of St. Anthony.

"Fredrika Bremer's New Scandinavia, Minnesota in 1850," *Minnesota History*, 31:148–57 (Sept., 1950). Reprints of significant sections of Miss Bremer's account of her visit to Minnesota in 1850. Taken from her *Homes of the New World*.

†* FRIDLEY, RUSSELL W., "The Beginnings of St. Paul," *Gopher Historian*, 14:1–4 (Spring, 1960).

HANSEN, MARCUS L., *Old Fort Snelling, 1819–1858*, pp. 187–201. Citizens and soldiers at Fort Snelling.

* HARTSOUGH, MILDRED L., *The Development of the Twin Cities as a Metropolitan Market*, pp. 21–29 (1924). The early growth of the Twin Cities.

*† HEILBRON, BERTHA L., *The Thirty-Second State*, pp. 58–69.

HOFFMANN, MATHIAS M., "New Light on Old St. Peter's and Early St. Paul," *Minnesota History*, 8:27–51 (March, 1927). Based on records of the visit of Bishop Loras in 1839.

HOLCOMBE, RETURN I., *Minnesota in Three Centuries*, 2:69–89, 105–24, 419–23.

NEWSON, THOMAS M., *Pen Pictures of St. Paul*, pp. 1–98 (1886). Clever descriptions of early St. Paul and its people by a pioneer editor.

* NUTE, GRACE LEE, "The Red River Trails," *Minnesota History*, 6:279–82 (Sept., 1925).

*† POATGIETER, A. H., and J. T. DUNN, *Gopher Reader*, pp. 108–10, 151–53. Two articles, one on St. Paul's beginnings, the other on the Selkirk colony.

PRITCHETT, JOHN P., "Some Red River Fur-Trade Activities," *Minnesota*

History, 5:401–23 (May, 1924). Settlement and the fur trade, especially the Selkirk colony and fur trade politics.

* Robinson, Edward Van Dyke, *Early Economic Conditions and the Development of Agriculture in Minnesota*, pp. 39–43. Settlement and the development of pioneer agriculture. Note the two maps on p. 42.

Shortridge, Wilson P., *The Transition of a Typical Frontier*, pp. 27–34.

Snelling, William Joseph, *Tales of the Northwest*. Note especially the story entitled "The Bois Brulé," pp. 77–169. The setting is the Red River Valley settlement. The action involves the rivalry between the Northwest Company and the Hudson's Bay Company.

Van Cleve, Charlotte O., *"Three Score Years and Ten,"* pp. 68–73. The Selkirk settlers.

* Wesley, Edgar B., "The Army and the Westward Movement," *Minnesota History*, 15:375–81 (Dec., 1934).

IV. THE PIONEERS ORGANIZE A TERRITORY AND THEN A STATE

11. *Creation of the Territory of Minnesota and the Securing of Indian Lands*

A. Jurisdictions over Minnesota

Jurisdictional status of Minnesota East, 1783–1848; of Minnesota West, 1803–46. Western Minnesota unorganized, 1846–49; eastern Minnesota unorganized, 1848–49.

B. The Southern and Eastern Boundaries

Proposals for the northern boundary of Iowa; for the western boundary of Wisconsin.

C. The Movement for a Territory

Frontier attitude toward government. The Stillwater Convention. Election of Sibley as delegate from the "remnant Wisconsin Territory."

D. The Territory Created

Sibley's reception by Congress. Stephen A. Douglas and Minnesota. Last-minute passage of a bill creating the Territory of Minnesota; its provisions. Extent of the territory. First counties. Officials.

E. The First Governor

Alexander Ramsey: earlier career, arrival in Minnesota. The beginnings of government. Early legislation. The Code of 1851. Politics during the first five years of the territory.

F. The Drive for More Land Cessions from the Indians

Extent of land opened to settlement by the treaties of 1837. Factors which steadily undermined belief in the permanency of the Indian boundaries as thus established. Three groups which pushed for further land cessions: land-hungry pioneers, fur traders, and the Indians themselves.

44

G. Treaties of Traverse des Sioux and Mendota, 1851

Luke Lea and Alexander Ramsey. Steps leading to the signing of the Treaty of Traverse des Sioux. Its provisions. The trick of the traders' paper. The Treaty of Mendota. Allegations of fraud. Amendments and ratification. Difficulty of securing Indian consent to amendments. Final settlements.

H. The Chippewa Treaties

The unratified Pembina treaty. Opening the northeast to miners: the Lake Superior Chippewa cession of 1854. Opening new pine regions to lumbermen: the Mississippi Chippewa cession of 1855. Prohibition of alcoholic liquor. Allotment of land. Reservation established by the two treaties.

I. Other Indian Relations

The Menominee and Winnebago reservations, a Chippewa-Sioux buffer state. The Menominee Reservation, 1847–54. The Winnebago: original home; removal to Watab; the Rice contract; the Blue Earth Reservation, 1855–63. The Lake Pepin half-breed tract. Attempts to obtain the land: Doty treaty, 1841; Ramsey treaty, 1849; Treaty of Mendota, 1851. The Rice act of 1854 providing for "half-breed" script. History of this script and of the Chippewa half-breed script.

J. The Aftermath

Amount of Indian land ceded. Influx of settlers. Establishing the Indians on their restricted lands. New Indian agencies. Fort Ridgely. The ethics of Indian treaty-making. The white ideal for the Indian: a self-support-ing, individualistic agriculturalist. Measures to put this ideal into effect. The actuality of treaty-making: intimidation, trickery, fastening indi-vidual debts upon the tribe, the annuity system and its evils. The effect of opening the lands upon settlement, the fur trade, and missionary work.

QUESTIONS AND SUGGESTIONS

1. Note that whereas Minnesota's boundaries were in part determined when Wisconsin and Iowa became states, the western boundary was not drawn until Minnesota received statehood.
2. Note the various proposals put forward in connection with the problem of drawing Iowa's northern boundary.
3. Topic: Stephen A. Douglas and Minnesota. Douglas visited Minnesota in 1847 and again in 1857.
4. It has been said that the events following the Stillwater Convention of 1848 "make up a strange tale of frontier audacity." Why? What was the "benign fiction" Folwell referred to in connection with the election of a territorial delegate? What connection did Henry M. Rice have with these developments?

5. Tell how the following were related to the attainment of territorial status for Minnesota: (a) Stillwater, (b) Henry H. Sibley, (c) the Delta Country, (d) Stephen A. Douglas, (e) Sections 16 and 36, (f) the Missouri River.

6. Distinguish between "organic act" and "enabling act."

7. Study the provisions of Minnesota's Organic Act (see any issue of the *Legislative Manual*).

8. How did Ramsey come to be chosen governor of Minnesota Territory?

9. What was the normal "news route" from Washington to St. Paul in 1849?

10. Compare the contemporary letter describing conditions in Minnesota in the summer of 1849 printed in *Minnesota History Bulletin*, 5:286–90 (Nov., 1923), with Folwell's imaginary letter in *Minnesota History*, 6:34–40 (March, 1925). Do you think it could be proved from internal evidence that Dr. Folwell's letter was not written in 1849? For almost any period in Minnesota history an interesting test of one's understanding of the situation is to try to do what Dr. Folwell did for the year 1849.

11. Note the extent of the three Minnesota judicial districts established in June, 1849.

12. The seal of Minnesota portrays an attitude which was strongly held by the pioneer settler. What attitude? If vigorously pressed how would this sentiment affect the "permanent Indian frontier"? For reproductions and descriptions of the seal, see Folwell, *History*, 1:459–62, and the *Legislative Manual, 1957–58*, pp. 8, 9. Worth noting are the motto of the 1849 seal and the poem by a pioneer writer, Mary H. Eastman, in which she interprets the seal. The key stanza of this poem is reprinted in a footnote in Folwell, *History*, 1:267.

13. With respect to the treaties of 1851: Why were two treaties negotiated, one at Traverse des Sioux, the other at Mendota? Note the course of the negotiations. What lands did the Sioux sell to the United States and on what terms? What lands were the Sioux to keep as a reservation? What were the accompanying "traders' papers"? Why did they leave a smoldering discontent among the Indians? Note the provisions relating to plans for civilizing the Sioux.

14. Delay in ratification of the treaties came when amendments were made by the Senate. Account for these amendments. By what means were the Sioux persuaded to accept the later amendments to the treaties?

15. Note that further delays came before the Sulands were legally open to sale. How were the following factors connected with this delay: survey, extension of the preemption privilege, opening of government land offices?

16. What interests were back of the Chippewa cessions of 1854 and 1855?

17. William L. Quinn, an interpreter, said of the Traverse des Sioux and

Mendota treaties, "They were as fair as any Indian treaties." This opinion may serve as the introduction to an examination of the entire problem of American Indian treaties and cessions.

18. Topics: The Menominee Reservation, the first Winnebago Reservation, the Blue Earth Reservation, the Half-Breed Tract.
19. What was half-breed script? To what uses was it put? Who benefited from it?
20. A map in Paullin, *Atlas*, Plate 47A, "Indian Cessions, 1750–1890," shows clearly how the westward surge of population pushed back the Indians. The greater part of Minnesota land was obtained during the period of 1851–70. Compare this map with those on Plates 58B–D and 59A, showing the public lands for each state and territory.
21. Map exercise: On a large outline map of Minnesota show the Indian cessions and reservations up to 1863.
22. Summarize Minnesota settlement at the end of the territorial period.

REFERENCES

* ANDERSON, WILLIAM, and ALBERT J. LOBB, *A History of the Constitution of Minnesota*, pp. 4–38 (1921). Note the maps showing the various boundaries proposed for Wisconsin and Iowa, and the map showing Minnesota East, West, and Northwest.

BERTHEL, MARY W., *Horns of Thunder: The Life and Time of James M. Goodhue Including Selections from His Writings*, pp. 201–16 (1948). Editorials by the editor of *Minnesota Pioneer* are here reproduced. They reflect the viewpoint commonly held by the pioneer settler.

* † BLEGEN, THEODORE C., *Building Minnesota*, pp. 129–42.

BLEGEN, THEODORE C., and PHILIP D. JORDAN, *With Various Voices*, pp. 82–88. The speech of Henry H. Sibley before the Committee on Elections of the House of Representatives pleading for territorial status. See pp. 43–61 for on-the-spot descriptions of treaty negotiations at Traverse des Sioux, as well as word pictures of both white and Indian participants.

CHRISTIANSON, THEODORE, *Minnesota*, 1:171–90.

DAVIS, SAMUEL M., "The Dual Origin of Minnesota," Minnesota Historical Collections, 9:519–48 (1901).

* FOLWELL, WILLIAM W., *History*, 1:231–65, making Minnesota a territory; note the map, p. 247, showing the original counties of Minnesota Territory, 1849–51, reproduced herewith, p. 48. 1:257–59, 266–326, 457–59, 462–86, Indian affairs, 1841–55; note the map, p. 324, showing Indian cessions to 1858, also reproduced herewith, p. 49.

*———"Minnesota in 1849: An Imaginary Letter," *Minnesota History*, 6:34–40 (March, 1925). Phrased as if written by a pioneer in 1849, this letter gives a valuable description of Minnesota at that time.

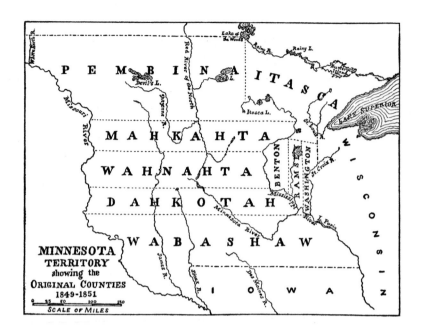

MINNESOTA TERRITORY showing the ORIGINAL COUNTIES 1849-1851

SCALE OF MILES

GOODHUE, JAMES M., "Indian Treaties," in William G. LeDuc, *Minnesota Year Book for 1852*, pp. 23–88 (1852), on the Traverse des Sioux negotiations.

HAMILTON, HOLMAN, "Zachary Taylor and Minnesota," *Minnesota History*, 30:97–110 (June, 1949). Onetime commander at Fort Snelling and in 1849 the President who appointed the first officers of Minnesota Territory.

* † HEILBRON, BERTHA L., *The Thirty-Second State*, pp. 70–85.

——— ed., *With Pen and Pencil on the Frontier in 1851*, pp. 145–89 (1932). The diary and sketches of Frank B. Mayer, who was at Traverse des Sioux in 1851.

——— "Frank B. Mayer and the Treaties of 1851," *Minnesota History*, 22:133–56 (June, 1941). A new version of the Mayer diary was unearthed in 1936. This article prints those portions of it not contained in the previous volume.

HOLCOMBE, RETURN I., *Minnesota in Three Centuries*. 2:335–469, the Wisconsin and Iowa boundaries of Minnesota, the creation of Minnesota Territory, and territorial politics to 1854. 2:207–18, 285–333, Winnebago, Sioux, and Chippewa relations with the government during the territorial period.

HUGHES, THOMAS, *Old Traverse des Sioux*, edited by Edward A. Johnson, pp. 33–102 (1929).

48

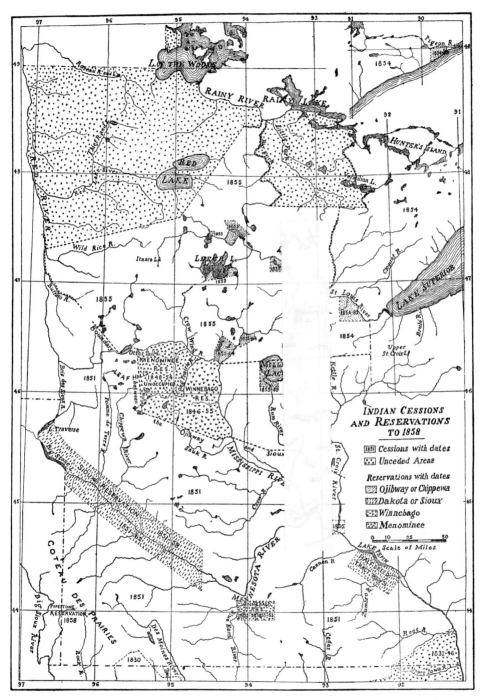

INDEX CESSIONS
AND RESERVATIONS
TO 1858

1851 Cessions with dates
Unceded Areas

Reservations with dates
Ojibway or Chippewa
Dakota or Sioux
Winnebago
Menominee

0   10   25   50
LAKE Scale of Miles

49

———— "The Treaty of Traverse des Sioux," Minnesota Historical Collections, vol. 10, part 1, pp. 101–29 (1905).

"Impressions of Minnesota in 1849," edited by Theodore C. Blegen, *Minnesota History Bulletin*, 5:286–90 (Nov., 1923). An Ohio visitor recorded his impressions in a letter home.

* KANE, LUCILE M., "The Sioux Treaties and the Traders," *Minnesota History*, 32:65–80 (June, 1951). Writing a century after the famous treaty, Miss Kane had new source material which led her to stress the interest which the fur traders had in the negotiations.

LYMAN, CLARA CROSS, "The World and Minnesota in 1849," *Minnesota History*, 30:185–201 (Sept., 1949). Pictures the international and national setting in which the territory was born.

Minnesota under Four Flags (1946). This pamphlet was prepared by Mary W. Berthel of the Minnesota Historical Society. Fifteen maps and text show successive changes from the Northwest Territory to Minnesota Territory.

MOSS, HENRY L., "Last Days of Wisconsin Territory and Early Days of Minnesota Territory," Minnesota Historical Collections, 8:67–88 (1898).

MURRAY, WILLIAM P., "Recollections of Early Territorial Days," Minnesota Historical Collections, 12:103–30 (1908).

"Organization of Minnesota Territory," Minnesota Historical Collections, 1:33–46 (1902 ed.). Details of the steps taken to secure the creation of Minnesota as a territory.

*† POATGIETER, A. H. and J. T. DUNN, *Gopher Reader*, pp. 33–35, 23–25. The series of treaties by which Minnesota's Indians sold their lands to the United States. Special attention is given to the Treaty of Traverse des Sioux in the second article.

Removal of the Winnebagoes (House Report No. 501, 31 Congress, 1 session, serial 585).

The Report of an Investigation of the Charges of Fraud and Misconduct in Office, Alleged against Alexander Ramsey, Superintendent of Indian Affairs in Minnesota (Senate Executive Document No. 61, 33 Congress, 1 session, serial 699).

RITCHEY, CHARLES J., "Martin McLeod and the Minnesota Valley," *Minnesota History*, 10:387–402 (Dec., 1929). How one fur trader regarded settlement.

ROBINSON, DOANE, *A History of the Dakota or Sioux Indians*, pp. 208–16. Treaties of Traverse des Sioux and Mendota.

ROYCE, CHARLES C., *Indian Land Cessions*, pp. 768–69, 780–81, 784–85, 792–97, 802–5. The land cessions of 1837, 1847, 1854, and 1855.

* SHORTRIDGE, WILSON P., *The Transition of a Typical Frontier*. Pp. 35–78, making the new territory. Pp. 91–119, the Indian problem.

SIBLEY, HENRY H., "Speech of Hon. H. H. Sibley, of Minn., before the Committee on Elections of the House of Representatives, Dec. 22, 1848," Minnesota Historical Collections, 1:47–54 (1902 ed.). Sibley skillfully presented the argument that a "Wisconsin Territory" existed after the admission of Wisconsin as a state. An interesting exposition of the frontier point of view.

Sioux Lands or Reservation in Minnesota Territory (House Report No. 138, 33 Congress, 1 session, serial 743). On the half-breed reservation.

* VAN KOUGHNET, DONALD E., "The Creation of the Territory," *Minnesota History*, 14:127–34 (June, 1933).

WINCHELL, ALEXANDER N., "Minnesota's Eastern, Southern, and Western Boundaries," Minnesota Historical Collections, vol. 10, part 2, pp. 677–87 (1905).

[IV. THE PIONEERS ORGANIZE A TERRITORY AND THEN A STATE]

12. *Rush for the "Suland": Land Laws and Protective Forts*

A. First Big Wave of Settlement

Increase in population, 1850–60. The two major streams of westward movement from the eastern seaboard: one to Kansas, one to Minnesota. States and foreign countries from whence these settlers came. Some factors promoting rapid settlement: organization of the territory, rich black dirt of "Suland," liberal land policies, boosting, increasing accessibility, organized settlement by companies, speculation, the wave of immigration to America, and the westward movement. Some factors hindering settlement: fear of the Minnesota winters, lure of California and other regions, geographical isolation of the Minnesota country. Securing the rich farm lands by purchase from the government or purchase from the speculator. Land laws in force: land acts of 1821 and 1841.

B. Modes and Routes of Travel to Minnesota

Steamboats on the Ohio and Mississippi. Trails, roads, covered wagon and stagecoach lines. Westward progress of railroad building. Completion of the Chicago and Rock Island Railroad to the Mississippi in 1854. The excursion of that year to St. Paul. Eastern visitors and their impressions. The Great Lakes.

C. Bringing in the People: The Program of Boosting and Promotion

Why advertising of the territory seemed necessary. Official promotion by the territorial government: distribution of pamphlets, the immigrant agent, the exhibition in New York's Crystal Palace. The rapid founding of newspapers, 1849–57; functions of the pioneer press (news organ, literary medium, boosting Minnesota, leadership in politics and culture); James M. Goodhue, origins, character, influence. Townsite speculation;

number of new towns platted; rivalries; dressing up the town (academies, mills, advertising brochures, newspapers); rise in land values; example of Ignatius Donnelly and Nininger City.

D. Characteristics of Territorial Settlement

Settlement by individuals and by organized groups. Districts settled: along the Mississippi River, along the Minnesota River, in the southeast triangle of the territory, in the "Delta Triangle." The organization of counties. New frontier military posts: Fort Ripley, 1849; Fort Ridgely, 1853; Fort Abercrombie, 1857. Temporary abandonment of Fort Snelling; sale to Franklin Steele, 1857; reoccupation during the Civil War. Agricultural development. Continuing importance of the three centers: Stillwater, St. Paul, St. Anthony–Minneapolis. Status of the squatter before and after 1854; the land-claim association and its relation to land survey and preemption. The beginnings of organization for the improvement of agriculture: the county agricultural societies, the territorial agricultural fair. The Panic of 1857 and the slowing down of settlement.

QUESTIONS AND SUGGESTIONS

1. Compare the population of Minnesota in 1850 and 1860 as to origins and distribution. If your ancestors came to Minnesota in this period try to find out why they came. Can you find any old letters or diaries telling of migration to Minnesota and early experiences here?

2. Note that the Homestead Act did not come until 1862, so that through the entire territorial period the settler had to buy his land, either under the terms of the land act of 1821 or from other individuals. Nor were railroad lands available until the 1860's. What were the provisions of the 1821 act? How much more would the settler be likely to pay if he bought his land from the speculator? In what way did the Preemption Act of 1841 affect the settler?

3. Describe the "ethics of the border" with reference to the acquisition of land by white settlers, taking illustrations especially from Minnesota history between 1849 and 1854. Compare the status of the squatter before and after 1854.

4. If you had come to Minnesota from Portland, Maine, in 1852 what route would you probably have followed? What methods of transportation might you have used in 1858?

5. Select a few issues of a newspaper published in the 1850's and classify their contents according to news (foreign, national, and local); editorials; literature (essays, poems, and stories); advertising (local and nonlocal). What proportion of the contents is political?

6. Subjects for investigation: The beginning of your town; an organized

colonization company project (e.g., Zumbrota, Excelsior, Garden City, Rolling Stone); the beginning of your county fair.

7. When did the "high tide" of American immigration in the 1850's occur? What nationalities contributed the greatest numbers to the American population between 1850 and 1860? Note the numbers of the leading foreign elements in Minnesota in 1860.

8. Why was the question of climate given so much attention in the official advertising of Minnesota in the 1850's?

9. Describe the work of the immigration agent stationed by the Territory of Minnesota at New York City.

10. "It is safe to say that in the three years from 1855 to 1857, inclusive, at least seven hundred towns were platted into more than three hundred thousand lots — enough for one and a half million people," states Dr. Folwell of the Minnesota situation (*History*, 1:362).

11. Nininger may be taken as an example of one of these "boom towns," a particularly good choice since so much has been written about it. Note the techniques of promotion used by the founders, its fabulous growth up to 1857, business and cultural institutions established or planned, the reasons why it faded and ultimately became a "ghost town." Remember that many another town succeeded.

12. Ignatius Donnelly reported that in that first year of growth of his boom town, Nininger City, he had reflected, "Here I am not yet twenty-six, and on the verge of a great fortune! How shall I ever be able to dispose of it?" Rather interesting in view of his activities for the next half century!

13. How did the Panic of 1857 affect Minnesota?

REFERENCES

APPEL, LIVIA, and THEODORE C. BLEGEN, eds., "Official Encouragement of Immigration to Minnesota in the Territorial Period," *Minnesota History Bulletin*, 5:167–203 (Aug., 1923). A collection of documents.

BABCOCK, CHARLES F., "Rails West: The Rock Island Excursion of 1854," *Minnesota History*, 34:133–43 (Winter, 1954). A newspaper reporter's account. About a thousand easterners made the trip to Minnesota Territory to publicize the first railroad contact with the Mississippi River.

BABCOCK, WILLOUGHBY M., ed., "Up the Minnesota Valley to Fort Ridgely in 1853," *Minnesota History*, 11:161–83 (June, 1930). A contemporary account of a steamboat trip up the Minnesota.

BALMER, FRANK E., "The Farmer and Minnesota History," *Minnesota History*, 7:199–217 (Sept., 1926). A good account of early agriculture.

BERTHEL, MARY W., *Horns of Thunder: The Life and Times of James M. Goodhue Including Selections from His Writings*. The best account of the stormy career of St. Paul's first newspaper editor. Extensive excerpts from the *Minnesota Pioneer* have been woven together by the author in the last part of the book and give an interesting report of conditions and events in and around St. Paul from 1849 to 1852.

* † BLEGEN, THEODORE C., *Building Minnesota*, pp. 143–51.

*———— *The Land Lies Open*, pp. 128–36. Town booming.

* BRAINARD, DUDLEY S., "Nininger, a Boom Town of the Fifties," *Minnesota History*, 13:127–51 (June, 1932).

* BROWN, RALPH H., "Fact and Fancy in Early Accounts of Minnesota's Climate," *Minnesota History*, 17:243–61 (Sept., 1936).

CHATELAIN, VERNE E., "The Federal Land Policy and Minnesota Politics, 1854–60," *Minnesota History*, 22:227–48 (Sept., 1941). Shows clearly the land laws in operation during the first great rush for land in the state.

* FOLWELL, WILLIAM W., *History*, 1:351–64, 2:64. Peopling the territory in the 1850's.

HARMON, RALPH L., "Ignatius Donnelly and His Faded Metropolis," *Minnesota History*, 17:262–75 (Sept., 1936).

* † HEILBRON, BERTHA L., *The Thirty-Second State*, pp. 86–93.

———— ed., "A 'Craven Lad' in Frontier Minnesota," *Minnesota History*, 27:281–99 (Dec., 1946). A firsthand report of conditions in territorial Minnesota by one who tried America for a few years and then returned to his British home.

† JOHNSON, H. NAT, *Minnesota Panorama*, pp. 18–26.

LARSEN, ARTHUR J., "Roads and Trails in the Minnesota Triangle," *Minnesota History*, 11:387–411 (Dec., 1930). The relation of roads to settlement.

LEDUC, WILLIAM G., "Minnesota at the Crystal Palace Exhibition, New York, 1853," *Minnesota History Bulletin*, 1:351–68 (Aug., 1916). A humorous and sprightly account. LeDuc had charge of the Minnesota exhibits at the Crystal Palace.

LOEHR, RODNEY C., "Franklin Steele, Frontier Businessman," *Minnesota History*, 27:309–18 (Dec., 1946). Lumberman, land speculator, townsite promoter, and frontier builder in early Minnesota.

MEYER, ROY W., "The Story of Forest Mills, a Midwest Milling Community," *Minnesota History*, 35:11–21 (March, 1956). Not all boom towns survived; some became ghost towns. Why? This article explains by taking one town and charting the changes.

PETERSEN, WILLIAM J., "The Rock Island Railroad Excursion of 1854," *Minnesota History*, 15:405–20 (Dec., 1934).

* † POATGIETER, A. H., and J. T. DUNN, *Gopher Reader*, pp. 79–80, 88–89, 98–101, 116–18. New frontier forts, promotional activity of land agencies, an open letter describing the territory and Minnesota's first editor, James M. Goodhue.

Prucha, F. Paul, "Fort Ripley: The Post and the Military Reservation," *Minnesota History*, 28:205–24 (Sept., 1947).

*———— "The Settler and the Army in Frontier Minnesota," *Minnesota History*, 29:231–46 (Sept., 1948).

Ritchey, Charles J., "Claim Associations and Pioneer Democracy in Early Minnesota," *Minnesota History*, 9:85–95 (June, 1928).

———— "Martin McLeod and the Minnesota Valley," *Minnesota History*, 10:387–402 (Dec., 1929). Traces the adaptation of a fur trader to the changing conditions caused by settlement.

Robinson, Edward Van Dyke, *Early Economic Conditions and the Development of Agriculture in Minnesota*, pp. 39–56. Settlement and the development of agriculture, 1838–60.

Roe, Herman, "The Frontier Press of Minnesota," *Minnesota History*, 14:393–410 (Dec., 1933).

Shortridge, Wilson P., *The Transition of a Typical Frontier*, pp. 70–90, 120–25. Note the two maps, p. 69 and 122, showing county boundaries in 1849 and 1855.

Snyder, Margaret, *The Chosen Valley: The Story of a Pioneer Town* (1948). A biography of Chatfield in southeastern Minnesota. Based on fact, it takes on the character of a novel because of the freedom with which the author interprets.

Tyler, Alice Felt, "William Pfaender and the Founding of New Ulm," *Minnesota History*, 30:24–35 (March, 1949). An excellent account of a group settlement.

Wesley, Edgar Bruce, *Owatonna: The Social Development of a Minnesota Community*. For an example of town building and speculation see pp. 8–24.

[IV. THE PIONEERS ORGANIZE A TERRITORY AND THEN A STATE]

13. *The Pioneer Commonwealth: Life, Customs, and Attitudes*

A. The Westward and Northern Movement of Minnesota's Frontier Line

Importance of recognizing that not all parts of the state had their "pioneer period" at the same time: the territorial period a pioneer period for the southeast triangle and the St. Croix triangle, with the frontier reaching the south central area, central region, southwest corner, Red River Valley, and northern Minnesota at different times from 1860 through the 1890's. Common features of all these pioneer areas. Justification then in using the territorial period as a pattern for all.

B. The Pioneer at Work and in the Home

Pioneer occupations: farming, lumbering, flour milling, merchandizing, the professions, and (in the 1880's and 1890's) mining. Dominance of the agricultural frontier. Need for adjusting to frontier conditions; self-sufficiency of each farm home unit; the farmer a jack-of-all-trades. Building the log cabin or sod house or frame home; home furnishings; frontier food; clothing; prices. Women and their tasks; child life. Transfer of eastern techniques and practices in virtually all occupations. Slow but steady improvement of conditions.

c. The Social and Cultural Life of the Pioneer

Isolation of the early agricultural frontier; loneliness. Frontier religion: lay preachers; early clergymen on circuit; erection of churches. Frontier education: territorial legislation for establishment and maintenance of common schools; the first country schools; training and pay of teachers; incorporation of the University of Minnesota, 1851; founding of Hamline, Macalester, St. John's, and other colleges; academies and seminaries. Prevalence of lyceums; their character and activities. Newspapers and books. The local newspaper as a cultural organ. Some early concerts: Ole Bull and Adelina Patti; musical troupes. Artists: Mississippi Valley panoramas. The church, school, and town as cultural centers. "Bridges Facing East": Minnesota's cultural contacts with the eastern United States. The stamp of New England upon Minnesota: strength of the Yankee influx during the territorial period; leadership of Yankees in town founding and governmental activity during the early period; New England social customs (the spelling bee, sewing circle, box social); piety and Puritanism (blue laws in pioneer days, the temperance movement).

D. Steamboats, Trails, and Roads

The rise of steamboating on the Mississippi, the St. Croix, and the Minnesota rivers: the *Virginia*, 1823, and the subsequent increase of steamboat traffic; cargoes up and down the Mississippi; excursions; lumber and logs; rafting on the St. Croix and Mississippi; steamboat companies; river towns (Stillwater, St. Paul, Winona); beginnings on the Minnesota River and settlement of the Minnesota River Valley. Trails to the northwest: trade relations between St. Paul and the Red River settlements; the Red River cart; the several trails; nature of the traffic; the railroad drives out the cart. Steamboats on the Red River: a brief period of activity because of difficulties of navigation and the coming of the railroad. Importance of the steamboat in the development of Minnesota: settlement; the lumber industry; opening the interior. The disappearance of the steamboat. Building a network of roads: the beginning of wagon roads in Minnesota; military roads — Mendota to Iowa, Mendota to Mankato, St. Paul to Superior; roads in southeastern Minnesota; importance of roads to the inland regions; pioneer demands for mail service and stagecoach communication; stagecoach lines and companies; express companies; the township district road act of 1858. National interest in railroad construction in the 1850's and the attitude of the pioneer in Minnesota toward the new mode of transportation; abortive railroad legislation of the 1850's and relation to the movement for statehood.

E. The Turner Interpretation of the Frontier as Applied to Minnesota Individualism. Attitude toward government. Pioneer democracy.

1. In what way would geography determine whether a pioneer settler might build himself a log cabin, sod house, or frame house?

2. Worth observing is pioneer self-sufficiency as revealed in the furnishing of the pioneer home and the provision for such needs as water, heat, lighting, beds, tables, chairs, varieties of food, and the preservation of food.

3. Contrast the sources and varieties of food used by the farmer of today with the pioneer settler of the 1850's.

4. The census of 1850 reports that the total number of servants in the territory was 15. The total population then was about 6,000. What does this tell about our pioneer population?

5. Was the pioneer sensitive to the need for education? How soon were school districts established? Schoolhouses? What was the length of the school year? How was the teacher paid? How much?

6. Could the newspaper in pioneer days serve as a social and cultural organ for both town and country? Explain.

7. With the phrase "personal journalism" as a point of departure, contrast the editorial policy of a pioneer newspaper with that of a modern newspaper. The Minnesota Historical Society has an outstanding collection of the state's newspapers, including, of course, many of the territorial papers. Perhaps your local library or newspaper has files which may be consulted.

8. What ties, economic, political, professional, and cultural, made the pioneer Minnesotan feel that he was an integral part of the nation, despite the fact that he lived on the western fringe of settlement?

9. How do you account for the fact that Minnesota, a frontier community, should have passed such laws as the territorial Sabbath law and the Maine law of 1852?

10. In an address before the Minnesota Historical Society, printed in the *Annals* for 1851, Governor Alexander Ramsey explained why it was not strange "that a Historical Society should have been formed in this Territory, less than a year after its organization . . . when the wilderness was . . . around us, when the smoke of Indian lodges still intercepted our view of the horizon, when our very name was so new that men dis-

puted as to its orthography and formed parties in contesting its literal meaning." The address is reprinted in Minnesota Historical Collections, 1:25–32 (1902).

11. Note the several trails commonly used by the pioneer in trade between Fort Snelling and the Red River region — Pembina and Fort Garry. See the map on p. 59 (from *Minnesota History*, September 1925).

12. What disadvantages for transportation existed in pioneer Minnesota? what advantages?

13. How extensive was the Mississippi River steamboat traffic to St. Paul before the Civil War?

14. What period is covered by the rise and decline of steamboating on the Minnesota River? What were the causes of the decline of that traffic?

15. What disadvantages did the upper Mississippi have as a commercial highway? Were these responsible for the decline of steamboat transportation?

16. The great classic on Mississippi steamboating is of course Mark Twain's *Life on the Mississippi*. An article by John T. Flanagan on Mark Twain's visits to the Minnesota region appears in the December, 1936, number of *Minnesota History* (17:369–84).

17. What are some of the characteristics of "frontier democracy"?

18. In Mr. Fish's article on "American Democracy" cited below, he speaks of three elements as having been deemed of prime importance in the American concept of democracy. What were they? Does it seem to you that Minnesota's pioneers regarded these as having equal importance?

19. The interpretation of American history advanced in 1893 by Frederick J. Turner in his famous essay on "The Significance of the Frontier in American History" should be examined by the student who wishes to understand the early history of this state. The essay, together with other notable studies, is included in Turner's *Frontier in American History* (1920). Note also Turner's article on "Middle Western Pioneer Democracy" in *Minnesota History*, 3:393–414 (Aug., 1920), and his volume on the *Significance of Sections in American History* (1920). In a brochure entitled *The Turner Thesis Concerning the Role of the Frontier in American History* (1949) and edited by George Rogers Taylor, the student will find nine articles by Turner, Paxson, Wright, and others on this theme.

REFERENCES

*† BABCOCK, WILLOUGHBY M., "The Historic Red River Trails," *Gopher Reader*, pp. 166–69.

——— "The St. Croix Valley as Viewed by Pioneer Editors," *Minnesota History*, 17:276–87 (Sept., 1936).

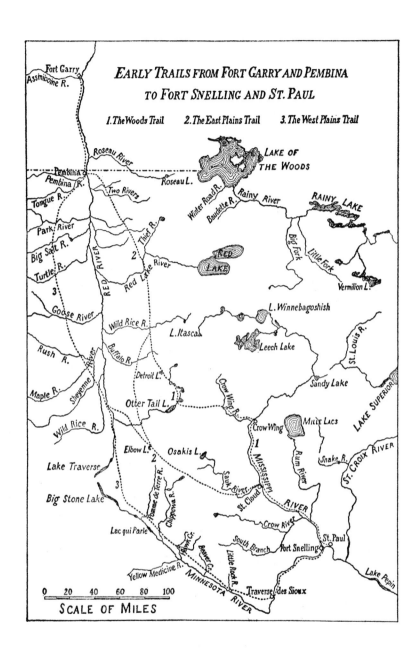

EARLY TRAILS FROM FORT GARRY AND PEMBINA
TO FORT SNELLING AND ST. PAUL

1. The Woods Trail   2. The East Plains Trail   3. The West Plains Trail

Fort Garry
Assiniboine R.

Roseau River
Pembina
Pembina R.
Two Rivers
Roseau L.
Tongue R.
Park River
Thief R.
Big Salt R.
Red Lake River
RED LAKE
Turtle R.
Goose River
Wild Rice R.
Rush R.
Buffalo R.
Sheyenne River
Maple R.
Detroit L.
Wild Rice R.
Otter Tail L.
Elbow L.
Osakis L.
Lake Traverse
Pomme de Terre R.
Chippewa R.
Big Stone Lake
Lac qui Parle
Hawk Cr.
Beaver Cr.
Little Rock R.
Yellow Medicine R.
MINNESOTA RIVER

LAKE OF THE WOODS
Winter Road R.
Baudette R.
Rainy River
RAINY LAKE
Big Fork
Little Fork
Vermilion L.

L. Winnebagoshish
L. Itasca
Leech Lake
St. Louis R.
Sandy Lake
Crow Wing R.
LAKE SUPERIOR
Crow Wing
MILLE LACS
Rum River
Snake R.
ST. CROIX RIVER
Mississippi
Sauk River
St. Cloud
RIVER
Crow River
South Branch
Fort Snelling
St. Paul
Lake Pepin
Traverse des Sioux

0   20   40   60   80   100
SCALE OF MILES

59

BELL, EDWIN, "Early Steamboating on the Minnesota and Red Rivers," Minnesota Historical Collections, vol. 10, part 1, pp. 91–100 (1905). Captain Bell ran the first steamboat to Fort Garry.

BERTHEL, MARY W., *Horns of Thunder*.

†———— "Minnesota's First Editor," *Gopher Historian*, 8:6–8 (Winter, 1953–54). A good brief account of Goodhue. The accompanying illustrations are excellent. Also found in Poatgieter and Dunn, *Gopher Reader*, pp. 116–18.

BLAKELEY, RUSSELL, "History of the Discovery of the Mississippi River and the Advent of Commerce in Minnesota," Minnesota Historical Collections, 8:375–418 (1898). Steamboating and related topics are discussed by a steamboat captain whose connection with the St. Paul traffic began in 1847. There are some illustrations of steamboats.

———— "Opening the Red River of the North to Commerce and Civilization," Minnesota Historical Collections, 8:45–66 (1898). A firsthand account.

* † BLEGEN, THEODORE C., *Building Minnesota*, pp. 152–86.

*———— "The Day of the Pioneer," *Minnesota History*, 14:134–42 (June, 1933).

———— "Henry H. Sibley, Pioneer of Culture and Frontier Author," *Minnesota History*, 15:362–94 (Dec., 1934).

*———— *The Land Lies Open*. Pp. 111–27, the taking up of land, and life in the early years. Pp. 137–50, contributions of the Yankees to Minnesota life.

*———— "Minnesota Pioneer Life as Revealed in Newspaper Advertisements," *Minnesota History*, 7:99–121 (June, 1926).

BLEGEN, THEODORE C., and PHILIP D. JORDAN, *With Various Voices*, pp. 216–22. Two brief but interesting accounts, one of St. Paul when the Territory of Minnesota was two years old, the other of how Minneapolis received its name.

BURRIS, EVADENE A., "Building the Pioneer Home," *Minnesota History*, 15:43–55 (March, 1934).

———— "Furnishing the Pioneer Home," *Minnesota History*, 15:181–93 (June, 1934).

*———— "Keeping House on the Minnesota Frontier," *Minnesota History*, 14:263–82 (Sept., 1933).

———— "Pioneer Food," *Minnesota History*, 14:378–92 (Dec., 1933). These four articles make fascinating reading. A scholarly and delightful study of everyday things.

CATHCART, REBECCA M., "A Sheaf of Remembrances," Minnesota Historical Collections, 15:516–52 (1915). Frontier society in St. Paul and Minneapolis.

Davis, LeRoy G., "Frontier Home Remedies and Sanitation," *Minnesota History*, 19:369–76 (Dec., 1938).

———— "Some Frontier Institutions," *Minnesota History*, 20:19–28 (March, 1939).

———— "Some Frontier Words and Phrases," *Minnesota History*, 19:241–46 (Sept., 1938).

Dingwall, Iva A., "Pioneers' Dinner Table," *Minnesota History*, 34:54–58 (Summer, 1954). The writer reminisces about foods and their preparation on a farm near Elk River in the 1870's and 1880's.

Dupre, Huntley, "E. D. Neill's Gospel of Minnesota (Including a Reprint of E. D. Neill's 'St. Paul and Its Environs')," *Minnesota History*, 30:202–19 (Sept., 1949). Dupre's sketch of this prominent early Minnesotan is good; so also is Neill's description of the capital in the middle 1850's.

Durant, Edward W., "Lumbering and Steamboating on the St. Croix River," Minnesota Historical Collections, vol. 10, part 2, pp. 663–72 (1905). Rafting logs and lumber.

* Eide, Richard B., "Minnesota Pioneer Life as Reflected in the Press," *Minnesota History*, 12:391–403 (Dec., 1931).

* Fawcett, Lois M., "Frontier Education," *Minnesota History*, 14:142–49 (June, 1933).

Fish, Carl R., "American Democracy," *Minnesota History Bulletin*, 3:251–72 (Feb., 1920).

Flanagan, John T., "Fredrika Bremer: Traveler and Prophet," *Minnesota History*, 20:129–39 (June, 1939). This Swedish novelist visited Minnesota in its first year as a territory. A report of that visit and of her impressions.

Flandrau, Charles E., "Reminiscences of Minnesota during the Territorial Period," Minnesota Historical Collections, 9:197–204 (1901). An interesting commentary on early social conditions, written by a notable pioneer personality.

Ford, Edwin H., "Early Newspapers: In Minnesota They Helped Prepare for Statehood," *Gopher Historian*, 6:6–7 (Jan., 1952).

———— "Southern Minnesota Pioneer Journalism: A Study of Four Newspapers of the 1850's," *Minnesota History*, 27:1–20 (March, 1946).

"Fredrika Bremer's New Scandinavia, Minnesota in 1850," *Minnesota History*, 31:148–57 (Sept., 1950). Reprints of significant sections of Miss Bremer's account in *Homes of the New World* of her visit to Minnesota in 1850.

* Gates, Charles M., "Bridges Facing East," *Minnesota History*, 16:22–34 (March, 1935). A thoughtful essay on cultural contacts between pioneer Minnesota and the East.

———— ed., "Tourist Traffic of Pioneer Minnesota," *Minnesota History*,

16:272–81 (Sept., 1935). Minnesota early became popular as a pleasure resort.

GOULD, EMERSON W., *Fifty Years on the Mississippi*, pp. 513–20, 572–90 (1889). Upper Mississippi packet companies. Discusses causes for the disappearance of the steamboats.

* HARTSOUGH, MILDRED L., *From Canoe to Steel Barge on the Upper Mississippi*, pp. 3–211 (1934). The whole book deals with the Mississippi River traffic. Pages 73–108 are especially valuable.

HEILBRON, BERTHA L., "Christmas and New Year's on the Frontier," *Minnesota History*, 16:373–90 (Dec., 1935). Charming descriptions of the two holidays as celebrated in pioneer Minnesota.

*† —— *The Thirty-Second State*, pp. 94–116.

HOLMES, FRANK R., *Minnesota in Three Centuries* (1908). 4:317–36, river and lake navigation. 4:307–16, 337–50, early roads, mail routes, and railroads.

HUGHES, THOMAS, "History of Steamboating on the Minnesota River," Minnesota Historical Collections, vol. 10, part 1, pp. 131–63 (1905).

KANE, LUCILE M., "Governing a Frontier City: Old St. Anthony, 1855–72," *Minnesota History*, 35:117–29 (Sept., 1956). St. Anthony merged with Minneapolis in 1872.

* LARSEN, ARTHUR J., "Early Transportation," *Minnesota History*, 14:149–55 (June, 1933). An excellent brief account.

* —— "Roads and Settlement of Minnesota," *Minnesota History*, 21:225–44 (Sept., 1940). Deals essentially with the first two decades of settlement.

* —— "Roads and Trails in the Minnesota Triangle," *Minnesota History*, 11:387–411 (Dec., 1930). The triangle is bounded by Iowa, the Mississippi, and the Minnesota–Blue Earth rivers. Mr. Larsen's maps are reproduced on p. 63.

—— ed., *Crusader and Feminist: Letters of Jane Grey Swisshelm, 1858–1865*, pp. 33–52 (1934). Central Minnesota life in the 1850's.

LOVELACE, MAUD and DELOS, *One Stayed at Welcome* (1934). A novel. It portrays pioneer life in Minnesota during the territorial period.

McDERMOTT, JOHN FRANCIS, ed., "Minnesota 100 Years Ago (Described and Pictured by Adolf Hoeffler)," *Minnesota History*, 33:112–25 (Autumn, 1952). A traveler's account.

*† McDONALD, SISTER GRACE, "Pioneer Churchman and Missionary to the Indians — Father Francis Pierz," *Gopher Historian*, 12:30 (Winter, 1957–58). A brief account of Pierz's work among the Indians and his promotion of settlement.

MATTSON, HANS, *Reminiscences: The Story of an Immigrant*, pp. 34–58

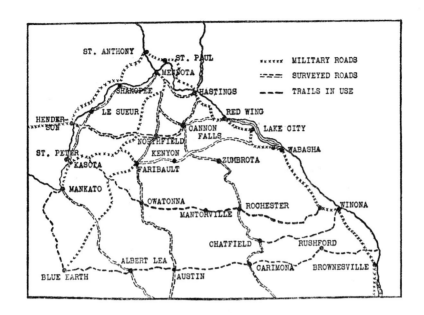

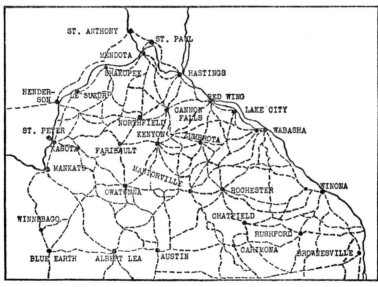

Roads in Southeastern Minnesota, 1854 (above) and 1860

(1892). A Swedish immigrant's experiences in founding a home in Minnesota.

MORTON, ZYLPHA S., "Harriet Bishop, Frontier Teacher," *Minnesota History*, 28:132–41 (June, 1947). A delightful sketch of this first teacher of an organized school in St. Paul.

* NUTE, GRACE LEE, "The Red River Trails," *Minnesota History*, 6:279–82 (Sept., 1925).

*———— "Wilderness Marthas," *Minnesota History*, 8:247–59 (Sept., 1927). Extremely interesting. Women and the home on the frontier, illustrated chiefly from the letters and diaries of missionaries.

PENDERGAST, WILLIAM W., "Sketches of the History of Hutchinson," Minnesota Historical Collections, vol. 10, part 1, pp. 69–78 (1905).

* PETERSEN, WILLIAM J., "The Early History of Steamboating on the Minnesota River," *Minnesota History*, 11:123–44 (June, 1930).

———— "Steamboating in the Upper Mississippi Fur Trade," *Minnesota History*, 13:221–43 (Sept., 1932).

*———— "The 'Virginia,' the 'Clermont' of the Upper Mississippi," *Minnesota History*, 9:347–62 (Dec., 1928). A highly interesting account of the first steamboat voyage to Fort Snelling.

*† POATGIETER, A. H., and J. T. DUNN, *Gopher Reader*, pp. 90–107, 160–71. Pioneer home life, education, and transportation.

POTTER, MERLE, "Joseph R. Brown and His Steam Wagon," *Gopher Historian*, 5:15–16 (May, 1951). Brown was a pioneer Minnesotan.

PRIMMER, GEORGE H., "Pioneer Roads Centering at Duluth," *Minnesota History*, 16:282–99 (Sept., 1935). Has an excellent map of pioneer roads centering at the head of Lake Superior.

PRUCHA, FRANCIS PAUL, "Minnesota 100 Years Ago, as Seen by Laurence Oliphant," *Minnesota History*, 34:45–53 (Summer, 1954). A highly readable account by an English writer and world traveler of his journey from Lake Superior down the Mississippi to St. Paul in 1854. Has sparkle, humor, keen observation, and prediction.

ROBINSON, EDWARD VAN DYKE, *Early Economic Conditions and the Development of Agriculture in Minnesota*. Pp. 27–32, canoe and steamboat transportation (note the map showing portages and canoe routes); the Red River cart. Pp. 33–38, wagons and railroads. Especially valuable for the maps.

SHIPPEE, LESTER B., "Steamboating on the Upper Mississippi after the Civil War: A Mississippi Magnate," *Mississippi Valley Historical Review*, 6:470–502 (March, 1920). The magnate was Commodore William F. Davidson, one of the most picturesque figures in the history of the river.

*† SPELTZ, FLORENCE, "Harriet Bishop, Frontier Teacher," *Gopher Historian*, 12:26 (Winter, 1957–58). A brief outline biography.

STEENSMA, ROBERT, "Rölvaag and Turner's Frontier Thesis," *North Dakota Quarterly*, 27:100–4 (Autumn, 1959).

TURNER, FREDERICK J., "Middle Western Pioneer Democracy," *Minnesota History Bulletin*, 3:393–414 (Aug., 1920).

[IV. THE PIONEERS ORGANIZE A TERRITORY AND THEN A STATE]

14. *Territorial Politics and the Movement for Statehood*

A. Frontier Politics

Two periods: 1849–54 characterized by lackluster partisanship, Democrats vs. Whigs; 1854–58, by lively partisanship, Democrats vs. Republicans. Preponderance of Democrats in territorial Minnesota; Sibley and Rice. Territorial governors, territorial delegates. National issues and developments: Kansas-Nebraska Act; formation of the Republican party. Public reaction in Minnesota to repeal of the Missouri Compromise. The slavery versus free land issue in the formation of the Republican party in Minnesota. The "friends of freedom" at St. Anthony. Organization of the Republican party; John W. North and Charles G. Ames. County and territorial conventions. Program of the party. Elements joining the new party.

B. Preliminaries to Statehood

Factors accounting for the movement: Northwest Ordinance of 1787, which furnished the pattern; growth of population and political maturity; federal land grants; railroad plans; political ambitions of certain leaders. Growing importance of railroad interests after the 1854 land-grant reversal. Rival schemes for state boundaries: a north-south vs. east-west state. The issues involved in the two proposals: railroads, politics. Seizure of initiative by Democrat Henry M. Rice. Rice's two bills: Enabling Act of February 25, 1857, and Act Chartering Six Minnesota Railroads, March 3, 1857.

C. A Frontier Farce

Willis A. Gorman and the St. Peter Land Company. Joe Rolette and the failure of the attempt to move the capital.

D. The Enabling Act

Provisions: boundaries of the state; election of delegates to vote on admission and to form a constitution; a census; reservation of public lands for schools, university, highways, and other purposes. Amount of public lands reserved. Modification of Enabling Act provisions by Gorman's special session of the territorial legislature. Beginnings here of a comedy of irregularities.

E. The Constitutional Convention

Election of delegates. Number elected and seated. Party affiliations. The two constitutional conventions and their work. Methods by which agreement was reached. The compromise committee and its work. One constitution, but two copies adopted.

F. The Election of October 13, 1857

Issues: adoption of the constitution and control of the state government. The Democratic victory. More irregularities: character of the ballot on ratification, fraudulent voting, election of three congressmen when population entitled Minnesota to only two. The census of 1857. The state legislature meets before Minnesota is admitted to the Union. Method of procedure. Measures. Amendments to the constitution before admittance. Election of Senators Rice and Shields.

G. Congress and the Act of Admission

The Kansas question and the delay in admitting Minnesota. Minnesota's senators and congressmen wait in Washington, D.C. Three congressmen cut to two. The debate on admission. The act passed, May 11, 1858. Minnesota's reception of the news of admission. The excluded area of Minnesota.

QUESTIONS AND SUGGESTIONS

1. Were party lines sharply drawn throughout the territorial period in Minnesota? Did the "fur" and "anti-fur" groups come into being because of attachment to national issues or local persons? Which party tended to wield greater power during the nine years of the territorial period? The passage by Congress of the Kansas-Nebraska Act (1854) affected politics markedly in the national sphere. How did it affect Minnesota politics?

2. The Republican party is the outstanding example of a third party which pushed aside one of the two major parties to become itself one of the country's two major parties. Were Minnesotans active in its beginnings? Who joined the new Republican party in Minnesota? What kind of platform did Minnesota Republicans draw up? What evidence is there of Puritanism in the early Republican party of Minnesota?

3. What factors or forces were responsible for the movement for statehood in Minnesota?

4. What advantages for railroad promoters did statehood have over a territorial status?

5. In 1821, following the Missouri Compromise, northern and southern states were balanced at twelve each. By 1848, three states had been added by each section. What states were admitted between 1848 and 1860? How many of these were free? How many slave? Did this have a bearing on Minnesota's movement toward statehood?

6. Note the sharp play of politics on the part of Henry M. Rice in his han-

dling of the two issues of boundaries and railroads in the Enabling Act and the Railroad Act of 1857.

7. What sectional, political, and economic rivalries were involved in the proposal to make Minnesota an east-west rather than a north-south state?

8. Note how extensive Minnesota's land grants were under the terms of the Enabling Act.

9. "The story of the entrance of Minnesota into the Union with its irregularities, procrastination, tricks, and blunders teaches the facility with which democracies may overcome such obstacles and reach their reasonable ends," writes Dr. Folwell. Give examples for each of the four categories named. Do you agree with Dr. Folwell's generalization?

10. Explain the partisan feeling in the election of delegates to the constitutional convention in the summer of 1857.

11. Be sure you understand why the convention split into two rival wings. What were the issues? compromise settlements?

12. Compare the rival conventions as to the geographical origins of the members.

13. Explain why "it is impossible today to print an absolutely correct text of the state constitution." Texts of the constitution are given in each issue of the *Legislative Manual* and in Anderson and Lobb, *A History of the Constitution of Minnesota*.

14. Would it be correct to say that Minnesota's constitution was an original document?

15. You have noted irregularities in Minnesota's convention of 1857. Were there irregularities in the first state election, that of October 13, 1857? in the first session of the state legislature which began meeting December 2, 1857 — "the ambiguous legislature"?

16. Why was the admission of Minnesota delayed from October 13, 1857 — the date of the adoption of the constitution by the Minnesota electorate — until nearly seven months later?

17. What parallels can you find between the excluded portion of Wisconsin in 1849 and the excluded portion of Minnesota in 1858?

18. Map exercise: Use two outline maps of the upper Mississippi area to depict (a) the several boundary proposals advanced during Iowa's movement toward statehood, including the one which finally fixed Minnesota's southern border, (b) the several boundary proposals advanced during Wisconsin's movement toward statehood, including the one which fixed Minnesota's eastern border. Consult Anderson and Lobb, *History of the Constitution of Minnesota*, pp. 15, 18, 20.

19. Map exercise: On an outline map of the upper Mississippi area draw in (a) two or three of the boundary lines proposed by those who wanted an

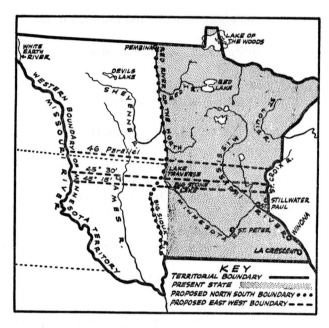

east-west line for Minnesota, (b) the north-south border originally proposed by Henry M. Rice and the line as actually drawn in the Enabling Act. Consult Anderson and Lobb, *History of the Constitution of Minnesota*, p. 48; Anderson, "Minnesota Frames a Constitution." A map from this latter article is reproduced above.

20. Map exercise: On an outline map of Minnesota show the routes of the six railroads chartered in Rice's act of 1857. Note the map on p. 105 of this outline.

REFERENCES

* ANDERSON, WILLIAM, "Minnesota Frames a Constitution," *Minnesota History*, 36:1–12 (March, 1958). The finest brief treatment available on the movement for the state constitution, by an eminent authority. Based on the Anderson and Lobb study cited below.

——— *Intergovernmental Relations in Review*, pp. 34–40 (1960). Emphasizes the play of the national government in Minnesota affairs, pre-territorial and territorial. Much attention is given to the movement for statehood. A brilliant interpretation.

ANDERSON, WILLIAM, with the assistance of WAITE D. DURFEE, JR., and staff, *Intergovernmental Fiscal Relations*, pp. 18–28 (1956). Research Monograph No. 8 in Intergovernmental Relations Series. Discusses financial support for Minnesota from the federal government during pre-territorial, territorial, and early statehood periods.

* Anderson, William, and Albert J. Lobb, *A History of the Constitution of Minnesota.* Pp. 29–55, territorial politics and plans for forming the new state. Pp. 55–143, an invaluable study of the constitution and the events preceding its adoption.

† Babcock, Willoughby M., "Distinguished Pioneer: Joseph Renshaw Brown," *Gopher Historian,* 12:19 (Winter, 1957–58). A brief outline biography.

* † Blegen, Theodore C., *Building Minnesota,* pp. 189–200.

Blegen, Theodore C., and Philip D. Jordan, *With Various Voices,* pp. 88–95. Southern opposition to statehood for Minnesota is revealed in this rabid speech by Senator John G. Thompson of Kentucky.

† Bray, Martha, "Franklin Steele," *Gopher Historian,* 12:21 (Winter, 1957–58). A brief outline biography.

Brown, Robert M., "Minnesota's Good Friend in Washington," *Gopher Historian,* 6:8, 9, 23 (Dec., 1951). Henry H. Sibley's work as territorial representative.

———"A Territorial Delegate in Action," *Minnesota History,* 31:172–78 (Sept., 1950). An account of Sibley's Washington, D.C., activities from 1849 to 1853.

Castle, Henry A., "General James Shields, Soldier, Orator, Statesman," Minnesota Historical Collections, 15:711–30 (1915).

Christianson, Theodore, *Minnesota,* 1:255–97.

"The Excluded Portion of Minnesota," *Minnesota History Bulletin,* 5:205–7 (Aug., 1932).

* Folwell, William W., *History.* 1:327–50, 365–87, railroad and other politics during the territorial period. 1:388–421, 486–502; 2:1–58, 355–61, statehood for Minnesota and state politics.

* Forrest, Robert J., "Mythical Cities of Southwestern Minnesota," *Minnesota History,* 14:243–62 (Sept., 1933).

Furness, Marion Ramsey, "Governor Ramsey and Frontier Minnesota: Impressions from His Diary and Letters," *Minnesota History,* 28:309–28 (Dec., 1947). The daughter of Minnesota's first governor here provides a fascinating description of the fifteen years following 1849. It is largely in Ramsey's own words, quotations from his diary and other papers.

"The Genesis of the Republican Party in Minnesota," *Minnesota History Bulletin,* 2:24–30 (Feb., 1917).

Gilfillan, Charles D., "The Early Political History of Minnesota," Minnesota Historical Collections (1901). 9:167–74, territorial politics. 9:174–80, constitutional conventions and early political figures.

* † Heilbron, Bertha L., *The Thirty-Second State,* pp. 117–24.

——— ed., "Minnesota Statehood Editorials," *Minnesota History,* 14:173–91 (June, 1933).

HOLCOMBE, RETURN I., *Minnesota in Three Centuries.* 2:435–513, territorial politics discussed by legislative sessions. 3:29–78, constitutional conventions and admission as a state.

HOLMQUIST, JUNE D., "Laws and Lawmakers," *Gopher Historian*, 5:20–21 (Feb., 1951). Some activities of the territorial legislature.

† JOHNSON, H. NAT, *Minnesota Panorama*, pp. 27–32.

* † JORSTAD, ERLING, "Henry Mower Rice," *Gopher Historian*, 12:18 (Winter, 1957–58). A brief outline biography.

———— "Personal Politics in the Origin of Minnesota's Democratic Party," *Minnesota History*, 36:259–71 (Sept., 1959). Territorial politics with particular attention to the Sibley-Rice rivalry.

* LARSEN, ARTHUR J., "Admission to the Union," *Minnesota History*, 14: 156–65 (June, 1933).

* † MARTINSON, FLORA P., "Minnesota's Territorial Legislature," *Gopher Historian*, 11:6–9 (Winter, 1956–57). A brief survey; readable. Contains illustrations. Also found in Poatgieter and Dunn, *Gopher Reader*, pp. 258–62.

MORAN, THOMAS F., "How Minnesota Became a State," Minnesota Historical Collections, 8:148–84 (1898).

* † POATGIETER, A. H., and J. T. DUNN, *Gopher Reader*, pp. 257–62, 263–65. Joe Rolette and the attempt to move the capital. Also activities of the territorial legislature.

* † QUALEY, CARLTON C., "Founder of Northfield — John Wesley North," *Gopher Historian*, 12:24 (Winter, 1957–58). A brief outline biography.

* ———— "John Wesley North and the Minnesota Frontier," *Minnesota History*, 35:101–16 (Sept., 1956). On one of the founders of the Republican party in Minnesota and of the town of Northfield.

SHORTRIDGE, WILSON P., *The Transition of a Typical Frontier*, pp. 120–31. Territorial growth and politics, with special reference to Sibley.

* † "The Story of Statehood," *Gopher Historian*, 12:1–27 (Fall, 1957). The entire issue is devoted to describing the movement for statehood. A timetable of key events, a map of the United States showing slave and free states in 1858, and a number of illustrations are included. Various phases of the movement are dealt with in the following articles: Philip D. Jordan, "The United States in 1858," pp. 1, 4. Russell W. Fridley, "Minnesota Starts on the Way to Statehood," pp. 5, 7, 8. "Electing the Men Who Made Minnesota's Constitution," p. 9. William Anderson, "Minnesota's Split Constitutional Convention," pp. 10–13. Erling Jorstad, "The Amazing Election for First State Governor," pp. 14–16. F. Sanford Cutler, "The State Legislature Which Had No State," pp. 17, 18. Frances Urevig, "Minnesota's First Senators and Representatives in Washington," pp. 19, 20. Jay Edgerton, "The North Star State Enters the Union," pp.

21, 22. Bertha Heilbron, "Glorious News! — a Century Ago," pp. 23, 24.
Roy P. Johnson, "Joe Rolette and the Capital Scandal," pp. 25–27.

[IV. THE PIONEERS ORGANIZE A TERRITORY AND THEN A STATE]

15. *The Government of Minnesota*

A. The Constitution

Similarity to other state constitutions. Similarity to the federal Constitution: the three departments (executive, legislative, and judicial);
checks and balances. Length as compared with that of the federal Constitution. The amending process — liberal up to 1898; tighter since 1898.
Extent of amendments. Importance of areas of government reserved to
states by the Tenth Amendment of the federal Constitution. Authority
exercised by the state in areas which come close to the lives of the people: marriage, education, health, morals, safety, the professions, and
many more.

B. The Legislative Department

The bicameral tradition. Frequency and length of sessions. Size of Senate and House compared with the two chambers of other states. Qualifications, length of term, and nonpartisan election of senators and representatives. Primary and general elections. The role of parties. Organization of the two chambers. How laws are made. Importance of committees.
Lobbying. Relation of the governor to the legislative process. Special
powers of the House; the Senate. The role of interim committees.

C. The Executive Department

A six-headed executive department established by the constitution and
administrative departments, boards, and commissions established by
legislative enactment. The governor, chief executive; his relationship to
the other five top executive officers different from that of the President
of the United States to his cabinet. Qualifications, election, and term of
office of the governor. His powers: administrative, legislative, judicial.
Variation in power and influence with each governor's interpretation of
his office. Duties of the five other members of the "top six." Evolution
of the administrative departments; importance of the Reorganization
Act of 1939 (amended in 1953); the five departments of administration,
public examiner, taxation, public welfare, and employment security.
Great power wielded by the Department of Administration and its head,
the commissioner of administration. The Department of Civil Service.

D. The Judicial Department

Original constitutional provisions modified by amendments; special importance of the amendment of 1956. The central system: one supreme
court and ten district courts. The local system: probate court, municipal

71

courts, justices of the peace. Relationship between the legislature and the judicial system. Judicial procedure.

E. Public Welfare Activities

Education: the public school system (types of school districts; the state Board of Education and the state Department of Education); school aids and the trust funds; the state colleges (the State College Board); the University of Minnesota (the Board of Regents). Health and correction: the state Board of Health; mental hospitals; state sanatorium; schools for the feeble-minded, blind, deaf; homes for children; reformatories and state prison. Conservation: Youth Conservation Commission; state parks and forests. Aid: old age, unemployment, maternity, crippled and handicapped children; relation to federal government.

F. Finances of the State Government

Variety of taxes: general property, individual income, corporate income, gasoline, tobacco, inheritance, gift, bank excise, iron ore occupation and royalty, gross earnings of certain industries, money and credits, and others. Relation to the federal tax program. Tax collection agency, the Department of Taxation. Other income: interest earned, department earnings, United States grants-in-aid. The question of dedicated taxes. Expenditures made under the watchful scrutiny of the Department of Administration.

G. Local Government

Units: township (town), county, village, city. Township government a heritage from New England. Officers of the township; the town meeting; extent of governmental authorization; trend toward decreasing activity. Counties: establishment by legislative enactment from 1851 to 1910; their number and size; the county board and its functions; the eleven county officers and their functions. Continuing importance of county government. Are there too many counties? Villages: the village code of 1949 established by the legislature; four patterns of government, one standard and widely used, the other three optional. Cities: the four classes; the forms of government — weak mayor council, strong mayor council, council-manager, and commission. The role of parties.

QUESTIONS AND SUGGESTIONS

1. The similarity of state constitutions, one to the other, would suggest a common ancestry. How far back in history would one go to find the original pattern?
2. The "bicameral tradition" is an example of what is suggested in question 1. Trace this feature to its origins.
3. Only one state has a unicameral legislature. Are the people of this state satisfied with the way it works?

4. The length of Minnesota's constitution could be compared with the federal Constitution by consulting the *Legislative Manual, 1957–1958*, pp. 382–400 and 409–16. Does the difference in length seem justifiable?

5. With reference to the amending process which Minnesota has had since 1898, it is said that a failure to vote on an amendment is tantamount to a "no" vote on that amendment. Explain.

6. Would you say that the sovereign powers of the state are "definitely prescribed" or "left fairly broad" by the Tenth Amendment to the federal Constitution?

7. From 1787 to the present, the trend in America's history has been for the national government to assume more and more power at the expense of the state government. Many are disturbed at this trend because they feel that democracy has its real strength in local government. Do you agree?

8. Every other year the state legislature has ninety days to do its lawmaking. Originally, the constitution set no time limit to legislative sessions. An amendment, ratified in 1860, set it at sixty days. The present ninety-day limit was set by amendment in 1888. Does a ninety-day session seem adequate today?

9. Why were primary elections introduced into the state?

10. Minnesota is unusual in that the members of its legislature are elected on a nonpartisan ballot. Yet, when each house organizes it breaks into Conservative and Liberal factions. Explain. If this were to be changed, would it be by constitutional amendment or legislative enactment?

11. How does the size of Minnesota's legislature compare with that of other state legislatures?

12. Trace a bill from its introduction into one of the chambers to its final signature by the governor.

13. Not all the machinery of government is set up by constitutional provision. Legislative enactment may account for a great deal of it. An example: the Reorganization Act of 1939 (modified in 1953). Its provisions radically altered the state administrative organization, and should be carefully studied.

14. What are the chief duties of the commissioner of administration?

15. How did the amendment of 1956 seek to modernize the judicial system of the state? This amendment replaced Article VI.

16. An excellent chart on state government income may be found in the *Legislative Manual, 1957–1958*, pp. 654–55.

17. With respect to the permanent trust funds of the state: (a) How did they come into being? (b) From what sources has the money come? (c) How and for what is this money used? (d) How did amendment Sec. 1A to

Article IX, adopted November 6, 1956, alter the manner in which proceeds from the iron ore occupation tax are to be used?

REFERENCES

ADRIAN, CHARLES R., "The Origin of Minnesota's Nonpartisan Legislature," *Minnesota History*, 33:155–63 (Winter, 1952).

ANDERSON, WILLIAM, *The Nation and the States, Rivals or Partners?* (1955). Mr. Anderson served on President Eisenhower's Intergovernmental Relations Commission. This is an expansion of his report to that commission. He supports the partnership theory and holds that there is no need to fear overcentralization or bigness so long as the people are in control of both federal and state governments.

———*Intergovernmental Relations in Review.* Pp. 53–64, national-state legislative relationships; the growing interdependence of national and state legislation; its meaning. Pp. 89–111, relations of the national government with smaller units of government within states. The treatment is not specifically on Minnesota but is applicable.

———"The Need for Constitutional Revision in Minnesota," *Minnesota Law Review*, 11:189–216 (Feb., 1927).

BLAKEY, ROY G., and ASSOCIATES, *Taxation in Minnesota* (1932). Some tax history, but primarily an analysis of the state's tax structure.

BROWN, ROBERT A., "The Great Seal of the State of Minnesota," *Minnesota History*, 33:126–29 (Autumn, 1952).

† FISHER, FRED W., "Leaders in Law," *Gopher Historian*, 5:11, 14 (Dec., 1950). Courts and lawyers of the territorial and early statehood period.

† GILLEN, ARTHUR, "A Day in the Minnesota Senate," *Gopher Historian*, 7:3–5 (Feb., 1953). A senator tells of the legislative process.

*† KISE, JOSEPH, *Minnesota's Government* (1958). Written to satisfy ninth-grade needs in the public schools. Pp. 70–155, aspects of state government. Pp. 18–69, local government. Brief, concise; the best treatment available on the structure of government.

* *Legislative Manual, State of Minnesota, 1957–1958.* This particular issue marked a new trend. The *Manual* ceased being a mere compilation of facts and became an informative volume on state government. Statements of functions and services are brief, but to the point. Consult pp. 19–32, 92–93, 134 for the legislature; pp. 135–36, 139–41, 143, 145–46, 148–49, 151, 154–55 for the "top six" executive offices; pp. 157–58 for the Department of Administration; pp. 250–53, 256–64 for the judiciary; pp. 285–94 for education; pp. 295–310 for conservation and state institutions; p. 447 for cities and villages; pp. 503–6 for political parties.

* *Legislative Manual, State of Minnesota, 1959–1960: Special Edition for Young Readers.* Contains the same material referred to in the volume

74

cited above brought together in a small pamphlet of 64 pages. Published primarily for school use. It is inexpensive, and several copies ought to be in each social studies classroom of the state.

* MITAU, G. THEODORE, *Politics in Minnesota*, pp. 34–79 (1960). The functioning of parties in elections and in sessions of the legislature. An excellent discussion of the practical workings of given phases of Minnesota government.

* NELSON, LOWRY, *The Minnesota Community: Country and Town in Transition*, pp. 99–113 (1960). The workings of local government — in county, town, incorporated village, and school district. Trends in local government.

O'BRIEN, C. D., III, "Who Owns Minnesota's Lakes? The Inter-action of Public and Private Rights," *Conservation Volunteer*, 7:6–10, 38–42 (Jan.–Feb., March–April, 1944). Mr. O'Brien was special counsel for the Department of Conservation of the state of Minnesota.

Report of the Constitutional Commission of Minnesota (1948).

* *Report of the Governor's Minnesota Tax Study Committee, 1956.* The essential tax changes through the state's history and a detailed analysis of the present tax structure.

SHORT, LLOYD M., CLARA PENNIMAN, and FLOYD O. FLOM, *The Minnesota Department of Taxation: An Administrative History* (1955).

*† "The State Capitol" and "Minnesota Emblems: The State Flag, the State Flower, the State Song, the State Tree, and the State and Territorial Seals," *Gopher Historian*, 12:5–14 (Winter, 1957–58).

The State You're In (1956). A pamphlet of 83 pages published by the League of Women Voters of Minnesota. Its main aim: to build a case in support of a convention to revise the state's constitution. Pages 1–21 give background on how Minnesota's constitution was formed. Pages 23–83 describe the various branches of government, with weaknesses always stressed in order to encourage sentiment in favor of revision. While written with this point of view always in mind, it is ably done.

* *You Are the Government: A Handbook of Minnesota Citizens*, (1949 and a thoroughgoing revision in 1958). Compiled by the League of Women Voters of St. Paul. Deals with the fundamentals of state and local government and the ways in which the citizen may play a proper role in his government.

[IV. THE PIONEERS ORGANIZE A TERRITORY AND THEN A STATE]

16. *Trials of the New State: Panic, Civil War, and Sioux Uprising*

A. Minnesota's Response to Slavery, Sectionalism, and the New Republican Party

Dred Scott at Fort Snelling; the Dred Scott Decision. Opinion on the slavery controversy in Minnesota. Negro slavery in Minnesota. Jane Grey Swisshelm, an antislavery crusader. Failure of the legislature elected in 1858 to meet. The campaign of 1859; Carl Schurz and other national figures visit Minnesota. Election of Ramsey as governor, Ignatius Donnelly as lieutenant governor. A Republican state legislature. The presidential campaign of 1860: issues, attitude toward Lincoln, visit of Seward, Republican efforts to capture the immigrant vote, results.

B. Economic Conditions in Minnesota on the Eve of the Civil War

Continuance of the depression of 1857. Its effect on the state's credit, immigration, town development, railroad building, and business. Ramsey's inaugural message of 1860. Legislative measures. Foreclosing on the railroads.

C. Minnesota's Role in the Civil War

National drift toward "the irrepressible conflict." Divergent views of Rice and Wilkinson in the Senate, 1860–61, with the state legislature supporting the position of Wilkinson. Ramsey's offer of men. The "First Minnesota." The contribution of the state to the military successes of the North. Volunteering. Training and outfitting the troops. The draft in 1864. The return of the troops. Politics during the war: elections of 1862 and 1863; presidential election of 1864 (Lincoln carries the state by an 8,000 majority); new governors (Stephen Miller and W. R. Marshall); new faces in Washington, D.C. (William Windom as representative, Ramsey as senator; Donelly as representative, Daniel S. Norton as senator).

D. The Sioux Uprising of 1862: Its Background and Immediate Causes

Two observations worthy of note: (1) The uprising was not an isolated event; there were others in the nation in the 1860's. (2) Today's interpretation of the episode is more charitable to the Indian than that of the frontiersman; it is now viewed as an aspect of a minority problem. Background factors: traditional Indian and land policy of the United States; unfairness of the treaty system as a means of dealing with the Indians; traders' papers; relentless push of whites for land to the destruction of the Indian's way of life; the agency system, in which agents were too often venal; demoralization of the Indians through liquor and sex; overconfidence of the Sioux, the Inkpaduta massacre, and absence of troops in the Civil War. Immediate causes: poverty and near starvation of the Indians; delay in annuity payments; demonstration at the Yellow Medicine (upper) agency; trouble at the Redwood (lower) agency; the Acton murders; the final order.

E. The Sioux Uprising of 1862: Its Course and Aftermath

Extent of the uprising. Massacres. The campaign of 1862. Fort Ridgely, New Ulm, Birch Cooley, Wood Lake. The outcome. The Indian prisoners and the military commission. The spirit of revenge; Bishop Whipple's attitude. Lincoln's order; the Mankato execution. The killing of Little Crow, 1863. Cancellation of reservations and of annuities. Removal of the Sioux. Removal of the Winnebago. Indian campaigns in the West, 1863–65. Importance of the Sioux War. Its place in the history of the American frontier.

F. Economic Transition during the War Years

Communication and the movement west: railroad building (first ten miles of track laid, 1862); telegraph reaches St. Paul, 1860; the advance farther west — Fisk expeditions of 1862–66. Money and banking: weaknesses of state banks; currency depreciation. National Banking acts of 1863 and 1865. Effect of the Civil War on prices and markets. Continuing settlement and growth in the state which the Sioux Outbreak failed to halt. The outlook in 1865.

G. Minnesota and Southern Reconstruction

President Johnson and the Radical Republicans. Minnesota's senators, Ramsey and Norton. The Ramsey dynasty. Norton's break with the Republican party. His attitude toward reconstruction. Ratification of the Thirteenth and Fourteenth amendments. Negro suffrage in Minnesota: attempts to amend the state constitution; success in 1868; ratification of the Fifteenth Amendment. Implications of the Seeger case and the McIlrath investigation.

H. The Chippewa and Sioux since 1862

Significance of 1862 and the almost complete removal of Sioux from the state. Early efforts to concentrate the Chippewa on reservations. Land sessions: 1837, 1854, 1855, 1863–64, 1866. Establishment of the White Earth Reservation (1867). Problems and progress. Impact of settler and lumberman. Indian grievances: land and timber frauds, damage to wild rice fields. Development of new Indian policies: end of the treaty-making policy (1871); growth of the allotment system; the Northwest Indian Commission (1886); the General Allotment Act (Dawes Act, 1887); the Nelson Act (1889). Establishment of the Red Lake Reservation (1889) and the Chippewa of Minnesota Fund. The Indian Reorganization Act (1934), the Indian's New Deal: end of allotment, strengthening of tribal authority, permitting of incorporation by tribes for business purposes. Effects of the new policy. The three agencies and their eight Chippewa reservations and five Sioux "communities." Indians off reservations. The Minnesota Indian today — a minority problem.

QUESTIONS AND SUGGESTIONS

1. In what ways did the state government attempt to combat the effects of the Panic of 1857? Would the same methods be used now?

2. Did the Civil War hinder or promote railroad building in Minnesota?

3. Note the Minnesota connections with the Dred Scott case.

4. A resolution was presented in the Minnesota House and a bill introduced in the Senate in March, 1860, "to permit owners to bring servants with them and hold them to service for a period of five months." See Folwell, *History*, 2:70. What do you make of this proposal?

5. Minnesota, as well as other states of the Upper Midwest, tended to welcome foreigners and to extend the franchise to them on easy terms. How do you account for this? Did the foreign-born citizen play any important role in the rivalry of the Democratic and Republican parties? In the elections of 1860 and 1864?

6. Compare the results of the presidential elections of 1860 and 1864 in Minnesota.

7. Compare the attitude of Minnesotans toward Lincoln in 1860 with that in 1864 and 1865.

8. Reports: Jane Grey Swisshelm; Minnesota women in the Civil War period; the history of a Minnesota regiment in the Civil War.

9. Compare the attitude of Rice toward secession with that of Wilkinson.

10. Note the terms of the Sioux land cession of 1858. See the map on p. 79, reproduced from Folwell, *History*, 2:110.

11. With respect to the Sioux Outbreak of 1862: (a) Draw up a list of general, or background, factors that help to explain the uprising. (b) Give the special, or immediate, causes for the outbreak. (c) Which list, in your judgment, goes farther toward explaining the violent action taken by the Indians?

12. What connection did the following have with the Sioux Outbreak of 1862: Andrew Myrick, Stephen Riggs, Henry H. Sibley, Charles E. Flandrau, Little Crow, John Other Day, Henry B. Whipple?

13. Whereas the military commission sentenced 307 persons to be hanged, only 38 were executed at Mankato. Explain this reduction in numbers.

14. Note how time has (a) corrected some of the exaggerations current in 1862 and 1863 with regard to the Sioux Outbreak, e.g., the number of white people who lost their lives and the extent of territory over which the Sioux carried on their depredations; (b) made possible the adoption of an interpretation which views the action of the Sioux in 1862 much less harshly than was true in the generation which followed the uprising.

15. Do you detect any inconsistency in the government's attitude toward the Indian when you reflect upon the manner in which the Sioux were treated following the outbreak? Were they dealt with as prisoners of war or as criminals? as members of a foreign nation or as subjects of the United States?

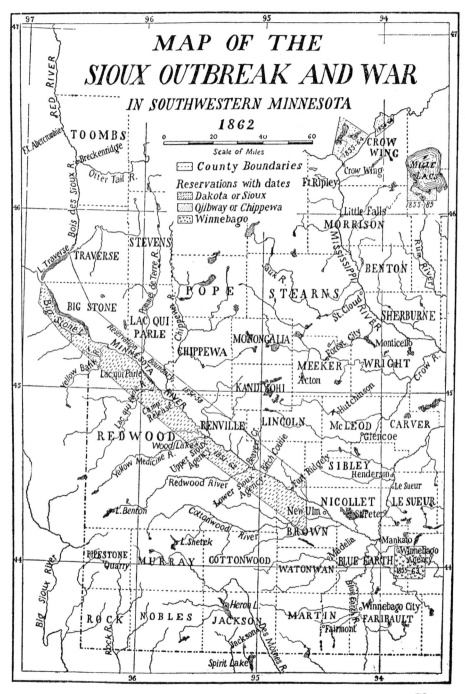

MAP OF THE
SIOUX OUTBREAK AND WAR
IN SOUTHWESTERN MINNESOTA
1862

Scale of Miles

0   20   40   60

County Boundaries
Reservations with dates
Dakota or Sioux
Ojibway or Chippewa
Winnebago

TOOMBS

Ft. Abercrombie
Breckenridge
Otter Tail R.
RED RIVER

CROW WING
1855-64
Crow Wing
MILLE LACS
1855-89
Ft. Ripley
Little Falls
MORRISON

STEVENS
TRAVERSE
L. Traverse
Bois des Sioux R.

Pomme de Terre R.
POPE
STEARNS
St. Cloud
BENTON
Rum River
Mississippi RIVER
SHERBURNE

BIG STONE
Big Stone L.
Sauk R.
Chippewa R.

LAC QUI PARLE
Reservation N.R.
MINNESOTA
Lac qui Parle
CHIPPEWA
MONONGALIA
MEEKER
Acton
WRIGHT
Monticello
Forest City
Crow R.

Yellow Bank
Lac qui Parle R.
Reservation Boundary 1857-8
KANDIYOHI
Hutchinson

Camp Release
REDWOOD
Wood Lake
Yellow Medicine R.
Upper Sioux Agency 1854-62
RENVILLE
Beaver Cr.
Birch Coulie
LINCOLN
Fort Ridgely
McLEOD
Glencoe
CARVER

Redwood River
Lower Sioux Agency 1854-62
SIBLEY
Henderson
Le Sueur
LE SUEUR

L. Benton
Cottonwood River
New Ulm
NICOLLET
St. Peter

L. Shetek
BROWN
Mankato
Winnebago Agency
1855-63

PIPESTONE
Quarry
MURRAY
COTTONWOOD
WATONWAN
Madelia
BLUE EARTH
Blue Earth River

Big Sioux River
Rock R.
ROCK
NOBLES
JACKSON
Heron L.
MARTIN
Fairmont
FARIBAULT
Winnebago City

Jackson
Des Moines R.
Spirit Lake

79

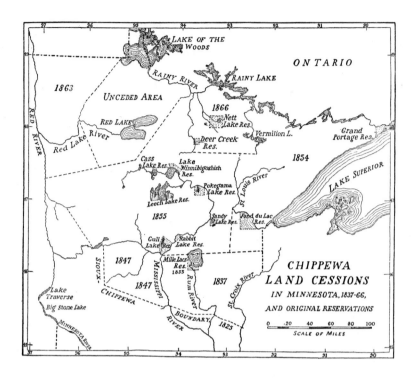

16. What benefits not previously obtainable did the Homestead Act confer upon the western settler?

17. How many homestead entries were made in Minnesota between 1863 and 1865? For how many acres? See Folwell, *History*, 2:331–33. Compare wheat production in Minnesota in the years 1860 and 1865.

18. Currency in circulation in Minnesota before 1865 was drastically different from that after 1865. Explain.

19. How long was settlement retarded by the Sioux War? What was the population of Minnesota in 1860 and in 1865?

20. Compare the attitudes taken by Senators Norton and Ramsey toward reconstruction problems. What was the popular reaction in Minnesota to Senator Norton's stand? Has there been any revision of judgment as to the wisdom of his acts since his time?

21. Describe the steps leading to the establishment of "free manhood suffrage" in Minnesota. How many Negroes were there in the state in 1870?

22. The map at the top of this page is a reproduction of one in Folwell, *History*, 4:191. It shows Chippewa cessions of land from 1837 to 1866.

23. What are some of the achievements of the Chippewa Indian? Describe some typical activities of today's Minnesota Chippewa.

24. To what extent do the Chippewa of today retain the language, customs, and beliefs of their ancestors?
25. What are some of the recreations of the Chippewa Indians today?
26. What is the present system of Indian government? In what ways does the Red Lake Reservation differ from the White Earth? Why did the plan to concentrate the Indians on a single reservation fail? Explain the causes of the failure to protect the Indian land holdings at the White Earth Reservation. What is the origin of the "Chippewa Fund"? To what uses is it put?
27. A thoughtful discussion of the state's "minority problem" is to be found in a publication of the Minnesota Legislative Research Committee: *Minnesota Indians*, Publication No. 27 (1950). This 140-page bulletin is a mine of information. It contains charts and maps difficult to find elsewhere. Its treatment of the current situation is factual and frank.

REFERENCES

* † BLEGEN, THEODORE C., *Building Minnesota*, pp. 201–28.

——— ed., "Campaigning with Seward in 1860," *Minnesota History*, 8:150–71 (June, 1927). From the diaries of Charles Francis Adams and Charles Francis Adams, Jr.

*——— "Guri Endreson, Frontier Heroine," *Minnesota History*, 10:425–30 (Dec., 1929).

BLEGEN, THEODORE C., and PHILIP D. JORDAN, *With Various Voices*, pp. 61–80. Aspects of the Sioux Uprising of 1862: a pioneer woman's account of her capture by the Sioux, an eyewitness description of the hanging at Mankato, and a defense of the Indians by Bishop Henry W. Whipple.

* BUCK, SOLON J., "Lincoln and Minnesota," *Minnesota History*, 6:355–61 (Dec., 1925). A very interesting short essay.

CHRISTIANSON, THEODORE, *Minnesota*. 1:386–87, the Chippewa during the Sioux Outbreak. 1:389–90, 392–98, Minnesota's expansion during the Civil War. 1:399–410, 440–44, the years of reconstruction.

* † CUTLER, F. SANFORD, "Bishop Henry B. Whipple," *Gopher Historian*, 12:28 (Winter, 1957–58). A brief biography with special mention of Whipple's aid to the Indians.

EDERER, BERNARD FRANCIS, *Birch Coulie* (1956). A novel. One of the major engagements of the 1862 Sioux Uprising was fought at Birch Coulie. The author spent his boyhood in close proximity to the battlefield.

FLANDRAU, CHARLES B., "The Ink-pa-du-ta Massacre of 1857," Minnesota Historical Collections, 3:386–407 (1880).

* FOLWELL, WILLIAM W., *History*. 2:33–36, 59–108, 302–27, 333–44, 450–52, the eve of the Civil War; the war and Minnesota's part in it. 2:328–33, 344–45, railroads, Homestead Act, and population increase. 2:109–301,

81

361–450, the best account of the Sioux Outbreak. 2:342; 3:3–17, 18–21, 76–77, 88–90, 325–32, 357–62, politics, legislative measures, and political morality. 2:374–82; 3:22–30, 4:190–329, 472–78, the Chippewa from 1837 to the present.

† GOVE, GERTRUDE, "St. Cloud Editor and Abolitionist — Jane Grey Swisshelm," *Gopher Historian*, 12:25 (Winter, 1957–58). A brief outline biography.

HARBISON, WINFRED A., "President Lincoln and the Faribault Fire-Eater," *Minnesota History*, 20:269–86 (Sept., 1939). An account of one newspaper editor's opposition to Lincoln during the course of the Civil War.

HECK, FRANK H., "The Grand Army of the Republic in Minnesota, 1866–80," *Minnesota History*, 16:427–44 (Dec., 1935). Origins of the G.A.R. in Minnesota.

*† HEILBRON, BERTHA L., *The Thirty-Second State*, pp. 127–55.

——— ed., "An English Visitor of the Civil War Period," *Minnesota History*, 9:271–84 (Sept., 1928).

HICKS, JOHN D., "The Organization of the Volunteer Army in 1861, with Special Reference to Minnesota," *Minnesota History Bulletin*, 2:324–68 (Feb., 1918).

History of the First Regiment Minnesota Volunteer Infantry, 1861–1864 (1916).

HOLCOMBE, RETURN I., *Minnesota in Three Centuries*. 3:217–425, a detailed account of the Sioux Outbreak. 3:79–126, politics, 1859–65. 3:447–61, politics, 1866–69.

HUBBARD, LUCIUS F., *Minnesota in Three Centuries*, 3:127–215 (1908). Governor Hubbard, who enlisted as a private and emerged as a brigadier general, tells of Minnesota troops in the Civil War.

HUGHES, THOMAS, "Causes and Results of the Inkpaduta Massacre," *Minnesota Historical Collections*, 12:263–82 (1908).

JORDAN, PHILIP D., *The People's Health: A History of Public Health in Minnesota to 1948*, pp. 220–42 (1953). Health conditions among Minnesota's Indians, particularly after 1862, and efforts to improve health.

† JORSTAD, ERLING, "Henry Hastings Sibley. First State Governor," *Gopher Historian*, 12:15–16 (Winter, 1957–58). A brief outline biography.

——— "Minnesota's Role in the Democratic Rift of 1860," *Minnesota History*, 37:45–51 (June, 1960). Strife among Democrats within the state organization in the election of 1860 epitomizes the national split.

KLEMENT, FRANK, "The Abolition Movement in Minnesota," *Minnesota History*, 32:15–33 (March, 1951). Seeks to show the attitude of Minnesotans on this issue before and during the Civil War. Based essentially upon editorial comment in contemporary newspapers.

82

* Kunz, Virginia Brainard, *Muskets to Missiles: A Military History of Minnesota*, pp. 76–112 (1958) . The Sioux War.

"Lincoln's Sioux War Order," *Minnesota History*, 33:77–79 (Summer, 1952). A reproduction of President Lincoln's order to execute the Sioux of Minnesota in 1862, with some commentary on his decision.

Larsen, Arthur J., ed., *Crusader and Feminist: Letters of Jane Grey Swisshelm*, pp. 1–32, 84–103.

Mittelholtz, Erwin F., and Rose Graves, *Historical Review of the Red Lake Indian Reservation* (1957). Poorly organized, but has some factual data of consequence.

Moyle, John B., "Minnesota's Famous Wild Rice," *Conservation Volunteer*, 20:38–44 (Sept.–Oct., 1957). Discusses the present-day popularity of wild rice; the relation of the industry to the Minnesota Indian.

——— "Wild Rice — Pioneer Food and Modern Delicacy," *Conservation Volunteer*, 19:11–14 (Jan.–Feb., 1956). Complementary to the article cited just above.

* Newson, Mary J., "Memories of Fort Snelling in Civil War Days," *Minnesota History*, 15:375–404 (Dec., 1934). A charming paper.

Oehler, C. M., *The Great Sioux Uprising* (1959). A lively, vivid account. Written for the general reader. The author has used personal reminiscences of victims to weave his story of blood, fire, and rapine. His criticism of Sibley's leadership is perhaps unjust. Location of the hanging of the thirty-eight Sioux was at Mankato, not South Bend.

* † Poatgieter, A. H., and J. T. Dunn, *Gopher Reader*, pp. 26–32. The Sioux Rebellion. Note the map on p. 26 and several fine illustrations.

Pritchett, John P., "Sidelights on the Sibley Expedition from the Diary of a Private," *Minnesota History*, 7:326–35 (Dec., 1926). The diary in question is published in full by Mr. Pritchett in the *North Dakota Historical Quarterly*, 5:103–29 (Jan., 1931).

Prucha, F. Paul, "Minnesota's Attitude toward the Southern Case for Secession," *Minnesota History*, 24:307–17 (Dec., 1943). Based on editorials appearing in Minnesota papers.

* *Report of the 1958 Minnesota Interim Commission on Indian Affairs* (1958). Problems confronting the present-day Indian of Minnesota and proposals for helping to solve them. An excellent study.

Riggs, Stephen R., *Mary and I*, pp. 138–92. A missionary's account of the Inkpaduta massacre and the Sioux Outbreak.

Robinson, Doane, *A History of the Dakota or Sioux Indians*, pp. 253–325. The historian of the Sioux records the Outbreak.

Robinson, Edward Van Dyke, *Early Economic Conditions and the Development of Agriculture in Minnesota*, pp. 60–61. Wheat-growing during the Civil War.

RODDIS, LOUIS H., *The Indian Wars of Minnesota* (1956).

* SHIPPEE, LESTER B., "Social and Economic Effects of the Civil War with Special Reference to Minnesota," *Minnesota History Bulletin*, 2:404–9 (May, 1918). The best study of this subject.

* SHORTRIDGE, WILSON P., *Transition of a Typical Frontier*, pp. 146–64. Sibley's part in the Sioux Outbreak.

"Slavery in Minnesota," *Minnesota History Bulletin*, 5:40–43 (Feb., 1923).

SWEET, GEORGE W., "Incidents in the Threatened Outbreak of Hole-in-the-Day and Other Ojibways at Time of Sioux Massacre of 1862," Minnesota Historical Collections, 6:401–8 (1894).

TRENERRY, WALTER N., "The Minnesota Rebellion Act of 1862: A Legal Dilemma of the Civil War," *Minnesota History*, 35:1–10 (March, 1956). On an act passed by the state legislature depriving southern rebels of the protection of the courts in civil cases. It was declared unconstitutional by the state's supreme court.

* UNDERHILL, RUTH M., *Red Man's America: A History of Indians in the United States*, pp. 320–41 (1958). A summary statement of trends in United States policy toward the Indians from 1607 to the present.

UREVIG, FRANCES, "Alexander Ramsey," *Gopher Historian*, 12:16, 17 (Winter, 1957–58). A brief outline biography.

*† "The White Earth Reservation," *Gopher Historian*, 14:21–25 (Fall, 1959). An excellent summary of this Chippewa reservation.

WILSON, QUINTUS C., "Joseph A. Wheelock, Pioneer Statistician," *Minnesota History*, 34:330–36 (Winter, 1955). A one-man crusade for state support in gathering statistics.

V. LAND OCCUPATION, POPULATION GROWTH, AND AGRICULTURAL DEVELOPMENT CHARACTERIZE THE STATE'S FIRST HALF CENTURY

17. *Population Influx and a Cosmopolitan People*

A. Minnesota's Rapid Growth

Increase by decades. The widening area of settlement: the prairie lands; the Red River Valley; the northeastern frontier. Factors explaining growth: end of the Civil War; Indian menace ended; the westward rush; fertile land; liberal land laws (the Homestead Act of 1862 and the Timber Culture Act of 1873); immigrants invited by the state; settlement promoted by railroads; promoters and workers attracted by the mining frontier.

B. Promotion of Settlement by State and Railroads

State's reasons for welcoming immigrants; methods used to encourage immigration; the Board of Immigration; Hans Mattson; state advertising; the question of climate; the policy regarding state-owned lands.

Railroads eager to use their extensive land grants; their methods of attracting immigrants; colonization departments and other agencies of the railroads; prices charged for railroad lands; colonies formed through railroad activity.

c. Changing Characteristics of the Population through the First One Hundred Years

Census figures reveal changing characteristics by decades, such as ratio of young to old, male to female, single to married, native born to foreign born, native increase to increase by immigration. Settlement by organized colonies in early decades. Changing rate of natural increase. The "old" and the "new" immigration as respects Minnesota. National immigration restriction. The census of 1950 — Minnesota more urban than rural for the first time.

d. Minnesota Racial Elements and Contributions

Early strains of immigration: The French-Canadian; the initial dominance of Yankee stock in politics, public affairs, education, religion, industry, and commerce; immigrants of British stock (Irish, Welsh, English, Scotch, Scotch-Irish). *The Germans:* Background of the immigrants; the New Ulm colony; German Catholics in the St. Cloud vicinity; other settlements; immigration figures decade by decade; work in agriculture; church preferences; political choices; social and cultural life; the *Turnverein*; the German-American press; contributions to Minnesota. *The "New Scandinavia," Norwegians, Swedes, Danes, and Icelanders:* Comparison of backgrounds; immigration figures decade by decade; regions settled; typical settlements, such as Vasa (Swedish), Spring Grove (Norwegian), Askov (Danish), Minneota (Icelandic); work on farm and in city; Scandinavians in special industries, for example lumbering; church affiliations; the place of the church in a typical settlement; social and cultural life; Scandinavian colleges (St. Olaf, Gustavus Adolphus, Augsburg, Concordia); the development of a Scandinavian press; special trends in each Scandinavian element; participation in Minnesota politics; westward spread; Rölvaag and other interpreters of Scandinavian-American life. *The Finns:* Old World background; immigration figures decade by decade; occupations; settlements; the mine worker seeks a farm; interest in politics; transplanted characteristics; heritage of folk music and poetry. *The Slavic peoples, Poles, Czechs, Slovaks, Russians, Ruthenians, Serbs, Croats, Slovenes, Lithuanians, Latvians:* Immigration causes and background; immigration figures decade by decade; activity in Minnesota mines, industry, agriculture, the professions, the arts; Silver Lake or New Prague, a New World Bohemia; other typical settlements; church affiliations; Old World cultural contacts; contributions to Minnesota. *Other racial groups:* Italians (special contributions to

85

Minnesota industry and life); Greeks (skill in operation of fruit and confectionery stores, religious affiliations); Dutch (typical communities and traits, Hollandale); Jews (influence on Minnesota business and cultural life, synagogues); Belgians; Roumanians; Hungarians; Mexicans (recent migration); Negroes (special centers, activities); the native Indian element.

E. Recent Tendencies and Contributions

Decreasing proportion of foreign born to native and increasing proportion of "new" immigration at the turn of the twentieth century. Early bilingualism followed by a decline of foreign languages in schools, churches, and press. Cultural activities and contributions in music, art, drama, fiction, education. Special organizations: Turner societies, *Bygdelags*, *Sokols*. Organizations such as the Sons of Norway, German-American Alliance, Polish-American Alliance, Bohemian National Alliance, Swedish Institute of Arts, Swedish Historical Society of America, and Norwegian-American Historical Association. The foreign-born element and Minnesota's liberal tradition in politics. Effect of the virtual cessation of immigration upon the solidarity of foreign groups in Minnesota. The leveling process of "Americanization" on the second and third generations. Minnesota's special position in the family of states from the point of view of racial elements and contributions. The "United Nations" aspect of Minnesota's population at the close of the first century of statehood.

QUESTIONS AND SUGGESTIONS

1. What were the unsettled regions of Minnesota in 1870? Shannon speaks of a "triangle of unsettled country" in 1870. Define this triangle. (See *Catholic Colonization on the Western Frontier*, p. 1.) What parts of these unsettled areas tended to be occupied first? Which next, and so on?

2. Notwithstanding the enormous immigration to Minnesota of non-English elements, the Yankee strain has, in the main, imposed its cultural forms upon the rest of the populace. Why has this been possible?

3. How important a part did the state play in the immigration of Europeans to Minnesota? the railroads?

4. Many pamphlets advertising the state were issued by the state Board of Immigration. Typical of them were *The Agricultural, Manufacturing and Commercial Resources and Capabilities of Minnesota* (1881) and *The Undeveloped Northern Counties of Minnesota* (no date). The legislature in 1865 awarded prizes for essays on the topic "Minnesota as a Home for Immigrants." These were printed. What other methods were used by the state to advertise its resources?

5. Many counties or sections in Minnesota put out their own publicity. Ex-

amples are C. A. Chapman, *Southwestern Minnesota, the Best Farming Section in the World* (no date); *Nicollet County, Minnesota, as an Agricultural and Dairying Section, and Saint Peter as a Manufacturing Center* (1884).

6. One of the appeals used to attract immigrants to the state was that of the therapeutic properties of the climate. An appeal was made especially to the tubercular. How did this policy embarrass the state? The answer is suggested in the title of Arthur J. Meyers' book, *Invited and Conquered.*

7. Compare the advertising activities of the state with those of the railroads, especially the Northern Pacific.

8. What fraction of Minnesota's land was given to the railroads? How did legislators of that day justify this lavish giving?

9. Why was it of concern to the railroads that settlement be promoted? What means other than advertising did they use to attract settlers?

10. How is the name of Hans Mattson associated with the campaign to attract settlers to Minnesota? Paul Hjelm Hansen?

11. Note the excellent series of maps in Nelson, Ramsey, and Toews, *A Century of Population Growth in Minnesota*, showing the distribution of various foreign-born groups in 1950.

12. What examples can you find of colonization companies in Minnesota?

13. The article by George M. Stephenson cited below deals with "America letters." What do you learn from these letters about the immigrant's impressions of this "Land of Canaan" and also about the type of person who left the Old World for the new? Similar letters may be read in Theodore C. Blegen, *Land of Their Choice: The Immigrants Write Home.*

14. The price which the settler paid for his land would vary with the agency from which he purchased it. Indicate what he might pay if he bought from the railroad, from the United States government, from the state of Minnesota, or from a land speculator. When considering purchase from the federal government you should remember that the federal land acts of 1820, 1862, and 1873 would be in effect at the same time.

15. Had the frontier in Minnesota disappeared by 1890?

16. O. E. Rölvaag's *Giants in the Earth* tells the saga of pioneer settlement on the prairies. Though the locale is South Dakota, the description applies to western Minnesota as well. Rölvaag's accuracy in describing pioneer conditions is attacked and defended in "The Study of Pioneer Life," *Minnesota History*, 10:430–35 (Dec., 1929); 11:63–74 (March, 1930); 11:185–87 (June, 1930).

17. Maps showing the percentage of foreign-born population in the total population of the United States, by twenty-year periods, and of the German-, Irish-, Swedish-, and Norwegian-born population are given in

Paullin, *Atlas*, Plates 71–76A. The density of population in the United States, 1790–1930, is shown on Plates 76B–79.

18. Some interesting facts may be gleaned about population changes in Minnesota in the ten years between 1940 and 1950 in the pamphlet *Migration in Minnesota, 1940–1950* by Ramsey, Orman, and Nelson. The most significant fact relates to the changing urban-rural relationship. Find out what the trend referred to is.

19. How important has Minnesota been as a source of emigration to other states and regions?

20. Graph exercise: Using statistics from the official census returns of the United States for 1950, prepare charts which would depict by decades various aspects of Minnesota's population changes in the first century of growth. Many of these census tables have been reproduced in Nelson, Ramsey, and Toews, *A Century of Population Growth in Minnesota*. The charts in this same pamphlet will also be found to be most helpful. The following would be worthy subjects for graphic presentation: (a) the population growth in Minnesota from 1850 to 1950 — urban, rural, and total; (b) the changing proportions by decades of those born in Minnesota, born in other states, and foreign born; (c) the percentage of foreign born from each country, with a separate pie graph for each decade, (d) the percentage of various age groups from 1880 to 1950.

21. The Festival of Nations, sponsored by the International Institute of St. Paul, is a colorful event which has been held every few years since 1932. The aim of each festival is to develop appreciation for the important contributions to American life made by each national group in the state's population. The story of the festival, with a vivid account of the many nationalities in one city, is told by Alice L. Sickels in *Around the World in St. Paul* (1945). A statement of the work and nature of both the institute and the festival may be found in "The International Institute," *Gopher Historian*, 14:22, 23 (Spring, 1960).

REFERENCES

ANDREWS, LYDIA B., *Pioneer of the North Woods Section of Minnesota: William H. Andrews* (1931). Early settlement in Cass and Crow Wing counties.

* BELL, IDA P., "A Pioneer Family of the Middle Border," *Minnesota History*, 14:303–66 (Sept., 1933). Recollections of a journey to southern Minnesota in 1860 and settlement there.

BERCOVICI, KONRAD, *On New Shores*, pp. 101–18 (1925). The Finns of Embarrass.

BISHOP, HARRIET E., *Floral Home*, pp. 133–47 (1857). "Claim making" and other aspects of pioneer settlement.

BJORK, KENNETH O., *Saga in Steel and Concrete* (1947). Contributions to engineering by Scandinavian-Americans.

—— *West of the Great Divide* (1958). Migration of Scandinavians from Minnesota and the Midwest to the Pacific coast.

* † BLEGEN, THEODORE C., *Building Minnesota*, pp. 229–36, 369–78.

—— *The Land Lies Open*, pp. 137–50, 196–216. Contributions of the Yankees to Minnesota life. Also a diary account of an 1873 covered-wagon journey from Wisconsin to southwestern Minnesota.

—— *Land of Their Choice: The Immigrants Write Home*. These letters were originally written in Norwegian and from many parts of the United States. They allow the reader to enter the homes and hearts of the pioneer settlers in a special way. Those from Minnesota are grouped under the heading "The Glorious New Scandinavia," pp. 419–46.

* —— "Minnesota's Campaign for Immigrants" and "Illustrative Documents," Year-Book of the Swedish Historical Society of America, 11:3–28, 29–83 (1926).

* —— *Norwegian Migration to America: The American Transition*, pp. 175–206.

BLEGEN, THEODORE C., and MARTIN B. RUUD, eds., *Norwegian Emigrant Songs and Ballads* (1936). This collection throws light on the human backgrounds of immigration.

* BRINGS, LAWRENCE M., ed., *Minnesota Heritage*: Val Bjornson, "Minnesota Melting Pot," pp. 120–27. Emphasizes the United Nations character of Minnesota's population. James P. Shannon, "Archbishop Ireland Colonizes," pp. 128–38. A brilliant condensation of Shannon's book on Catholic colonization cited below.

CHRISTENSEN, THOMAS P., "Danish Settlements in Minnesota," *Minnesota History*, 8:363–85 (Dec., 1927). An excellent account of this racial group.

CHRISTIANSON, THEODORE, *Minnesota*, 1:416–19; 2:102–5. Discusses the promotion of immigration.

CLAPESATTLE, HELEN, "When Minnesota Was Florida's Rival," *Minnesota History*, 35:214–21 (March, 1957). Develops the point that through much of the 1860's and 1870's Minnesota was viewed as a health haven. Malaria sufferers and consumptives came in large numbers.

COLUMBUS MEMORIAL ASSOCIATION OF MINNESOTA, *Dedication of the Columbus Memorial*, pp. 58–79 (1931). Contains information about the Italians in the various communities of Minnesota.

DAY, FRANK A., and THEODORE M. KNAPPEN, *The Life of John Albert Johnson*, pp. 13–70 (1910). Environment and early life of a governor whose parents were immigrants.

EDGAR, MARJORIE, "Finnish Folk Songs in Minnesota," *Minnesota History*, 16:319–21 (Sept., 1935).

FOLWELL, WILLIAM W., *History*, 2:331–33, 344–45; 3:1–2, 58–60, 62–65, 73, 139–41, 192–93. Census figures, 1865–90.

GJERSET, KNUT, "A Norwegian-American Landnamsman: Ole S. Gjerset," *Minnesota History*, 10:273–93 (Sept., 1929). An especially interesting story of an immigrant family and its Minnesota experiences.

GUSTAFSON, ERNEST B., "The Swedes in Minnesota," Year-Book of the Swedish Historical Society of America, 10:45–113 (1925). An account of the Swedish settlements of Marine and of Vasa.

HAGG, HAROLD T., "Bemidji: A Pioneer Community of the 1890's" *Minnesota History*, 23:24–34 (March, 1942). Establishment of a town on one of the last of Minnesota's frontiers.

* HEDGES, JAMES B., "The Colonization Work of the Northern Pacific Railroad," *Mississippi Valley Historical Review*, 13:311–42 (Dec., 1926). An excellent study.

*† HEILBRON, BERTHA L., *The Thirty-Second State*, pp. 156–63.

HOLBROOK, STEWART H., *The Yankee Exodus: An Account of Migration from New England* (1950). See Chapter 3 entitled "Pioneers in Minnesota," pp. 166–86.

HOLMES, FRANK R., *Minnesota in Three Centuries*, 4:27–31. Minnesota in 1870.

*† HOLMQUIST, JUNE D., "East-Central Minnesota: Swedeland, U.S.A.," *Gopher Historian*, 13:19–21 (Spring, 1959). A fine brief account of heavy settlement in the early period by one nationality.

HOLT, ANDREW, "Characteristics of the Early Swedish Settlers in Minnesota," Year-Book of the Swedish Historical Society of America, 7:7–23 (1921–22).

* JARCHOW, MERRILL E., *The Earth Brought Forth*, pp. 41–79. Various ways by which a settler could obtain land. An excellent, concise treatment.

JERABEK, ESTHER, "Antonin Jurka, a Pioneer Czech Schoolmaster," *Minnesota History*, 13:269–76.

*——— "The Transition of a New-World Bohemia," *Minnesota History*, 15:26–42 (March, 1934). The story of the Czechs in the Silver Lake community.

† JOHNSON, H. NAT, *Minnesota Panorama*, pp. 33–36.

JOHNSON, HILDEGARD BINDER, "Eduard Pelz and German Emigration," *Minnesota History*, 31:222–30 (Dec., 1950). For twenty years this citizen of Germany regarded it as his "mission" to encourage Germans to emigrate to Minnesota.

KOLEHMAINEN, JOHN ILMARI, "The Finnish Pioneers of Minnesota," *Minnesota History*, 25:317–28 (Dec., 1944).

LARSON, LAURENCE M., "The Norwegian Element in the Northwest," *American Historical Review*, 40:69–81 (Oct., 1934).

Lawson, Victor E., "The First Settlements in the Kandiyohi Region and Their Fate in the Indian Outbreak," Year-Book of the Swedish Historical Society of America, 10:19–44 (1924–25).

Lucas, Henry S., ed., "Early Dutch Settlements in Minnesota (Including a Sketch by Herman Borgers Entitled 'The Hollanders in Minnesota, 1856–97')," Minnesota History, 28:120–31 (June, 1947).

Marin, William A., "Sod Houses and Prairie Schooners," Minnesota History, 12:135–56 (June, 1931).

Mattson, Hans, Reminiscences, pp. 97–137. Mattson's work abroad in promoting emigration.

Moro, Arthur R., "The English Colony at Fairmont in the Seventies," Minnesota History, 8:140–49 (June, 1927).

Moynihan, James H., The Life of Archbishop John Ireland, pp. 20–32 (1953). An account of efforts to establish Irish colonies in Minnesota — group planting.

* Murchie, R. W., and M. E. Jarchow, Population Trends in Minnesota (1936). A fine treatment of the subject, based upon the United States census of 1930. This is the first study in a series issued by the Minnesota Agricultural Experiment Station.

Myers, Arthur J., Invited and Conquered: Historical Sketch of Tuberculosis in Minnesota, pp. 15–33 (1949). Many victims of consumption were attracted to the state because of its beneficent climate.

——— "Invited and Conquered," Gopher Historian, 5:18–19 (Jan., 1951).

* Nelson, Lowry, The Minnesota Community, pp. 39–53. National backgrounds of Minnesota's people and the play of language, religion, and Old World customs.

* Nelson, Lowry, Charles E. Ramsey, and Jacob Toews, A Century of Population Growth in Minnesota (1954). A brilliant pamphlet, the finest on the subject. Based upon the United States census of 1950. Has valuable charts, tables, and maps. It is the third study in a series issued by the Minnesota Agricultural Experiment Station.

Nute, Grace Lee, "The Lindbergh Colony," Minnesota History, 20:243–58 (Sept., 1939). Description of an example of group settlement, including a letter from the leader of the group.

Orfield, Matthias N., Federal Land Grants to the States, with Special Reference to Minnesota, pp. 145–255 (1915). The administration of public lands in Minnesota.

Paullin, Charles O., Atlas of the Historical Geography of the United States, Plates 71–76A, 76B–79. Note also the accompanying text.

*Peterson, Harold F., "Early Minnesota Railroads and the Quest for Settlers," Minnesota History, 13:25–44 (March, 1932).

—————"Some Colonization Projects of the Northern Pacific Railroad," *Minnesota History*, 10:127–44 (June, 1929).

PLAUT, W. GUNTHER, *The Jews in Minnesota* (1959).

* QUALEY, CARLTON C., *Norwegian Settlement in the United States*, pp. 97–129 (1938). Emphasis is on the years before 1880.

*—————"Pioneer Norwegian Settlement in Minnesota," *Minnesota History*, 12:247–80 (Sept., 1931).

*—————"Some National Groups in Minnesota," *Minnesota History*, 31:18–32 (March, 1950). Emphasizes that the state's population finds its sources in many nations and regions.

* RAMSEY, CHARLES E., ALLAN D. ORMAN, and LOWRY NELSON, *Migration in Minnesota, 1940–1950*. An excellent study, based upon the United States census of 1940, with significant tables and maps. It is the second study in a series issued by the Minnesota Agricultural Experiment Station.

RÖLVAAG, O. E., *Giants in the Earth* (1927). Commonly recognized as one of the great American novels. While its setting is the Dakota frontier, its portrayal of frontier life fits the Minnesota scene as well.

SCHULTZ, FERDINAND P., *History of the Settlement of German Mennonites from Russia at Mountain Lake, Minnesota* (1938). An excellent study of group settlement.

SHANNON, JAMES P., "Bishop Ireland's Connemara Experiment," *Minnesota History*, 35:205–13 (March, 1957). The Catholic group settlement program was in the main highly successful. Shannon here tells of one which failed, the group from Connemara, Ireland, which settled at Graceville in Big Stone County.

—————*Catholic Colonization on the Western Frontier* (1957). In the decade following 1875 John Ireland established ten colonies in Minnesota which remain to this day flourishing Catholic centers. The story is well told.

SIRJAMAKI, JOHN, "The People of the Mesabi Range," *Minnesota History*, 27:203–15 (Sept., 1946). Emphasizes the diverse make-up of the population attracted to northern Minnesota because of the iron industry. Also, shows the play of the old *and* the new immigration.

SMITH, ALICE E., "The Sweetman Irish Colony," *Minnesota History*, 9:331–46 (Dec., 1928).

STEPHENSON, GEORGE M., *John Lind of Minnesota* (1935), pp. 3–14. The backgrounds of a future governor.

*—————*The Religious Aspects of Swedish Immigration* (1932), pp. 397–476. The Americanization of the Swedish immigrants.

*—————"When America Was the Land of Canaan," *Minnesota History*, 10:237–60 (Sept., 1929). A brilliant article based upon new original research. "America letters" and their effect on emigration.

TWEET, ROALD, "The Mountain Lake Community: A Radio Script," *Minnesota History*, 27:221–27 (Sept., 1946). A highly readable script about the group Mennonite settlement of a western Minnesota town.

UPHAM, WARREN, "The Settlement and Development of the Red River Valley," Minnesota Historical Collections, 8:18–24 (1898).

VAN CLEEF, EUGENE, *The Finn in America* (1918). Excellent on the Finns in Minnesota.

WASATJERNA, HANS R., *Minnesotan Suomalaisten Historia* (1957). Finnish settlement.

WESLEY, EDGAR B., *Owatonna: The Social Development of a Minnesota Community* (1938).

[V. LAND OCCUPATION, POPULATION GROWTH, AND AGRICULTURAL DEVELOPMENT CHARACTERIZE THE STATE'S FIRST HALF CENTURY]

18. *Becoming an Agricultural State*

A. Pioneer Agriculture

Early agricultural activity of fur traders and soldiers at Fort Snelling. Farming in the St. Croix Triangle and southeastern Minnesota. Features of pioneer agriculture: clearing away the trees; use of forests for cabin, fuel, and fences; inadequacy of transportation; self-sufficiency of each farm unit; early diversity; new land under cultivation; infrequent and simple social activities. Advertising of resources: Le Duc and the Crystal Palace Exhibition, 1853. Spread of agricultural settlement. Agricultural products. Fairs. Horticultural Society, 1866. Minnesota predominantly agricultural by 1860.

B. Mechanization: A Trend in the Pioneer Period, a Major Development after 1860

Early implements of pioneer farmer often wooden, often homemade — plow, drag, cradle, flail. The introduction in the 1850's of iron or steel plow, breaking plow, reaper, thresher, and well-digging machine. Increased use of the manufactured hoe, scythe, rake, spades, axes, wagons, and sleighs. Civil War labor shortage an impetus to mechanization. Steady improvement of reapers, threshers, drills, plows, and rakes. Local manufacture of farm implements. The high cost of mechanization.

C. When Wheat Was King, 1860–80

Growth of wheat farming. Reasons for the predominance of wheat: rise in price, 1860–65; introduction of machinery; the railroads bring virgin areas within the reach of markets; the rise of and improvements in the flour industry. Bonanza farming.

D. New Factors in Wheat Farming

A shift in the center of production to the Red River Valley. Minneapolis and Duluth become important primary wheat markets. New milling processes make spring wheat more important. Line elevators develop for local markets. The southeastern section of the state loses its primacy in the wheat trade. Factors explaining the movement away from the one-crop emphasis toward diversification: soil depletion, price drop, the move westward, more scientific farming, the beginnings of dairying.

E. Some Problems and Some New Developments for the Farmer

Natural plagues: grasshoppers, hail, fire, frost, diseases. Experimentation: Wendelin Grimm and alfalfa, Peter M. Gideon and the Wealthy apple. Introduction of new crops. Morrill Land Grant College Act of 1862 and beginnings of agricultural education.

QUESTIONS AND SUGGESTIONS

1. To what extent did fur traders, missionaries, and soldiers in Minnesota carry on agriculture?

2. Why was it felt necessary to advertise the agricultural possibilities of the state?

3. How do you explain the one-crop system in Minnesota in the 1860's and 1870's? What were the effects of this kind of farming? Account for the failure of this pattern of farming to continue.

4. In his book on agriculture in Minnesota (cited below), Merrill E. Jarchow entitles one of his chapters "Wheat: King or Tyrant?" Why?

5. Decline of the one-crop emphasis would, of course, mean diversification. What parts of the state began diversifying earliest? What manner of diversification took place? What progress had been made in diversification by 1890?

6. What were the causes of the shift in wheat farming from the southeastern to the northwestern part of the state?

7. The grasshopper invasions of 1873–77 gave rise to a considerable literature. Two contemporary pamphlets are David R. Breed, *The Locust-Scourge in Minnesota* (1878), and John S. Pillsbury, Charles V. Riley, and Pennock Pusey, *The Rocky Mountain Locust* (1876).

8. Bonanza farming is sometimes called "factory farming." Why? What conditions would have to prevail to make this kind of farming possible? What parts of Minnesota satisfied these conditions?

9. Compare the production of wheat in 1859, 1879, and 1899 with that of oats, barley, rye, corn, potatoes, and hay. Tables showing the production in these years are given in Robinson, *Early Economic Conditions and the Development of Agriculture*, pp. 48–54, 89–99, 118–30. Tables, charts, and maps may also be found in Schrimper, *Minnesota Agriculture — Crops, 1858–1958*, a compilation issued by the State-Federal Crop and Livestock Reporting Service.

10. What agencies in the state were interested in the improvement of agriculture by 1875?
11. Reports: Wendelin Grimm, Peter Gideon, William G. Le Duc, the grasshopper invasions of 1873–77, the blizzard of 1873.

REFERENCES

BALMER, FRANK, "The Farmer in Minnesota History," *Minnesota History*, 7:199–217 (Sept., 1926). A portrayal of early attempts at farming by Indians, fur traders, missionaries, and soldiers.

*† BLEGEN, THEODORE C., *Building Minnesota*, pp. 237–42.

BLEGEN, THEODORE C., and PHILIP D. JORDAN, *With Various Voices*, pp. 310–15. A concise but graphic description of the grasshopper plague of 1873–77. Told by a farmer who knew it too well.

CHRISTIANSON, THEODORE, *Minnesota*, 1:458–60, 467–76; 2:91–92. Bonanza farming, agricultural calamities, diversification.

EDWARDS, EVERETT E., and HORACE RUSSELL, "Wendelin Grimm and Alfalfa," *Minnesota History*, 19:21–33 (March, 1938).

* FOLWELL, WILLIAM W., *History*, 3:65–67, 93–111, 157–58, 251–52. Bonanza farming, the grasshopper invasions, and wheat raising. Notice the maps of the grasshopper invasions.

HAMILTON, LAURA M., "Stem Rust in the Spring Wheat Area in 1878," *Minnesota History*, 20:156–64 (June, 1939).

HAVIGHURST, WALTER and MARION, *Climb a Lofty Ladder: A Story of Swedish Settlement in Minnesota* (1952). Setting: wheat lands of Minnesota Valley in the 1890's.

*† HEILBRON, BERTHA L., *The Thirty-Second State*, pp. 164–74.

HILL, JAMES J., "History of Agriculture in Minnesota," Minnesota Historical Collections, 8:275–90 (1898).

HOLMES, FRANK R., *Minnesota in Three Centuries*, 4:107–16, 211–22, 389–400. Grasshopper invasions, cyclones, the development of agriculture.

* JARCHOW, MERRILL E., *The Earth Brought Forth*, pp. 3–26, 80–261. The finest treatment on the subject. If this volume is not available, some of the same material may be found in the following articles by Mr. Jarchow in *Minnesota History*: "Farm Machinery in Frontier Minnesota," 23:316–27 (Dec., 1942). "Livestock in Frontier Minnesota," 26:106–25 (June, 1945). "The Beginnings of Minnesota Dairying," 27:107–21 (June, 1946). " 'King Wheat,' " 29:1–28 (March, 1948).

LAMPHERE, GEORGE N., "History of Wheat Raising in the Red River Valley," Minnesota Historical Collections, vol. 10, part 1, pp. 12–32 (1905).

LARSON, HENRIETTA M., *The Wheat Market and the Farmer in Minnesota, 1858–1900* (1926). An excellent study of the wheat farmer and his problems in marketing his grain.

LOEHR, RODNEY C., "Minnesota Farmers' Diaries," *Minnesota History,*
18:284–97 (Sept., 1937). The farmers themselves speak through their
diaries of the details of farm life.

PETERSON, FRANK, "Early Days on the Minnesota Prairies," Year-Book of
the Swedish Historical Society of America, 8:7–25 (1922–23).

POATGIETER, A. H., and J. T. DUNN, *Gopher Reader,* pp. 122–23. The "Three
G's of Minnesota Agriculture": Grimm, Gideon, and Gregg.

* ROBINSON, EDWARD V., *Early Economic Conditions and the Development
of Agriculture in Minnesota,* pp. 57–106. The period of specialized wheat
farming.

SCHRIMPER, RICHARD J., *Minnesota Agriculture — Crops, 1858–1958* (1958).

UPHAM, WARREN, "The Settlement and Development of the Red River Valley," Minnesota Historical Collections, 8:18–24 (1898).

[V. LAND OCCUPATION, POPULATION GROWTH, AND AGRICULTURAL
DEVELOPMENT CHARACTERIZE THE STATE'S FIRST HALF CENTURY]

19. *Politics: Republican Party Dominance and the Rise of Third-Party
Movements of Protest*

A. The Republican Party Establishes a Dynasty within the State as in the
Nation

Commanding position of the Republican party: Republican governors
win all elections from 1859 to 1898 and 1900 to 1904; Republican candidates for president of the United States receive the greatest number of
votes in all elections from 1860 to 1908; congressional delegations are
under the control of Republicans from 1860 to 1912 except from 1887 to
1889 and 1891 to 1893; Republicans are in clear control of the state legislature from 1860 to 1890.

B. Minnesota in the Forefront of the Nation's Agrarian Crusade

Basis of farmer discontent not to be found in poor land, poor crops, or
a "down and out" situation, but rather in the conviction that the farmer
was not getting his fair share. Markets, prices, mortgages. Complaints
against railroads, middlemen, monopolies. Grievances: discriminatory
practices of railroads and elevators, excessive rates, unfair grading of
grain, high interest rates, an unfair tax system. Attitude of corporate
interests. Bird's-eye view of the protest movement: rise of two nonpolitical farm organizations — Patrons of Husbandry (Grange) and Alliance; the formation of three political parties — Anti-Monopoly party,
Greenback party, and Populist party.

C. Grangers and Politics in the Seventies

Oliver H. Kelley. The National Grange: origin, growth, social and educational program, intended nonpolitical character. Donnelly and the

Anti-Monopoly party, 1873–76: formation of the party from Granger elements; fusion with Democrats and the liberal Republican rump. Granger strength in the state government, 1874. Granger laws of 1871, 1874, 1875. Reaction to Granger laws. The Panic of 1873 and its effects. Supreme Court decision in *Munn vs. Illinois*. Rise of the Greenback party and its role in Minnesota. The Merrill Textbook Law, 1878. Decline of the Grange. Significance of the Granger movement. Revival of the Grange in recent times. Contemporary Republicans: Horace Austin, William Windom, Cushman K. Davis, John S. Pillsbury. The Donnelly-Washburn campaign of 1878.

D. The Farmers' Alliance and Politics in the Eighties and Nineties

The Alliance launched in Chicago in 1880. Minnesota's 80 Alliance locals in 1881 grow to almost 1,000 by 1890. Alliance activities at first nonpolitical with a drift to indirect political action by the mid-eighties. Cooperation with the Knights of Labor — a farmer-labor tie. The Wabash Case, 1886. Effective work by the Alliance bloc in the legislature of 1887; ineffective in legislature of 1889. Legislative enactments: establishment of Railroad and Warehouse Commission, 1885; Bureau of Labor Statistics, 1887; Australian ballot, 1889. The appearance of Knute Nelson in Minnesota politics. The Alliance enters politics directly as a third party in 1890. Election of 1890: Sidney M. Owen and Donnelly; election of two congressmen by the Alliance and a "balance of power bloc" in legislature. Inept legislative work by the Alliance bloc in the 1891 session. Donnelly's use of the literary medium as an outlet for protest: *Caesar's Column, Doctor Huguet, Golden Bottle,* and other works. National action and the formation of the Populist (People's) party. Influence of Populism on the Republican party. Election of Nelson as governor in 1892. Enactment of agrarian reforms: local elevators subjected to state inspection, public grading of grain, creation of pools and trusts made illegal, a state elevator authorized, regulation of working conditions in factories. The silver issue after the Panic of 1893. Populism turns to national issues. Nelson elected United States senator in 1894. The free silver campaign of 1896: John Lind, fusion candidate of Populists and Democrats defeated by David M. Clough, Republican. Lind again a fusion candidate in 1898 and this time victorious. Decline of the Populist party. Significance of the agrarian revolt, and the "persistence of Populism."

QUESTIONS AND SUGGESTIONS

1. How do you account for the predominance of the Republican party in the post-Civil War generation in Minnesota?

2. The policies and accomplishments of successive Republican governors of

97

Minnesota may be gleaned from citations listed below by Castle, Christianson, Folwell, and Holmes.

3. With respect to the "Agrarian Crusade" of 1865–1900: (a) What Minnesota conditions explain the farmers' revolt? (b) Were complaints of the farmers justified?

4. Apropos of the Patrons of Husbandry (the Grange): (a) What Minnesota connections did its founder, Oliver Kelley, have? (b) How prominent a part did Minnesota play in the activities of this organization? (c) What were its best years in Minnesota? (d) What happened to the organization?

5. What grievances led farmers to ask for the Granger acts? Minnesota's three Granger laws of 1871, 1874, and 1875 proved to be disappointing. Why?

6. Why was the Supreme Court decision in the *Munn vs. Illinois* case (1876) of such importance to state legislation of the Granger law type? the Wabash case (1886)?

7. What reforms did the Greenback party advocate? How firm was the support it received in Minnesota?

8. Give reasons for the decline of the Grange. What were its main achievements?

9. When one of the Granger leaders did some reminiscing in the late 1870's, she insisted that, at least, the movement had brought "poetry" into the lives of the farmers. What did she mean?

10. Characterize Governor Pillsbury's administration.

11. In organizational development both the Grange and the Alliance owed much to Ignatius Donnelly. Explain. What were the *Anti-Monopolist* and the *Representative?*

12. Among the specific reforms asked for by the parties of the protest movement were the continued issuance of greenbacks and the unlimited coinage of silver, initiative and referendum, direct election of senators, and an income tax. Could you point to grievances which led to these requests for reform?

13. Explain why the Alliance bloc in the state legislature failed to accomplish much by way of reform legislation despite the fact that they held the balance of power, especially in 1887 and 1891.

14. Point to examples where the Republicans seemed to have been influenced by third-party principles in that they carried through reform legislation.

15. You should be able to identify the following personalities: Oliver H. Kelley, Horace Austin, Ignatius Donnelly, Knute Nelson, John Lind, and Sidney M. Owen.

16. Why is importance attached to the 1892 (national) platform of the Populist party?
17. You should be able to explain what is meant by initiative, referendum, recall, direct election of senators, primary election, Australian ballot.
18. The year 1896 is, in a sense, a dividing line in the history of both the Republican and the Democratic parties. How so?
19. What did the political developments of 1896 mean to the Populist party? Who were the "Middle-of-the-Roaders"? the Fusionists?
20. The Populist party hoped to replace one of the two major parties, even as the Republican party had done in 1854. It failed to do so. Would you say that the whole movement was, therefore, a failure?
21. It is said that the spirit of independence in voting is strong in Minnesota, and that this characteristic has stemmed from its strong third-party movements. Political scientists hold that this is both good and bad. Give pros and cons.
22. The Farmer-Labor party was not organized until the twentieth century. What examples of political cooperation between farmers and laborers could you point to during the last half of the nineteenth century? Do you find support for the thought that the Farmer-Labor party has its roots in the soil of third-party protest activity of the post-Civil War period?
23. For third-party movements of protest in the twentieth century see topic 34.

REFERENCES

ADAMS, ELMER E., "The Nelson-Kindred Campaign of 1882," *Minnesota History Bulletin*, 5:89–107 (May, 1923).

* † BLEGEN, THEODORE C., *Building Minnesota*, pp. 295–306.

———— ed., "Campaigning with Seward in 1860," *Minnesota History*, 8:150–71 (June, 1927). From the diaries of Charles Francis Adams and Charles Francis Adams, Jr.

*BRINGS, LAWRENCE M., ed., *Minnesota Heritage*: Theodore Fenske, "From Furs to Farming," pp. 159–62. The agrarian crusade of the post-Civil War period. These pages contain a reprint of an article by Theodore C. Blegen which appeared originally in the *Minnesota Alumni Weekly*.

* BUCK, SOLON J., *The Agrarian Crusade: A Chronicle of the Farmer in Politics* (1920). An admirable survey of both the Granger and Alliance movements, and their political counterparts.

———— *The Granger Movement* (1913 and reprint 1921). A more extensive treatment than the volume cited just above.

*———— "Lincoln and Minnesota," *Minnesota History*, 6:355–61 (Dec., 1925). A very interesting short essay.

CASTLE, HENRY A., "Reminiscences of Minnesota Politics," *Minnesota Historical Collections*, 15:553–91 (1915). Political annals, 1880–90. Castle was editor of the *St. Paul Dispatch* from 1876 to 1885.

CHATELAIN, VERNE E., "The Federal Land Policy and Minnesota Politics, 1854–60," *Minnesota History*, 22:227–48 (Sept., 1941). One theory as to why Minnesota went Republican in the national election of 1860.

* CHRISLOCK, CARL H., "The Alliance Party and the Minnesota Legislature of 1891," *Minnesota History*, 35:297–312 (Sept., 1957).

*——— "Sidney M. Owen, an Editor in Politics," *Minnesota History*, 36: 109–26 (Dec., 1958).

CHRISTIANSON, THEODORE, *Minnesota*. 1:445–58, 464–65; 2:9–64, 81–91, 99, 107–19, politics from 1869 to 1880. 2:121–29, 142–89, politics 1880–1890. 2:191–206, 231–41, 251–65, Governors Nelson, Clough, and Lind.

FOLWELL, WILLIAM W., *History*. 3:14–18, 32–57, 66–68, 73–92, politics in the 1870's. 3:116–18, 143–53, 168–74, 184–87, politics in the 1880's. 3:187–90, 195–206, 219–23, 241–55, 474–79, politics in the 1890's. The treatment is essentially chronological. Some attention is given to third parties, but not as a central theme in this post-Civil War survey.

*† FRIDLEY, RUSSELL W., "Oliver H. Kelley: Founder of the National Grange," *Gopher Historian*, 10:12–13 (Winter, 1955–56). Also found in Poatgieter and Dunn, *Gopher Reader*, pp. 124–25.

* HICKS, JOHN D., "The Origin and Early History of the Farmers' Alliance in Minnesota," *Mississippi Valley Historical Review*, 9:203–26 (Dec., 1922).

*——— "The People's Party in Minnesota," *Minnesota History Bulletin*, 5:531–60 (Nov., 1924).

*——— "The Persistence of Populism," *Minnesota History*, 12:3–20 (March, 1931).

*——— "The Political Career of Ignatius Donnelly," *Mississippi Valley Historical Review*, 8:92–132 (June–Sept., 1921).

*——— *The Populist Revolt: A History of the Farmers' Alliance and the People's Party* (1931). Pp. 54–185, farmers' grievances; the Farmers' Alliance and its activities. Pp. 205–423, the best account of the Populist party.

HOLMES, FRANK R., *Minnesota in Three Centuries*, 4:33–106, the administrations of Austin, Davis, and Pillsbury. 4:131–88, the administrations of Hubbard, McGill, and Merriam. 4:189–209, political history, 1893–1900.

HOLMQUIST, JUNE D., "Convention City: The Republicans in Minneapolis, 1892," *Minnesota History*, 35:64–76 (June, 1956). A national party convention has been held in Minnesota only once.

Johnson, Hildegard B., "The Election of 1860 and the Germans in Minnesota," *Minnesota History*, 28:20–36 (March, 1947).

Larson, Henrietta M., *The Wheat Market and the Farmer in Minnesota, 1858–1900*, pp. 75–117, 166–219. Monopoly and the Grange; reforming the grain market.

Lawson, Victor E., "The Farmers' Alliance in Kandiyohi County," *Minnesota History Bulletin*, 4:337–39 (Aug.–Nov., 1922).

Merrill, Horace Samuel, *Bourbon Democracy of the Middle West, 1865–1896* (1953).

* Naftalin, Arthur, "The Tradition of Protest and the Roots of the Farmer-Labor Party," *Minnesota History*, 35:53–63 (June, 1956). An excellent survey of the rise of agrarian and labor organizations of the nineteenth century and of their political activity.

Odland, Martin W., *The Life of Knute Nelson*, pp. 159–223 (1926). Nelson as governor; his campaign for the senatorship.

Preus, Jacob A. O., "Knute Nelson," *Minnesota History Bulletin*, 5:329–47 (Feb., 1924). Governor Preus began his political career as Nelson's secretary.

* † Ridge, Martin, "Ignatius Donnelly," *Gopher Historian*, 12:31 (Winter, 1957–58). A brief outline biography of this spokesman for discontented farmers and workers.

Saby, Rasmus S., "Railroad Regulation in Minnesota, 1849–1875," *Minnesota Historical Collections*, 15:70–86, 120–51 (1915). The Grange and railroad legislation.

Shannon, Fred A., *The Farmers' Last Frontier, 1860–97*, pp. 291–348 (1945). The Granger and Alliance movements.

Smith, Donnal V., "The Influence of the Foreign-Born of the Northwest in the Election of 1860," *Mississippi Valley Historical Review*, 19:192–204 (Sept., 1932).

Stephenson, George M., *John Lind of Minnesota*. The best biography of this Minnesotan. Pp. 28–82, Lind's congressional career. Pp. 83–190, the farmers' struggle for equality in the 1890's and Lind's part in that struggle.

VI. MINNESOTA SHARES IN THE NATION'S POST-CIVIL WAR INDUSTRIAL ADVANCE

20. The Development of a Railroad System

A. Minnesota and the 1865–1900 Industrial Revolution in the United States
Minnesota's participation in the Industrial Revolution is healthy, but less rapid and not as intensive as in East. Factors influencing degree of industrial advance: youth of state, sparseness of population, preoccupa-

tion with frontier demands, tardiness in unearthing mineral resources, need of capital. The four major industries of the period: railroading, lumbering, flour milling, iron mining. Quiet but steady growth of many smaller industries. Special character of railroading — serves all other industries.

B. Pioneer Enthusiasm and Early Disappointments

A national policy set by the pattern of land grants to the Illinois Central of 1850 and the resultant fever for railroad building. Minnesota memorializes Congress for a railroad land grant, 1851. Isaac I. Stevens and his survey. The railroad charter of 1854 — and miscarriage. Growing demand for improved transportation. Problem of getting wheat to market in Minnesota. The federal Land-Grant Act of 1857: extent of grant; the six routes and four companies chartered. Effect of the Panic of 1857 on proposed railroad building in Minnesota. The "5 million dollar loan" fiasco.

C. Rapid Construction, 1862–73

Minnesota's land-grant railroads of 1857 reorganized. The first ten miles in Minnesota: St. Paul–St. Anthony, 1862. The beginnings of the Northern Pacific. Connection with Chicago, 1867 and 1871. The Lake Superior and Mississippi. The main trunk lines begin to take shape. The railroad system in 1873. Connections east and south. Decline of steamboat and stagecoach. Stimulus to agriculture and industry.

D. Renewed Expansion, 1877–93

Effects of the Panic of 1873: a temporary check to building and encouragement of a consolidation trend. Main trunk lines essentially completed. Filling in with "feeder" lines. James J. Hill: interest in the Red River Valley, relations with the Canadians, emergence of the Great Northern. Henry Villard and the Northern Pacific. The Soo Line and the millers. Iron range railroads. Emergence of the Twin Cities as a railroad center, a consequence of the 1857 charter pattern; Duluth a second center. Importance to a community of securing railroad connection; competition of towns. Railroad finance: lavish government land grants; gifts of money or depot sites; extension of credit by local government units; railroad bonds, defaults, and reorganization. Railroads as agents of settlement and colonization. Change in public attitude toward railroads with consolidation and concentration of control; the great systems emerge; railroad abuses and growing demand for regulation.

E. Building toward Saturation Point in Trackage, 1897–1920

Another panic (1893), and again a construction slowdown and more consolidation. James J. Hill's absorption of Henry Villard's Northern Pacific. The Northern Securities Company, 1901; James J. Hill and J. P. Morgan.

Completion of track coverage of the state and linkage with all parts of the nation.

F. Retrenchment, 1920–

World War I and the interlude of management by the federal government. Postwar return of roads to private management. Serious problems for the railroads: competition from the automobile, truck, bus, and later the airplane; point of diminishing returns; overcapitalization; bankruptcies and reorganization; government regulation and fixed rates. Talk of government ownership. Meeting the new difficulties by improved services, streamlined trains, diesel engines, more favorable passenger accommodations and rates, emphasis on freight and long-distance travel. The role of the railroads in Minnesota's first century of growth.

QUESTIONS AND SUGGESTIONS

1. Account for the sudden interest in railroad building in pioneer Minnesota, as well as the rapidity with which a railroad system came to be built.

2. Henry M. Rice's railroad land-grant act of 1857 set the stage for railroad building in Minnesota. What were the terms of this act? What pattern did it set for the state's railroad lines?

3. By what route and by what means of conveyance would a letter from Fort Snelling have reached Washington, D.C., in 1825? in 1845? in 1865?

4. How important a role did railroads play in the economic life of the prairie regions? List ways in which the railroads might affect the farmer. How did panics affect railroad construction?

5. Show how railroad building was financed.

6. Why were flour millers interested in a railroad east through Sault Ste. Marie?

7. What effect did iron mining in northern Minnesota have upon railroad development?

8. A study of the life of James J. Hill will give a fair picture of railroad development in Minnesota. Points worthy of note in such a study: What led him to enter the field of railroad building? How important a role in his remarkable career was played by capital, government land grants, organizational talent, Minnesota iron, immigration influx?

9. In what way were the following men connected with Minnesota railroad development: Jay Cooke, Henry Villard, Norman Kittson, Donald Smith.

10. Despite the interest and support which farmers gave the coming of railroads, it was not long before they demanded regulation of railroads. Explain. For more detailed suggestions on this subject see topic 19.

11. Note in Robinson, *Early Economic Conditions and the Development of*

Agriculture in Minnesota, pp. 35, 37, the map of the Mississippi showing railroads and river ports in 1860, and of railroads in operation in Minnesota in 1869.

12. The relation of Minnesota railroad building, 1860–70, to that of the nation is shown on Plates 139B and 140A in Paullin, *Atlas.* The relation of federal land grants for the construction of railroads and wagon roads in Minnesota to the grants made in other states is illustrated by Plate 56D. The James J. Hill railroads in 1914 are shown on Plate 141G.

13. What manner of financial assistance, direct or indirect, has Congress through the years accorded to trucks, buses, and airplanes? How do railroads today feel about this aid?

14. Special study project: The story of railroading in your home community — beginnings; extent of local financial assistance; government grants of land and sale of these lands; trunk and feeder-line services; meaning to community; significant changes through the years.

15. Map exercise: On an outline map of the state show, in black, the railroad system as proposed in 1857. Trace, in color, the lines completed by 1873.

16. Map exercise: On a series of outline maps of the state show railroad lines as they were in (or near) 1873; 1893; and 1920.

REFERENCES

BISHOP, JUDSON W., "History of the St. Paul and Sioux City Railroad, 1864–1881," Minnesota Historical Collections, vol. 10, part 1, pp. 399–415 (1905). Bishop was chief engineer for the railroad.

*† BLEGEN, THEODORE C., *Building Minnesota,* pp. 243–50.

BLEGEN, THEODORE C., and PHILIP D. JORDAN, *With Various Voices,* pp. 177–90. James J. Hill's own account of the development of the Great Northern system.

*† CHAMBERLIN, THOMAS W., "The Railroads of Minnesota," *Gopher Historian,* 11:21, 22 (Spring, 1957). A brief, good portrayal of the status of railroading in Minnesota after one century. Also found in Poatgieter and Dunn, *Gopher Reader,* pp. 172–73.

CHRISTIANSON, THEODORE, *Minnesota,* 1:421–40; 2:65–80. The railroad era.

CROOKS, WILLIAM, "The First Railroad in Minnesota," Minnesota Historical Collections, vol. 10, part 1, pp. 445–48 (1905). The Minnesota and Pacific Railroad Company.

FOLWELL, WILLIAM W., "The Five Million Loan," Minnesota Historical Collections, 15:189–214 (1915).

*——— *History,* 1:327–50; 2:37–60, 328–30; 3:2–3, 60–62, 141–42, 441–74. Railroads, railroad legislation, and politics. Dr. Folwell's map of "The Railroad Situation" is reproduced on the facing page.

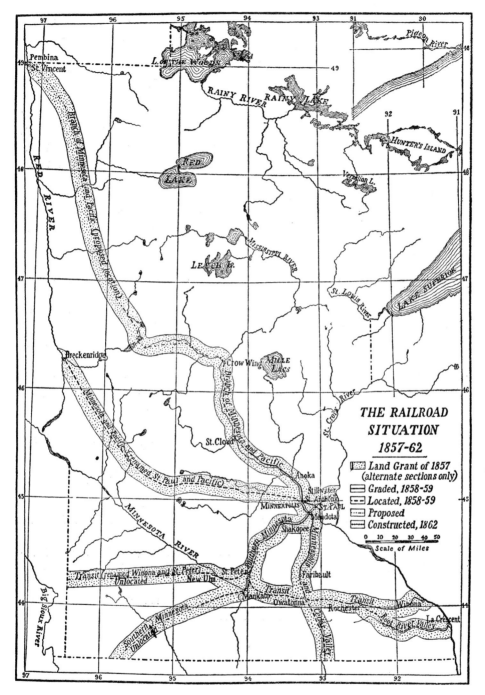

THE RAILROAD
SITUATION
1857-62

▨ Land Grant of 1857
(alternate sections only)
▭ Graded, 1858-59
▭ Located, 1858-59
▭ Proposed
▭ Constructed, 1862

0 10 20 30 40 50
Scale of Miles

105

HARTSOUGH, MILDRED L., *The Development of the Twin Cities as a Metropolitan Market*, pp. 72–112. Transportation and rates in the development of the Twin Cities.

*————— "Transportation as a Factor in the Development of the Twin Cities," *Minnesota History*, 7:218–25 (Sept., 1926).

HEILBRON, BERTHA L., *The Thirty-Second State*, pp. 188–92.

————— ed., "Isaac I. Stevens and the Pacific Railroad Survey of 1853," *Minnesota History*, 7:127–49 (June, 1926). Excerpts from Stevens's *Narrative and Final Report* skillfully woven together and edited. An illustration shows St. Paul in 1853 as drawn by an artist on the Stevens expedition.

* HOLBROOK, STEWART H., *James J. Hill, a Great Life in Brief* (1955). Perhaps the best treatment of Hill available, even if not extensive.

*————— "The Legend of Jim Hill," *American Heritage*, 9 (no. 4):10–13, 98–101 (June, 1958). Brief but excellent. Based upon his earlier biography. The illustrations are apt.

HOLMES, HAROLD R., *Minnesota in Three Centuries*, 4:337–73. The railroad era in Minnesota.

PETERSON, HAROLD F., "Early Minnesota Railroads and the Quest for Settlers," *Minnesota History*, 13:25–44 (March, 1932).

————— "Some Colonization Projects of the Northern Pacific Railroad," *Minnesota History*, 10:127–44 (June, 1929).

*† POATGIETER, A. H., "The First Train Trip in Minnesota," *Gopher History*, 11:12–15, 23 (Spring, 1957). Also in Poatgieter and Dunn, *Gopher Reader*, pp. 174–78. A play based upon newspaper accounts of the initial trip on Minnesota's first ten miles of track.

PYLE, JOSEPH G., "James J. Hill," *Minnesota History Bulletin*, 2:296–302 (Feb., 1918).

————— *Life of James J. Hill*, 2 vols. (1917). Highly laudatory.

RANDALL, JOHN H., "The Beginning of Railroad Building in Minnesota," Minnesota Historical Collections, 15:215–20 (1915).

* SABY, RASMUS S., "Railroad Legislation in Minnesota, 1849 to 1875," Minnesota Historical Collections, 15:1–188 (1915).

* SHIPPEE, LESTER B., "The First Railroad between the Mississippi and Lake Superior," *Mississippi Valley Historical Review*, 5:121–42 (Sept., 1918). A model brief account of one railroad.

* SHORTRIDGE, WILSON P., *The Transition of a Typical Frontier*, pp. 132–45. The coming of the railroad to Minnesota.

[VI. MINNESOTA SHARES IN THE NATION'S POST-CIVIL WAR INDUSTRIAL ADVANCE]

21. *The Lumber Industry*

A. Minnesota Lumbering: An Epic

The state's pristine forest endowment; kind and amount of virgin timber; importance of white pine; rivers and lakes in relation to the lumber industry; water power. Conquest of the forest frontier an aspect of the nation's westward movement and a spur to settlement in Minnesota. The dramatic role of both the lumber magnate and the lumberjack.

B. Pioneer Period (1837–70)

Beginnings: the soldiers' mill at St. Anthony Falls; Treaty of 1837 and the opening of the St. Croix Delta to lumbering; entry of lumbermen from the East, especially Maine and New England; French-Canadian, Scotch, and Scandinavian influx. Survey of Delta lands and purchase by lumbermen. Small-scale logging operations with primitive equipment and techniques; the one-room Maine shanty. Early sawmill centers: Marine and Stillwater on the St. Croix River, Anoka on the Rum River, Winona and St. Anthony on the Mississippi River. One sawmill in 1839, 207 in 1870. Markets dependent upon the westward movement of the United States; importance of the Mississippi River. Rafting.

C. Broadened Markets (1870–90)

Continuing demand for lumber from down-river Mississippi. New markets in the wake of railroads and settlement of trans-Mississippi areas: southwestern, western, and northern Minnesota and the neighboring Dakotas, Montana, Iowa, Kansas, and Nebraska. Railroads and the speed-up of shipments — taking loads of lumber out to these areas, bringing wheat on the return trip. Spread of logging operations northward and farther from the river banks. Increased size of logging camps, improved equipment, wider division of labor in camps. Improvements in sawmill machinery and techniques of operation. Growth in state of allied industries using lumber. Decline of sawmills on the Mississippi River below the state line; end of rafting.

D. Maturity: Peak Production (1890–1905)

Decline of production in Michigan and the opening of the eastern markets to Minnesota lumber. Invasion of Minnesota by Michigan lumbermen and capital; new methods and a quickened tempo. Frederick Weyerhaeuser and the trend toward larger companies; consolidation; lumbering as big business. Great increase of lumber production in the 1890's; Minneapolis becomes the top lumber market of the world. Rise of new and important mill centers: Duluth, Cloquet, and the range towns. Continuing importance of western and northwestern Minnesota and of the

Dakotas as markets; shipment east via the Great Lakes. Concentration of timberlands of northern Minnesota in hands of a few. Fraudulent manipulation of land laws. Life of the lumberjack; work, wages, camp cabins, cookhouse, camp store, recreation, and colorful language.

E. Period of Retreat, 1905–

Dwindling timber supply; ruthless cutting; fires; closing of sawmills. Problems attendant upon decline: unemployment, failures in farming cutover lands, tax delinquency, relief rolls. The beginning of a new cycle: gradual regrowth of timber resources although of different tree varieties; establishment of federal and state forests and parks; a replacement for sawmilling with the rise of new forest products industries — pulpwood and paper, firewood, insulation board, matchwood, Christmas trees and wreaths. Capital of lumber kings available for new industries and for philanthropies.

QUESTIONS AND SUGGESTIONS

1. How large an area of the state was forested originally? How large an area is forested at present? See the report of the state Planning Board.
2. Suggest some ways in which the climate and geography of the state tended to promote lumbering.
3. If you view the story of lumbering in Minnesota as a part of the nation's history, you will realize that it is an aspect of the westward movement — the Maine lumber frontier moving to New York, to Michigan, to Wisconsin, and then to Minnesota.
4. Give some reasons for considering lumbering a typical pioneer industry.
5. In what ways was Minnesota lumber important in the building of the West?
6. Compare the production of lumber in 1870 with that in 1890; in 1905; in 1930; in 1950.
7. Did the lumbermen have any connection with the Indian cession treaties of 1837, 1854, and 1855?
8. Two distinct phases of the lumber industry were "logging" and "lumber milling." Be sure that you can distinguish between them.
9. Terms to identify: go-devil, peavey, spring drive, timber cruiser, road monkey, raft pilot.
10. Persons to identify: Daniel Stanchfield, John McKusick, Samuel F. Hersey and Isaac Staples, Dorilus Morrison, W. H. Laird, Frederick Weyerhaeuser.
11. Contrast logging operations of the pioneer period with lumbering at its height. Do the same for milling.
12. Show how seasonal changes affected lumbering activities. How did this in turn affect the annual work pattern of the lumberjack?

13. When lumbering reached its peak in the state, how did Minnesota compare with other states on such points as amount of board feet cut, value of product, and number of men employed?
14. As Minnesota's lumber was marketed it was scattered far and wide over the country. What areas in particular used Minnesota's lumber? Indicate the different types of uses to which this lumber was put in each of these areas.
15. List the main steps in the transformation of a stand of white pine in the St. Croix Delta to finished lumber at the St. Louis market. You should be able to describe at least four main steps.
16. What native and foreign-born groups played significant roles in the development of the state's lumber industry? What special contributions did each group make?
17. Build a case *for* and another *against* the following statement: Stripping the state of its timber resources in the short span of seventy years by the lumber barons of Minnesota can only be viewed as unmitigated tragedy. Consult the article by Leona T. Rienow cited below.
18. What measures have been taken to protect and restore timber resources?
19. Report: The Paul Bunyan myths. Have these myths any significance beyond being amusing and entertaining? There is an extensive literature developing around Paul Bunyan. Not a little of it is manifestly modern and spurious; that is, it attempts to fasten upon the lumberjack many tales which he never invented.

REFERENCES

BACHMAN, ELIZABETH M., "Minnesota Log Marks," *Minnesota History*, 26:126–37 (June, 1945).

* BARDON, JOHN A., "Early Logging Methods," *Minnesota History*, 15: 203–6 (June, 1934).

* † BLEGEN, THEODORE C., *Building Minnesota*, pp. 253–60.

BLEGEN, THEODORE C., and PHILIP D. JORDAN, *With Various Voices*, pp. 124–42. A traveler's account of lumbering activity along the Rum River in 1868.

† BUCKMAN, CLARENCE B., "Lumbering and the Pine Forests," *Gopher Historian*, 13:9–13 (Spring, 1959). Discusses beginnings and present-day forestry practices. There are ten excellent photographs.

CHRISTIANSON, THEODORE, *Minnesota*, 2:207–13. The pine land investigation.

DELAITTRE, JOSEPH A., as told to Calvin L. DeLaittre, *A Story of Early Lumbering in Minnesota* (1959). Personal recollections graphically told. Photo documentation is of a high order.

DURANT, EDWARD W., "Lumbering and Steamboating on the St. Croix

River," Minnesota Historical Collections, vol. 10, part 2, pp. 645–75 (1905).

FOLWELL, WILLIAM W., *History*, 1:227–29, 307–8, 356–58, 470–78; 2:332; 3:60, 63, 141, 208n, 252, 500–15. Some aspects of the history of lumbering in Minnesota.

GLASER, EMMA, "How Stillwater Came to Be," *Minnesota History*, 24:195–206 (Sept., 1943). Lumbering founds a town.

HAGG, HAROLD T., "The Beltrami County Logging Frontier," *Minnesota History*, 29:137–49 (June, 1948). One of the last lumbering frontiers — northwest Minnesota.

———— "The Lumberjack's Sky Pilot," *Minnesota History*, 31:65–78 (June, 1950). Deals with an aspect of lumbering not commonly considered — his spiritual welfare.

* HEILBRON, BERTHA L., *The Thirty-Second State*, pp. 175–79.

HOLCOMBE, RETURN I., *Minnesota in Three Centuries*, 2:135–42. The beginning of the lumber industry.

HOLMES, FRANK R., *Minnesota in Three Centuries*, 4:401–17. Lumbering in the St. Croix Valley.

† * KANE, LUCILE, "Isaac Staples, Pioneer Lumberman," *Gopher Historian*, 7:7–9 (Jan., 1953). Brief, but highly illuminating.

KAUFERT, FRANK H., "Minnesota's Forests and Forest-Products Industries," *Minnesota's Tomorrow: The Economic Future of Our Region* (1956). A publication of the Social Science Research Center of the Graduate School of the University of Minnesota. Presents an optimistic view of the newer uses of Minnesota's forests.

* LARSON, AGNES, *History of the White Pine Industry in Minnesota* (1949). The standard work on this subject. From beginnings, through peak, to decline. Illustrated.

*———— "On the Trail of the Woodsman in Minnesota," *Minnesota History*, 13:349–66 (Dec., 1932). A spirited account of the lumberjack and his life.

*———— "When Logs and Lumber Ruled Stillwater," *Minnesota History*, 18:165–79 (June, 1937).

† LEE, MARJORIE W., "Early Beginnings of Stillwater," *Gopher Historian*, 7:3–5 (Jan., 1953). By a native of the town. Her father was a Stillwater pioneer and local historian.

LOEHR, RODNEY C., "Caleb D. Dorr and the Early Minnesota Lumber Industry," *Minnesota History*, 24:125–41 (June, 1943). Presents a picture of beginnings.

NELSON, ALFRED L., "Paul Bunyan — The Great Logger," *Conservation Volunteer*, 21:1–6 (July–Aug., 1958). Very brief. Gives a taste of the Paul Bunyan tales.

110

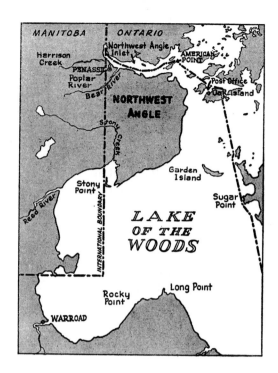

NELSON, LOWRY, *The Minnesota Community*, pp. 126–46. Discusses the problems of the cutover region of Minnesota.

NEVUE, WILFRED, "A Winter in the Woods," *Minnesota History*, 34:149–53 (Winter, 1954). This lumberjack's experiences in a camp came late, when the industry was at its peak (winter of 1905–6). The scene: far north in the state. The author's photographs are excellent.

ORCUTT, WRIGHT T., "The Minnesota Lumberjacks," *Minnesota History*, 6:3–19 (March, 1925).

ORFIELD, MATTHIAS N., *Federal Land Grants to the States, with Special Reference to Minnesota*, pp. 168–218. Timber lands, Chippewa half-breed, scrip, and frauds.

Minnesota at Midpoint: An Economic Survey of Minnesota at the Turn of the Half-Century, 1950, pp. 9–14 (1950). A publication of the state Department of Business Research and Development.

Minnesota's Wood Pile (1954). A publication of the Office of Iron Range Resources and Rehabilitation of the state of Minnesota. This pamphlet has valuable data and graphs which seek to give an appraisal of the state's timber resources.

† POATGIETER, A. H., and J. T. DUNN, *Gopher Reader*, pp. 232–38. A brief

account of the state's golden age of lumbering, log branding, and the diverse origins of her lumberjacks.

RIENOW, LEONA T., "Lament for Minnesota; One Hundred Years of Pillage," *Harper's Magazine*, 216:57–59 (May, 1958). A scathing indictment of the decimation of the state's timber and mineral resources. For rebuttal read Agnes Larson, *History of the White Pine Industry in Minnesota*, pp. 403–15.

SHEPHARD, ESTHER, *Paul Bunyan* (1924). Perhaps the best collection of Bunyan yarns.

STANCHFIELD, DANIEL, "History of Pioneer Lumbering on the Upper Mississippi and Its Tributaries," Minnesota Historical Collections, 9:325–62 (1901). By a pioneer lumberman.

WALKER, THOMAS B., "Memories of the Early Life and Development of Minnesota," Minnesota Historical Collections, 15:455–78 (1915). Written by one of the lumber kings.

WELSH, THOMAS J., "Logging on the Northwest Angle," *Minnesota History*, 34:1–8 (Spring, 1954). The Northwest Angle was the scene of some very late cutting. A map of the Angle from this article is reproduced on p. 111.

[VI. MINNESOTA SHARES IN THE NATION'S POST-CIVIL WAR INDUSTRIAL ADVANCE]

22. *Flour Milling: Vanguard of Minnesota Manufacturing*

A. Small Beginnings

Army grist mill at St. Anthony Falls, 1823. Mills of the territorial period: use of grinding stones; power sources (horses, wind, water); types. Difficulties: lack of wheat, of machinery, of millwrights. Eighty-one mills by 1860. Hard spring wheat and expansion to 507 mills by 1870. Drift to merchant milling and improved processes. Lead of southeastern Minnesota. Minneapolis beginnings: Nicollet Island mill; C. C. Washburn and the Washburn B mill, 1866; John Crosby; John S. Pillsbury.

B. The "Milling Revolution," 1870–90

Minneapolis becomes the "Mill City." Factors explaining the rapid rise of milling in Minneapolis: St. Anthony Falls; available capital; work of George Christian, Edmund La Croix, James S. Bell, and others; the middlings purifier; the Hungarian roller process; acknowledged quality of the product; large-scale production; concentration of ownership; development of national and export markets. Subsidiary influences: barrel and bag manufacturing, rise of Minneapolis as center of banking and finance.

C. Minneapolis: "Flour City" of the world, 1890–1920

Features of Minneapolis milling: adoption of scientific methods of test-

112

ing wheat and flour; bleaching; efforts to control or manage elevators and railroads in marketing and shipping of grain; diversification of products (dark bread, macaroni, breakfast foods). Drive for wider markets: heavy advertising; use of brand names and slogans. Decline of some smaller Minnesota mills away from Minneapolis; continuing growth of others. Factors leading to a drop in Minneapolis production after 1915: unfavorable railroad rate decisions, higher freight rates; a decreasing supply of hard red spring wheat; competition of Canadian wheat and the transfer of export trade to Buffalo; the rise of other milling centers; a deliberate effort to decentralize; the increasing supply of good wheat in Kansas and elsewhere; the drop in demand for high-quality flour with the development of wholesale bakeries and the decline of home baking, the rise of chain groceries, and the reducing fad.

D. The Building of a National Milling Empire, 1920–
Turmoil of World War I and its critical aftermath. New leaders: James Ford Bell, Harry A. Bullis, Donald Davis. Expansion of the Washburn Crosby Company with mills at Chicago and Kansas City in 1922, and a packaged food plant at Chicago in 1923. Advertising on a grand scale: WCCO radio, 1924; Betty Crocker; "Breakfast of Champions." Washburn Crosby Company joins three other widely scattered milling firms to form General Mills, Inc., a holding company controlling 27 operating companies in 16 states; the world's largest miller. Weathering the depression of 1929–33. Emphasis on packaged foods like Bisquick and Cheerios. General Mills changes from a holding company to an operating company in 1937. Research intensified during and after World War II: the soybean and its diverse products, Softasilk and the many cake mixes, Crustquick, and Brown'n Serve rolls.

E. Unspectacular but Steady Growth to 1900 in Minnesota Manufacturing Other Than Flour
Flour milling not the only area of manufacturing. Other industries mostly small; single proprietorships or partnerships in the main; generally dependent upon local markets. Pottery works, woolen mills, sash and door factories, furniture and cabinet making, cooperies, foundries and machine shops, breweries, brickmaking, stone quarries, stockyards. Census figures.

QUESTIONS AND SUGGESTIONS

1. What factors in pioneer Minnesota were favorable to the development of flour milling? What factors were unfavorable?
2. Early Minnesota mills first used "toll grinding," then "merchant milling." Distinguish between them.
3. Indicate the relationship between the lumber and the flour industries.

4. How important a factor was flour milling in the growth of Minneapolis?
5. The wheat kernel has four parts. Of what concern was each of these parts to the miller of good flour?
6. What was the "milling revolution" that was of such importance to the Minneapolis millers? Explain why Minnesota's brand of wheat made this revolution necessary.
7. You should know the meaning of such terms as middlings and middlings purifier, high grinding and low grinding, gradual reduction.
8. How were the following connected with milling in Minnesota: George Christian, Edmund La Croix, William H. Dunwoody, James S. Bell?
9. Minneapolis' leadership in flour milling became not only state-wide but nation-wide. Explain.
10. What connection was there between the Minneapolis millers and the Soo Railroad?
11. To ensure a steady supply of wheat the millers helped make Minneapolis the primary grain market of the Northwest. What part in this development was played by the Minneapolis Millers' Association, 1869; the Minneapolis Chamber of Commerce, 1881; the construction of "elevator chains"? How did Minnesota farmers view these developments?
12. Show how the flour-milling industry was related to various other phases of Minnesota's economic development.
13. Explain the establishment by the Minneapolis millers of a mill in Buffalo, New York. Show how freight rates and "bonded wheat" entered the picture.
14. What role was played by James Ford Bell in the establishment of General Mills, first as a holding company, then as an operating company?
15. Would it be correct to say that despite the nation-wide spread of General Mills plants this corporation remains essentially a Minnesota concern?
16. How did World War I affect the millers of Minneapolis? World War II?
17. Select one of the important flour-milling families and trace its ramifications in the economic, social, and political life of Minnesota.
18. Trace changes in type and number of products placed upon the market by the millers of Minneapolis from "beginnings" to "empire" activity of the mid-twentieth century.
19. Map project: On an outline map of the United States locate the following facilities of General Mills in 1952: flour mills, package food plants, grain elevators, feed mills, soybean processing plants, research laboratories, and mechanical plants. Consult James Gray, *Business without Boundary*, the map between pp. 210 and 211.
20. Study project: Develop the story of small manufacturing as you may find it in your home community or perhaps better in one of the larger

114

towns of Minnesota, such as Austin, Albert Lea, Mankato, or St. Cloud. Pay special attention to the period down to 1900.

REFERENCES

* Blegen, Theodore C., *Building Minnesota*, pp. 261–69.

Blegen, Theodore C., and Philip D. Jordan, *With Various Voices*, pp. 164–68. The La Croixs and the development of the middlings purifier.

Christianson, Theodore, *Minnesota*, 1:460–64, 479–80. Events connected with the milling industry.

Folwell, William W., *History*, 3:66–70, 131–38. Grain elevators, flour-milling improvements, and the mill explosion of 1878.

* Fossum, Paul R., "Early Milling in the Cannon River Valley," *Minnesota History*, 11:271–82 (Sept., 1930).

* Gray, James, *Business without Boundary: The Story of General Mills* (1954). Begins with the story of the rise of milling in Minneapolis, giving special attention to the Washburn Crosby Company, pp. 1–89. Then describes the formation of General Mills and nation-wide expansion under that corporation, pp. 90–256. Perhaps too laudatory, but told in an absorbing fashion.

Holmes, Frank R., *Minnesota in Three Centuries*, 4:419–30. The flour-milling industry.

* Kuhlmann, Charles B., *The Development of the Flour-Milling Industry in the United States, with Special Reference to the Industry in Minneapolis*, pp. 104–82, 212–323 (1929). Flour milling in Minnesota.

——— "The Influence of the Minneapolis Flour Mills upon the Economic Development of Minnesota and the Northwest," *Minnesota History*, 6:141–54 (June, 1925).

*† Poatgieter, A. H., "The Story of Milling in Minnesota," *Gopher Historian*, 6:1–4 (Dec., 1951). Gives a clear picture of the main trends. Written by the magazine's editor with assistance from C. K. Mitchener, editor of the *Northwest Miller*. Brief. Also found in Poatgieter and Dunn, *Gopher Reader*, pp. 228–30.

Storck, John, and Walter Dorwin Teague, *Flour for Man's Bread: A History of Milling* (1952). See especially pp. 185–212, 241–45, 283–86, 318–21.

[VI. MINNESOTA SHARES IN THE NATION'S POST-CIVIL WAR INDUSTRIAL ADVANCE]

23. *The Iron Mining Industry*

A. Geological History and Early Interest in the Mining Area

Formation of iron deposits, the geological story. Minnesota's three ranges. Iron deposits of Michigan, Wisconsin, and Minnesota and the importance of Minnesota's ranges in the picture of natural resources in the nation. Ramsey's idea of the mineral wealth in the north; Peter Mitchell. Henry H. Eames report, 1865; the Vermilion Lake gold rush. Newton H. Winchell surveys, 1878 and 1880. Other searchers for iron deposits during the 1880's.

B. Vermilion, the First Range to Be Opened

Surveys and explorations, 1875 and 1880: George R. Stuntz, George C. Stone, and Albert H. Chester. Investment in ore lands by Charlemagne Tower and Samuel Munson. Soudan mine opened in 1882; the Minnesota Iron Company. Securing a state grant of land for a railroad; building the railroad, Tower to Two Harbors, 1884; Charlemagne Tower, Jr. Boom in mining companies, 284 by 1890. High quality of ore. Tower, Ely, and other towns. Charlemagne Tower's loss of control of the Minnesota Iron Company to a syndicate of eastern capitalist and steel interests, 1887. The Federal Steel Company.

C. Mesabi Range, Giant of the Nation's Iron Fields

The Merritts and their search for ore. J. A. Nicols and the discovery of the Mountain Iron mine, 1890. Open-pit mining. The Biwabik mine, 1891. Frank Hibbing. The range opened: towns, railroads. Edmund J. Longyear. Archibald M. Chisholm, 1896. Production records. The Merritts lose control to Rockefeller. Henry W. Oliver: lease of mines of Lake Superior Consolidated Company and formation of a fleet of Great Lakes freighters. Importance to steel industry of the Great Lakes. Consolidation trend; United States Steel Corporation organized, 1901. James J. Hill and his bargain with United States Steel.

D. The Cuyuna Range and Minor Deposits of Southern Minnesota

Discovery by Cuyler Adams, 1895. Kennedy mine opened, 1911. High manganese content of the ore. Discovery of ore in Fillmore County, 1884 and 1930. Small-scale production. Growing emphasis on research by the industry: grading of ores to secure evenness of quality, analysis of chemical content, beneficiation of low-grade ores.

E. The Iron Range Country: Social and Economic Developments

Speedy transfer of ore lands to private ownership; federal land laws and their evasion; previous holdings of lumber interests; soldier and half-breed scrip. Influx of population; diverse national origins. Development and character of range towns; lavish schoolhouses, libraries, and other public buildings. Local taxation policies; Victor Power of Hibbing. The miner and the problem of unemployment. Growth and development of the ore ports: Two Harbors, Duluth, Superior. Ore carriers and terminal docks.

116

F. Two World Wars and the Dwindling of High-Grade Ore

Minnesota iron and victories in two world wars. Effect on prices and production. Near exhaustion of best areas. Low-grade ore and Oliver Mining's first beneficiating plant, 1907. State royalty and occupation taxes; relationship to permanent trust funds of the state. The depression of 1929 and unemployment. Expanded use of labor-saving machinery, check in population growth of mining areas, marketing problems. Critical picture of the 1950's: dwindling supply of high-quality iron ore reserves and competition from Venezuela, Brazil, and Quebec-Labrador. Growing interest in taconite; vast reserves; finding an economically feasible method of beneficiation; lengthy experimentation of E. W. Davis; magnetic and nonmagnetic taconite. State and local tax policies: stifle or encourage taconite processing? Reserve Mining Company at Babbitt and Silver Bay, 1952; Oliver Iron Mining Company at Mountain Iron and Virginia, 1953; Erie Mining Company at Hoyt Lakes and Taconite Harbor, 1957. Climbing production. The outlook. Company sponsorship of new modern towns.

QUESTIONS AND SUGGESTIONS

1. Is there any geological relationship between the iron ranges of Minnesota and those of Wisconsin and Michigan? Of what importance to the United States in its post-Civil War industrial advance was the iron of these three states? of Minnesota alone?
2. Can you see any explanation for the tardiness in opening Minnesota's iron mines?
3. Describe early efforts to find minerals in the northeast area.
4. Who were the "Seven Iron Men" described by Paul de Kruif?
5. How did the state "lose" the Mountain Iron mine?
6. What connection did the following men have with the development of the iron mining industry in Minnesota: George C. Stone, Charlemagne Tower, Charlemagne Tower, Jr., Henry W. Oliver, John D. Rockefeller, James J. Hill, Leonidas Merritt?
7. Iron ore formations may vary considerably. How about differences which prevailed in Minnesota's three ranges? Did these differences affect methods of mining? cost?
8. You ought to know the meaning of the following terms: overburden, sampling, Bessemer process, manganiferous ore, concentration.
9. Of what significance to the iron industry were the Great Lakes? How does coal enter this picture?
10. How did the Merritts lose control of their Mesabi interests? to whom?
11. Did capital from Minnesota play as big a role in the development of mining as it did in flour milling?

12. Distinguish between "royalty" and "occupation" taxes. How were these related to the permanent trust funds of the state for some three decades before 1956? What was the development in 1956 that changed this picture?

13. As range towns grew in northeastern Minnesota, they seemed to take on characteristics which were different from towns in other parts of the state. What were some of these characteristics? Consider such points as national origins of population, housing, permanence of location, tax base, use of that tax base, labor problems.

14. Study project: The early appearance of a monopoly trend in Minnesota iron mining.

15. Study project: The state's tax policy on iron mining — significant features and variations through the decades.

16. Study project: Examine the financial records of the state for several given years to find (a) the proportion of the total tax revenue which comes from taxes on iron ore, (b) fluctuations since 1920.

17. Study project: Search for data which will show (a) the tonnage of annual shipments of iron from Minnesota ports since 1945, and (b) the tonnage of annual importation of iron ore from foreign countries since 1945.

18. Map exercise: On an outline map show the iron ranges of Minnesota and the railroads which serve them.

19. Graph exercise: Charts may be prepared which will show (a) a comparison of the output of the Vermilion and Mesabi ranges by decades, (b) the total shipment of ore from Minnesota ports since 1900, (c) changing amounts of estimated ore reserves in the state, especially since 1950 (see the *Minneapolis Star*, December 10, 1958, 4B), (d) growth in taconite production by year since 1950.

20. What part did Minnesota iron play in winning World Wars I and II?

21. Describe the essential steps of the E. W. Davis process in transforming taconite to iron pellets. May both magnetic and nonmagnetic ore be used? What problems relative to finance, water supply, and mining activity explain the hesitance of corporations to embark upon the beneficiation of taconite?

22. Contrast the attitude of the mining companies of the 1950's (which engaged in taconite processing) with that of the mining companies of the 1880's, 1890's, and early 1900's in the matter of housing for employees and in labor relations.

23. When Minnesota celebrated her statehood centennial in 1958 most of her high-grade iron ore had been consumed. What factors or conditions would help determine whether taconite might keep Minnesota in the forefront as a supplier of ore for the steel industry?

REFERENCES

* † A series of articles on Minnesota iron appeared in the *Gopher Historian*, 6:1–13 (April, 1952): George M. Schwartz, "The History behind Our Iron Ranges," pp. 1–2. "How Did Nature Make Minnesota's Iron?" pp. 3–4. Text and charts with the advice of George A. Thiel. William Johnson and Treffle Daniels, "Taconite — New Hope for the Mesabi," pp. 5, 24. Grace Lee Nute, "Charlemagne Tower, Developer of the Vermilion Iron Range," pp. 6, 7, 16. Janna P. Burgess, "Pioneers as Seekers," pp. 8–10, 20. The Merritt brothers. Catherine Munch, ed., "Man-Made Grand Canyon," pp. 12–13.

* †BLEGEN, THEODORE C., *Building Minnesota*, pp. 272–81.

* BRIDGES, LEONARD HAL, *Iron Millionaire: Life of Charlemagne Tower*, pp. 135–283 (1952). An excellent biography of a financier who never visited Minnesota, but whose capital made possible the opening of the first iron range in the state and whose name was affixed to a mining town. There is here an account of acquisition of ore lands, building a railroad and securing land grants for that railroad, mining operations, and highly involved financial dealings.

CHRISTIANSON, THEODORE, *Minnesota*, 2:215–29.

DAVIS, EDWARD W., "Pioneering with Taconite: The Birth of a Minnesota Industry," *Minnesota History*, 34:269–83 (Autumn, 1955). In recognition of his engineering contributions to the industry, the great taconite plant at Silver Bay is called the E. W. Davis Works. While the language of the article is at times technical, the pains of birth are vividly described.

——— "Taconite: The Derivation of the Name," *Minnesota History*, 33: 282–83 (Autumn, 1953).

DE KRUIF, PAUL, *Seven Iron Men* (1929). A dramatic and popular account of the Merritt brothers.

* FOLWELL, WILLIAM W., *History*, 4:1–59. The Minnesota iron mines. His map is reproduced on p. 120.

HEILBRON, BERTHA L., *The Thirty-Second State*, pp. 179–83.

* HODGES, LEROY, "Immigrant Life in the Ore Region of Northern Minnesota," *Survey*, 28:703–9 (Sept. 7, 1912). Living conditions and wages.

HOLBROOK, STEWART H., *Iron Brew: A Century of American Ore and Steel*, pp. 79–147 (1939). Chapters 7 to 15 are of particular interest to Minnesotans.

HOYT, M. H., "Making Americans in Minnesota," *Educational Review*, 58:15–20 (June, 1919). The public schools of Virginia.

NUTE, GRACE LEE, ed., *Mesabi Pioneer: Reminiscences of Edmund J. Longyear* (1951).

"Oliver Mining Company Number," *U.S. Steel News* (June, 1937).

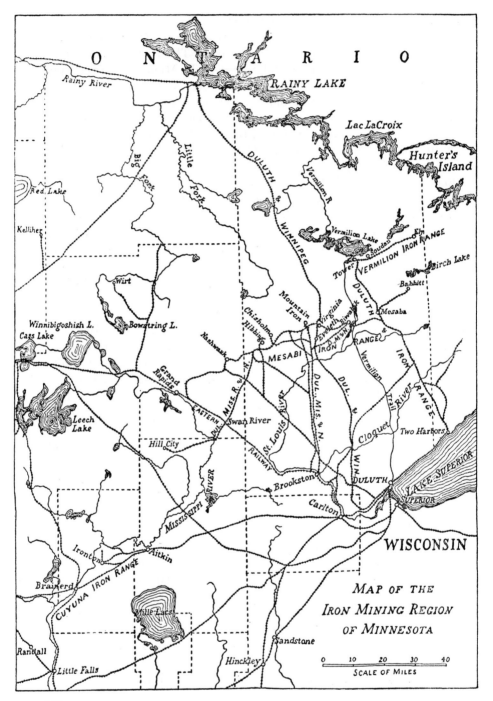

MAP OF THE
IRON MINING REGION
OF MINNESOTA

0   10   20   30   40
SCALE OF MILES

ORFIELD, MATTHIAS N., *Federal Land Grants to the States, with Special Reference to Minnesota*, pp. 219–34. Mineral lands in the state. Loss of the Mountain Iron mine.

PALMER, C. B., "Into the Wilderness: The Taconite Trail," *New York Times Magazine*, Nov. 11, 1956, pp. 14, 15. Enthusiastic portrayal of the beginnings at Silver Bay. Fine illustrations.

* PEDERSON, C. A., "Southern Minnesota's Iron Mines," *Conservation Volunteer*, 21:48–50 (March–April, 1958). A good brief account of how the steel demands of World War II led to the development of Fillmore County iron.

PFEIFFER, C. W., "From Bohunks to Finns," *Survey*, 36:8–14 (April 1, 1916).

* † POATGIETER, A. H., and J. T. DUNN, *Gopher Reader*, pp. 217–27. Geology of the ranges, working the Mesabi, the activities of the Merritt brothers and Charlemagne Tower.

VORSE, M. H., "Mining Strike in Minnesota," *Outlook*, 113:1036, 1045–48 (Aug. 30, 1916). The 1916 strike was important.

WINCHELL, NEWTON, "The Discovery and Development of the Iron Ores of Minnesota," Minnesota Historical Collections, 8:25–40 (1898).

WIRTH, FREMONT P., *The Discovery and Exploitation of the Minnesota Iron Lands* (1937). Discusses fraud and bribery associated with the acquisition of iron ore lands.

——— "The Operation of the Land Laws in the Minnesota Iron District," *Mississippi Valley Historical Review*, 13:483–89 (March, 1927).

[VI. MINNESOTA SHARES IN THE NATION'S POST-CIVIL WAR INDUSTRIAL ADVANCE]

24. *The Rise of Cities and of Labor Organizations*

A. Concomitants of Industrialization

In the state as in the nation the rate of urbanization and extent of labor activity related to speed and intensity of industrialization. City growth in Minnesota less rapid than in the eastern United States; development of labor organizations tardier. In 1860 only 9.4 per cent of the state's population urban and only 3 towns of 2,500 or over; in 1950, 53.9 per cent urban and 90 cities of 2,500 or over. Labor unions few in number before 1880; more than 200 by 1900; state's labor force over 35 per cent unionized by 1954.

B. Pattern for City Growth in Minnesota

In 1950, only 3 cities above 100,000; only 5 between 20,000 and 30,000; 14 between 10,000 and 20,000; preponderance of cities between 2,500 and 10,000, 68. Varying rates of growth in transition from pioneer towns to cities of first, second, third, and fourth class. Rivalry. Factors affecting rate of growth. A noteworthy trend since 1940: growth of suburban communities — St. Louis Park, Bloomington, Roseville, Rosemount, Robbinsdale, and others.

c. The Three Cities of the First Class

St. Paul: An early start by reason of being the head of Mississippi River navigation, the territorial and state capital, a railroad hub, a leading retail and wholesale center by 1872. Nineteenth-century manufacturing: shoes, doors, agricultural implements, cigars, liquor, printing, clothing. Twentieth-century manufacturing: meat packing, chemicals, adhesive tapes, abrasives, electrical equipment, calendars. Population doubled in first four successive decades; 133,156 by 1890; 311,613 by 1950. The capitol buildings and the capitol approach. *Minneapolis:* Favorable location, at the power site of St. Anthony Falls. Establishment of two towns: St. Anthony on the east bank of the Falls and Minneapolis on the west bank. Their merger in 1872. Nineteenth-century industrial emphasis: sawmilling, flour milling, sash and door factories, metal works, grain marketing, banking, wholesale and retail trade in groceries, drugs, furniture, clothing, and hardware. Twentieth-century manufacturing: flour milling, agricultural machinery, industrial machinery, electronic equipment, electronic controls, packaged foods, printing, clothing. Population growth surpasses St. Paul by 1880; 164,738 by 1890; 521,718 by 1950. *The "Twin Cities":* The development of a marketing area. Expansion of credit facilities; banks and other financial agencies; the Ninth Federal Reserve District. Development of large-scale production. The Midway District. The Twin Cities as a cultural, educational, and religious center: University of Minnesota, liberal arts colleges, Minneapolis Symphony, art galleries and museums, libraries, Minnesota Historical Society. *Duluth:* Modest beginnings tied to lumber and railroad promotion. Boom following development of iron mining. Importance of location: harbor at the head of the Great Lakes; railroad connections with the Pacific coast, Canada, and southern and eastern United States. Nineteenth-century shipments: lumber, grain, iron ore. Erection of ore docks, grain elevators, storage warehouses. Twentieth-century shipments second highest tonnage in the nation. Slow growth in population to 1880; jump from 3,483 in 1880 to 33,115 in 1890; 101,463 by 1930; 104,511 by 1950. Extension of Atlantic seacoast inland 1,500 miles by the St. Lawrence Seaway System; erection of municipal marine terminal and expansion of other port facilities by private corporations. Meaning of Seaway to Duluth. Meaning of taconite development to Duluth.

D. The Less Populous Cities: Their Main Streets and Industrial Establishments

Cities with 10,000 to 20,000 population not numerous. Trade centers and social and cultural capitals for surrounding area. General factors favoring growth. Reasons for special development of certain areas, such as Rochester, South St. Paul, St. Cloud, Winona, Mankato, Austin, Red Wing, Le Sueur, Northfield, Virginia. Cities under 10,000: their great number; role in Minnesota life; retail activity; relation to farming area. The "Main Street" outlook.

E. Governing the Cities and Expanding Services

Problems: water supply, fire and police protection, sanitation, streets, schools, parks and playgrounds, housing. Increasing severity of problems with growth in size of cities. Corruption in city government — in nation and in Minnesota. Organization of the League of Minnesota Municipalities, 1913: its publication and advisory services; its attitudes toward the three main types of city government.

F. Cities and the Beginnings of the Labor Movement

Urbanization and economic change: from self-sufficiency of pioneer period to diverse specialization of urban period; increased interdependence of all aspects of economic life; small shop to large factory; large-scale production and large labor force; the large corporation with management separate from ownership; growing inpersonal treatment of labor. Labor's goals; inability to attain them except through organization. Effect of free land upon the early development of the labor movement; of universal manhood suffrage; of the foreign-born worker. Early labor conditions. Unions and strikes of the 1850's, 1860's, and 1870's, few and weak; threat of blacklisting and strike. The Panic of 1873, a setback to union activity. The Anti-Monopoly party upsurge of 1880's. Appearance of city centrals: Trades and Labor Assembly of St. Paul, 1882; Minneapolis Trade Assembly, 1883; Labor Day, 1885. The Knights of Labor in Minnesota, 1878; Terence V. Powderly; experimenting with cooperatives; the state Board of Labor Statistics, 1887. Decline of the Knights of Labor, 1887 and on. Labor and the Farmers' Alliance. Le Grand Powers: "Apostle of Labor," a man ahead of his time. Formation of the Eight Hour League, 1889; its ineffectiveness.

G. The AFL in the Nation and in the State

The parent organization, 1881; its emphasis on craft unionism; horizontal organization. Formation of the Minnesota Federation of Labor, 1890; program, rapid growth, dominant position in early decades. Long-term presidencies of E. G. Hall, 1911–35, and R. A. Olson, 1938–. Labor gains. Issues: closed shop, union shop, socialism, communism. The Minneapolis Truck Drivers' Strike of 1934. Labor outside the AFL: unorganized labor in industry, the farm laborer, the seasonal worker, the I.W.W., independent unions. A labor press: *Minnesota Union Advocate*, St. Paul, 1896; *Labor World*, Duluth, 1896; *Labor Review*, Minneapolis, 1907.

H. The CIO in the Nation and in the State

National appearance of the Committee on Industrial Organization, 1935; its emphasis of vertical organization, by industries; sensational growth in recovery years of the 1930's; relationship to AFL. CIO beginnings in Minnesota, 1936–37; notable strength in towns or cities of strong industries like Hibbing and Virginia (mining), Austin and South St. Paul (meat packing). Gains in hours, wages, fringe benefits. Merger in 1956 with AFL into the Minnesota AFL-CIO Federation of Labor. Unionization of public employees like the police and firemen; the question of propriety. Labor press: *Austin Unionist, Minnesota Public Employee, Minnesota Federationist*, and others.

I. Labor and Politics since 1890

Fusion of workers and farmers in the Populist Revolt. Official attitude of the AFL toward direct party action. Types of approved political action: endorsement of candidates, lobbying, drafting legislative program. Labor legislation: Child Labor acts, 1878, 1895, 1912; Nine Hour Law for Women, 1913; Workmen's Compensation Act, 1913; eight-hour day for state employees, 1918; labeling of "prison made" goods, 1929 and 1935. Labor and World War I. The Nonpartisan League; labor setbacks and unrest of the 1920's. The state Department of Labor and Industry, 1921; the Industrial Commission. The crash of 1929 and the Farmer-Labor party. Labor gains of the 1930's: NRA, the Wagner Act, and labor's right to organize. Labor in World War II and after. The Minnesota Labor Relations Act, 1939, with its ten-day waiting period preceding a strike. Political influence in post-World War II years; the Democratic-Farmer-Labor party.

QUESTIONS AND SUGGESTIONS

1. According to the state's classification, what are cities of first, second, third, and fourth class? After one hundred years of Minnesota development which class of cities did Minnesota have in greatest number?
2. Stillwater, Marine Mills, St. Paul, and Mendota all began as early Minnesota towns and at approximately the same time. How do you account for the fact that St. Paul outstripped them all in population? How do you explain that Stillwater and Marine Mills had larger populations at one time than they do now?
3. List factors which explain the singular growth of Minneapolis; of Duluth; of Rochester; of Austin.
4. Suggest reasons for the development of St. Paul as a commercial center and of Minneapolis as an industrial center.
5. Why did St. Paul become the railroad center of the Northwest?
6. Note the nature of the census quarrel between St. Paul and Minneapolis

that reached a climax in 1890. Three interesting pamphlets relating to this quarrel are Charles W. Johnson, comp., *A Tale of Two Cities: Minneapolis and St. Paul Compared* (1885), which was issued at the time of the state census in 1885, when Minneapolis had a population of 129,200 and St. Paul of 111,397; the same author's *Another Tale of Two Cities* (1890); and Harry P. Robinson's *Federal City: Being a Remembrance of the Time before St. Paul and Minneapolis Were United* (1891). Postdated at "Federal City, March 15, 1916," twenty-five years after the census controversy, Robinson's pamphlet made a plea for unity of the two cities, stressed their common interests, and forecast their future development into a single urban district. Dr. Folwell in his *History*, 4:479–89, relates the extraordinary story of the federal census of Minneapolis and St. Paul in 1890.

7. What does Professor Gras mean by a *metropolitan center*? A *metropolitan area*? How does he interpret the history of Minnesota and the Northwest? Answers may be found in *An Introduction to Economic History*.

8. List the features that make the Twin Cities a metropolitan center. A complete picture would call for a delineation of characteristics in manufacturing, trading, banking, and cultural affairs.

9. Support or attack the viewpoint of Professor Gras that if a city is the economic capital of a surrounding region it is to be expected that it will also be that region's cultural capital.

10. Which grew relatively faster between 1860 and 1890, the Twin Cities or the rural regions of the state? between 1890 and 1950?

11. Select one of the smaller cities like Rochester, St. Cloud, or Mankato and study it to determine whether it serves as a trade center for the area around it; as a social and cultural center.

12. Report: Analyze your home town, giving particular attention to its dominant economic activities, dependence upon some larger center like Minneapolis or Duluth, labor union organization, record in strikes.

13. Graph exercise: A series of graphs may be drawn, all of them dealing with certain aspects of population change in Minnesota through the state's first century of growth. United States census figures suggest that this be done by decades. (a) A line graph depicting changes in the urban-rural composition of the state. (b) A bar graph depicting the proportion of the population to be found in Minneapolis, St. Paul, Duluth, and other urban centers. (c) A bar graph which will show that beginning with 1940 there has been a marked rate increase in population growth of suburban centers about the Twin Cities. Consult Nelson, Ramsey, and Toews, *A Century of Population Growth in Minnesota*, pp. 4–7 and 35–37.

14. For the years 1858 to 1900 did Minnesota experience as much activity in

labor organization as did the nation as a whole? for the years 1900 to 1958?

15. What changing conditions of the post-Civil War years help to explain the rise of a labor movement?
16. Are you aware of any classes of labor that seemed less likely than others to organize?
17. How vital was labor's part in the Farmer-Labor party election victories of the 1930's?
18. Were legislative gains secured for labor during those years of the 1930's when the Farmer-Labor party showed such great strength at the polls?
19. How effective has the Minnesota Labor Relations Act of 1939 been?
20. You should be able to differentiate between the vertical and horizontal types of union organization advocated by the CIO and the AFL, respectively.
21. What influence, if any, has been exerted by the League of Minnesota Municipalities in the adoption of the council-manager form of city government?
22. There are many histories or historical sketches of villages, cities, and counties of Minnesota. During the centennial year of 1958 great numbers of pamphlets, books, special newspaper editions, and monographs appeared. They vary greatly in quality and interest. Too numerous to be included in this publication, the titles of some of the more valuable of them may be found in the 1958 and 1959 issues of *Minnesota History*. Consult the section of this magazine entitled ". . . On the Minnesota Horizon."

REFERENCES

BISHOP, HARRIET E., *Floral Home*, pp. 151–68, 172–81, 191–211, 226–37 (1857). Early Minnesota towns.
* † BLEGEN, THEODORE C., *Building Minnesota*, pp. 282–92.
BLEGEN, THEODORE C., and PHILIP D. JORDAN, *With Various Voices*, pp. 229–40. Unknown authors report their impressions of Duluth in 1869 and the Twin Cities in 1880.
BRINGS, LAWRENCE M., ed., *Minneapolis, City of Opportunity: A Century of Progress in the Aquatennial City, 1856–1956* (1956). A lively, episodic survey of Minnesota's largest city. Not intended as a studied, continuous history, it nevertheless has carefully written, if brief, sketches of many aspects of the rise of Minneapolis. The numerous illustrations are especially good. The text is scattered among much advertising material.
—— ed., *The Story of Minneapolis in Pictures* (1954).
The Challenge of Metropolitan Growth (1958). Report No. 1 of the Twin Cities Metropolitan Planning Commission. Deals with the Twin Cities:

people, land, economy, government; growth problems; and future planning.

CHRISTISON, MURIEL B., "LeRoy S. Buffington and the Minneapolis Boom of the 1880's," *Minnesota History*, 23:219–32 (Sept., 1942). A period of great growth for Minneapolis and the role of a famous architect in that growth, a man called the "father of the skyscraper."

ENGBERG, GEORGE B., "The Knights of Labor in Minnesota," *Minnesota History*, 22:367–90 (Dec., 1941). While this one organization is stressed, the story of labor generally is carried to about 1895.

——— "The Rise of Organized Labor in Minnesota," *Minnesota History*, 21:372–94 (Dec., 1940). Deals with the beginnings down to 1885.

ENGEBRETSON, BETTY L., "Minnesota's Largest City: Minneapolis," *Gopher Historian*, 10:14–16 (Spring, 1956). Note also the two succeeding articles: "How Minneapolis Grew" and Lucile M. Kane, "The Early Government of Minneapolis."

FOLWELL, WILLIAM W., *History*, 3:30–31, 67, 252–53, 333–47, 479–89, development of St. Anthony, the railroad village, the Twin Cities, preservation of the Falls of St. Anthony, the census of 1890. 4:425–34, 448–59, accounts of Charles M. Loring and Le Grand Powers.

GRAS, NORMAN S. B., *An Introduction to Economic History*, pp. 295–314 (1922). The Twin Cities as a metropolitan area.

*——— "The Significance of the Twin Cities for Minnesota History," *Minnesota History*, 7:3–17 (March, 1926). A stimulating essay in economic history.

HARTSOUGH, MILDRED L., *The Development of the Twin Cities as a Metropolitan Market*, pp. 38–193.

*——— "Transportation as a Factor in the Development of the Twin Cities," *Minnesota History*, 7:218–25 (Sept., 1926).

*† HEILBRON, BERTHA L., *The Thirty-Second State*, pp. 201–31.

HOLLOWAY, ROBERT J., *A City Is More Than People: A Study of Fifteen Minnesota Communities* (1954). The fifteen are that middle group of cities ranging in population from 10,000 to 30,000. A general analysis.

LARSON, HENRIETTA M., *The Wheat Market and the Farmer in Minnesota, 1858–1900*, pp. 118–35, 220–52. Marketing wheat in Minnesota.

LAWSON, GEORGE W., *History of Labor in Minnesota* (1955). A lengthy and detailed treatment. The author was secretary-treasurer of the Minnesota Federation of Labor for forty years.

MACDONALD, DORA MARY, *This Is Duluth* (1950). Especially good on the founding and early days of Duluth. The later section tends to be a compilation of factual data without effort to trace major trends. In the author's own words, it is because of the inclusion of anecdotes "a story of and stories about Duluth."

*† *Minneapolis, Its People, History, Resources, and Government* (1959). Written for ninth-grade social studies classes in the schools of Minneapolis. Valuable for the adult reader as well.

Minnesota AFL-CIO Federation of Labor, Official Year Book, pp. 37–79 (1958). Largely a condensation of Lawson's history cited above.

* MITAU, G. THEODORE, *Politics in Minnesota*, pp. 87–90. Lobbying activities of the Minnesota AFL-CIO Federation of Labor.

SCARBOROUGH, RAY J., "The Lesser Cities of Minnesota," *Journal of Geography*, 14:233–36 (Feb., 1916).

SMITH, G. HUBERT, "Minnesota Potteries from Pioneer Craft to Modern Factory," *Minnesota History*, 33:229–35 (Summer, 1953). A brief survey of pottery manufacture throughout the state, with prime attention to Red Wing.

SNYDER, MARGARET, *The Chosen Valley: The Story of a Pioneer Town*. A biography of the town of Chatfield in southeastern Minnesota.

STEFFENS, LINCOLN, *The Shame of the Cities*, pp. 63–97 (1904). An account of corruption in Minneapolis city government during the 1890's.

† TOOLE, ROBERT C., "Saint Paul: Upper Midwest Market Center," *Gopher Historian*, 14:24–27 (Spring, 1960). Pictures the wholesale and retail trade area served by this city. Note the map.

† "The Towns of Southeastern Minnesota," *Gopher Historian*, 13:27–35 (Winter, 1958–59). Short accounts of the founding, development, and present-day industries by the editor, A. H. Poatgieter. For towns of east-central Minnesota see the *Gopher Historian*, 13:14–18 (Spring, 1959); for northwestern Minnesota see the *Gopher Historian*, 14:26–35 (Fall, 1959); for southwestern Minnesota see the *Gopher Historian*, 14:15–27 (Winter, 1959–60). Ten issues of the *Gopher Historian*, beginning with the winter, 1958–59, issue, deal with as many sections of the state. Town biographies may be found for any part of the state in these ten issues.

"Twin Cities," *Fortune*, 13:112–19, 186, 190, 193–94, 197; 14:86–88, 142 (April, July, 1936). Attempts an interpretation of trends in the Twin Cities. Should be read critically.

VAN CLEEF, EUGENE, "Minnesota Cities: Duluth and the Range Towns," *Journal of Geography*, 14:230–33 (Feb., 1916).

WALKER, CHARLES R., "Minneapolis," a series of three articles in the *Survey Graphic*, vol. 25 (Oct.–Dec., 1935). An account of the truck drivers' strike in Minneapolis in 1934. A pro-striker bias is in evidence. Much of the same material may also be found in his book *An American City* (1937).

WESLEY, EDGAR B., *Owatonna: The Social Development of a Minnesota Community*.

VII. MINNESOTA BUILDS CULTURAL, SOCIAL, AND RECREATIONAL INTERESTS

25. *The Advance of Minnesota Education*

A. The Federal Government, the State Government, and Education

The Tenth Amendment of the federal Constitution makes education a state matter. Northwest Ordinance of 1787. The Organic Act of 1849 and sections 16 and 36. The state constitution of 1858, Article VIII: assumption of responsibility for education by the state; permanent trust funds. The growth of the idea of education for all children at the public expense.

B. The Public School System: Establishment and Growth

Authorization of the common school district, 1849 and 1851; suitability to pioneer conditions. Frequent legislation and resultant complexity in types of school districts: common, special, independent, unorganized, county. Offices of state and county superintendent. Edward D. Neill, Minnesota's "Apostle of Education." Pioneer period one of slow growth, the "old schoolhouse," short terms. Teacher training. Later expansion to 72 districts in 1858, 7,606 in 1947. Secondary school beginnings: private ventures, college preparatory departments, academies; authorization of the public high school, 1865; 39 high schools by 1881. High school attendance 5 per cent by 1900, 60 per cent by 1930, 87 per cent by 1950. Some trends and issues: textbook legislation, compulsory education, religion in the schools, kindergarten, federal aid. Creation of the state Department of Education under the Board of Education, 1919; the commissioner of education; supervision of elementary and secondary schools. Consolidation of districts: 1911 authorization and meager results; 1947 Reorganization Act and effective consolidation. Increased state aid to schools; impressive growth of permanent school fund; complexity in patterns of state aid; the simplified pattern of 1947. Increase in amount of teacher preparation. The junior college movement, a twentieth-century development. Early junior colleges: Rochester, 1915; Hibbing, 1916; Eveleth, 1919. Increase to a total of nine in 1957. Legislation of 1959. Financing education: proportionate support from governments, with 67.8 per cent local, 27.6 per cent state, 3.1 per cent county, 1.5 per cent federal (1956–57 figures); the permanent school fund the second largest in the nation; 1956 amendment and diversion of iron ore tax to the general fund; distribution of state aid. Area vocational-technical schools, 1945. Place of the nonpublic schools: elementary and secondary parochial schools of the Roman Catholic, Lutheran Missouri Synod, and Seventh Day Adventist churches. The M.E.A.: teacher welfare and professional growth.

C. Higher Education: Normal Schools to Teachers Colleges to State Colleges

The need. National attention to teacher training. Creation of normal school board and authorization of three normal schools by state in 1858. Establishment of normal schools: Winona, 1860, the first west of the Mississippi and the thirteenth in the nation; Mankato, 1868; St. Cloud, 1869; Moorhead, 1888; Duluth, 1902; Bemidji, 1919. Curriculum growth from the essentially secondary school character of normal schools in the early decades to the limitation of enrollment to high school graduates in 1917. Achievement of teachers college status, 1921; authorization of four years of college and the bachelor's degree. Broadened service as area colleges and in offering liberal arts. Authorization of fifth year (graduate) and the master's degree, 1953. Post-World War II surge in enrollment. Teachers colleges designated state colleges in acknowledgment of broadened functions.

D. Higher Education: the University of Minnesota

Foundations: legislation of 1851; the university land grant; picking a site; beginnings as a preparatory school; difficulties of the 1850's and 1860's; John S. Pillsbury, "Father of the University"; the presidency of William Watts Folwell and solid beginnings, 1869–84. Expansion under the presidency of Cyrus Northrop, 1884–1911: colleges of agriculture, law, medicine, mines, dentistry, pharmacy, education, graduate studies. George E. Vincent, 1911–16: the Mayo Foundation; Guy Stanton Ford and the Graduate School; John B. Johnston and the Arts College. Lotus D. Coffman, 1920–38: improvement of the physical plant; establishment of the General College and the Center for Continuation Study; the struggle with the state for autonomy — the "Chase case." James L. Morrill, 1945–60: campus expansion; post-World War II climb in enrollment; Duluth Teachers College becomes Duluth Branch of the University of Minnesota in 1947; broadened offerings. Growth in fame; recognized as one of the world's great universities. Varied services: KUOM, University of Minnesota Press, Northrop Auditorium concerts and lectures, persistent research in many areas, Agricultural Experiment Station.

E. Higher Education: Liberal Arts Colleges

Denominational character. Function of the denominational college. Early church attention to the academy, then to the college and seminary. Early difficulties: finding funds, obtaining students, securing faculties, providing campuses and buildings. Establishment of institutions: Hamline, 1854; St. John's, 1857; Gustavus Adolphus, 1862; Carleton, 1866; Augsburg, 1872; St. Olaf, 1874; Macalester, 1885; St. Thomas, 1885; Concordia, 1891; St. Catherine, 1906; St. Teresa, 1907; St. Scholastica, 1912; St. Benedict, 1913; St. Mary's, 1913. The junior college movement: Dr. Martin Luther, 1884; Concordia, 1905; Bethany, 1926; Bethel, 1931.

Seminaries. Some trends and issues: decline of the academy; coeducation; expanding curriculums; growth of enrollments; gaining accreditation; new campuses and building programs; varying strength of the tie with the supporting denomination; promotion of music, art, drama, forensics, athletics; limiting enrollments; mid-twentieth-century boom in enrollments and campus expansion; and the growth of curriculum offerings.

QUESTIONS AND SUGGESTIONS

1. What is the historical basis in the United States for the concept that education is essentially the concern of the state rather than of the federal government? Has this concept been strengthened through the years?
2. How would you explain the twentieth-century drive for "federal aid" to education? Why are many opposed to federal aid?
3. Would you say that Minnesota was "in step" or "out of step" with national trends in the matter of support for (a) public elementary schools during the first half century of statehood? the second half century? (b) public high schools during the first half century of statehood? the second half century? (c) teacher training institutions during the first half century of statehood? the second half century?
4. Would it be correct to say that the development of higher education in Minnesota was, for a time, held back because of the tardy development of the public high school?
5. Show how Minnesota's permanent trust funds came into being and how they grew. How do Minnesota's funds of this type compare with those of other states? What effect did the 1956 amendment to the state constitution have upon the growth of the permanent school fund?
6. Describe the several sources of state aid to the public schools of Minnesota and the manner of distributing this aid.
7. For a tabulation and distribution of types of public schools in Minnesota consult *A Handbook for Minnesota Teachers*, the table on p. 37.
8. How would you account for the change of normal schools to teachers colleges? of teachers colleges to state colleges? Did these changes follow a national pattern?
9. What is meant by the term "area college"? May it be said that area colleges have developed in Minnesota?
10. The University of Minnesota had to struggle for existence in the early decades. Why? What role was played by John S. Pillsbury in putting it on its feet? by William Watts Folwell?
11. Cyrus Northrop served as president of the University of Minnesota for better than a fourth of a century. What were the features of growth under his leadership?

12. What significance did the administration of the University of Minnesota attach to the "Chase case"?
13. Services rendered to the people of Minnesota by their state university are numerous and most impressive. Draw up a list of as many services as you can discover.
14. Explain the early appearance of denominational schools in Minnesota.
15. Denominational leaders hold that private schools have a special place in society and that they have particular functions to perform. Explain.
16. What proportion of Minnesota's youth are educated in the private colleges and what proportion in the publicly supported institutions of higher learning? Try to obtain figures for given years, such as 1890, 1920, and 1950, to see whether this proportion has changed.
17. Account for the upsurge in demand for a college education that came in the wake of World War II. How did this trend affect Minnesota institutions of higher learning?
18. A class might attempt to write a history of its own school, using school records, local newspapers, and other printed or manuscript records, and also interviewing persons who attended or taught in the school in its earlier period.
19. Among many subjects that might profitably be studied through class or individual investigation are the following: the story of one of the state teachers colleges; the history of St. Olaf, Carleton, Hamline, or any other small college of the state; the biography of an educational leader; Dr. Folwell as an educational seer; the story of some influential teacher such as Maria Sanford; the expansion of the University of Minnesota.

REFERENCES

* Asher, Hellen D., "A Frontier College of the Middle West: Hamline University, 1854–69," *Minnesota History*, 9:363–78 (Dec., 1928).

Barry, Colman J., O.S.B., *Worship and Work: Saint John's Abbey and University, 1856–1956* (1956). The author is a member of the community at Collegeville. He portrays the first hundred years of development of these two institutions. The abbey is the largest Benedictine abbey in the world. Illustrated.

Benson, William C., *High on Manitou: A History of St. Olaf College, 1874–1949* (1949). Written by a member of the college's faculty on the occasion of the seventy-fifth anniversary of the founding of the school.

* † Blegen, Theodore C., *Building Minnesota*, pp. 307–18.

*——— *The Land Lies Open*, pp. 151–95. The establishment of the state university. Birth pangs, early trials, attainment of sure footing.

Bliefernicht, Edmund R., *Brief History of Dr. Martin Luther College* (1934).

* BRINGS, LAWRENCE M., ed., *Minnesota Heritage*: Grace Orr Armstrong, and Bernice Dainard Gestie, "Education in Minnesota," pp. 177–86. Not so much a historical survey as a picture of beginnings and of recent (1959) conditions. Discusses elementary and secondary schools, teacher preparation, and teacher certification. Ruth E. Eckert and R. Edith Stedman, "Public Higher Education in Minnesota," pp. 218–40. On junior colleges, state colleges, and the university. Gives historical background, the current picture, enrollments, and other data. Leal A. Headley, "Private Liberal Arts Colleges," pp. 187–217. An introductory statement; then a portrayal of each institution.

BUCK, SOLON J., ed., *William Watts Folwell: The Autobiography and Letters of a Pioneer of Culture* (1933).

CARMICHAEL, OLIVER C., "The Roots of Higher Education in Minnesota," *Minnesota History*, 34:90–95 (Autumn, 1954). A general treatment. Refers to the origins of the denominational colleges, the five state colleges (then teachers colleges), and the University of Minnesota.

DUPRE, HUNTLEY, *Edward Duffield Neill: Pioneer Educator* (1949). A brief sketch of the founder of Macalester College. Neill's interests were many, but his promotion of education is here emphasized. Written on the occasion of the seventy-fifth anniversary of the establishment of the college.

* † —— " 'Minnesota's Apostle of Education' — Edward Duffield Neill," *Gopher Historian*, 12:27 (Winter, 1957–58). A brief outline biography.

ENGELHARDT, FRED, *Minnesota Public Schools*, pp. 3–15, 29–30, 113 (1934). A history of the public school system.

* † FAWCETT, LOIS M., "Pioneer Education," *Gopher Historian*, 5:9–10 (Dec., 1950).

FIRKINS, OSCAR, *Cyrus Northrop: A Memoir*, pp. 311–407 (1925). Northrop as president of the University of Minnesota.

* FOLWELL, WILLIAM W., *History*, 3:253–54; 4:60–189, 434–48, 459–65, 478–85.

—— *University Addresses* (1909). Folwell's far-reaching ideas on education are given here.

FUNK, HENRY D., *A History of Macalester College*, pp. 29–230 (1910).

* GRAY, JAMES, *The University of Minnesota, 1851–1951* (1951). The fullest account of the subject. An extensive treatment, with emphasis on the last fifty years of the university's first century.

* —— *Open Wide the Door: The Story of the University of Minnesota* (1958). Essentially the same as the above, although considerably abridged.

* *A Handbook for Minnesota Teachers* (Commission on Teacher Education and Professional Standards, M.E.A.), pp. 1–79 (1950). The development,

organization, and financing of education in Minnesota. Brief, precise, authoritative.

HOFFMANN, ALEXIUS, *St. John's University, Collegeville, Minnesota: A Sketch of Its History* (1907).

HURLEY, SISTER HELEN ANGELA, *On Good Ground: The Story of the Sisters of St. Joseph in St. Paul* (1951). Depicts not merely the growth of a college (St. Catherine), but the promotion by this religious community of academies, hospitals, and elementary schools.

IVERSON, SAMUEL G., "The Public Lands and School Fund of Minnesota," *Minnesota Historical Collections*, 15:287–314 (1915).

KAGIN, EDWIN, *James Wallace of Macalester* (1957). The story of the rise of Macalester College is intimately associated with the life of this man.

KEENAN, EDWARD, *Story of St. Thomas College* (1936).

KREY, AUGUST C., "Names and Personalities in Minnesota Education," *Minnesota Journal of Education*, 17:205–8, 210 (Jan., 1937).

Legislative Manual, State of Minnesota, 1957–1958, pp. 285–94. The public school system, the state colleges, and the university. A very brief description.

LEONARD, DELEVAN L., *The History of Carleton College* (1904).

LEONARD, WILLIAM E., "Early College Silhouettes," *Minnesota History*, 16:178–86 (June, 1935). The University of Minnesota in the seventies.

McDONALD, SISTER GRACE, "A Finishing School of the 1880's: St. Benedict's Academy," *Minnesota History*, 27:96–106 (June, 1946).

MELLBY, CARL A., *St. Olaf College through Fifty Years* (1925).

MINNESOTA COMMISSION ON HIGHER EDUCATION, *Higher Education in Minnesota* (1950): Edgar M. Carlson and Mother Antonius, "Problems Facing Minnesota's Private Colleges," pp. 191–209. Ruth E. Eckert and John E. Dobbin, "An Overview of Higher Education in Minnesota Today," pp. 52–77. Ruth E. Eckert, Robert J. Keller, and W. Donald Olsen, "Development of the Junior College in Minnesota," pp. 119–44. Ruth E. Eckert and T. R. McConnell, "The University of Minnesota: Its Programs, Services, and Problems," pp. 317–46. O. W. Snarr, "The State Teachers Colleges in Minnesota's Program of Higher Education," pp. 239–52.

MITAU, G. THEODORE, *Politics in Minnesota*, pp. 97–99. Political activities of the M.E.A.

MORTON, ZYLPHA S., "Harriet Bishop, Frontier Teacher," *Minnesota History*, 28:132–41 (June, 1947). A delightful sketch of this first teacher of an organized school in St. Paul.

* NELSON, LOWRY, *The Minnesota Community*, pp. 83–98. A sociologist's interpretation of educational trends. The emphasis is on the twentieth

134

century. Especially interesting is the discussion of the poor record of attendance by the state's rural youth in high school and college.

ORFIELD, MATTHIAS N., *Federal Land Grants to the States, with Special Reference to Minnesota*, pp. 235–55. The permanent trust funds. University lands.

PACE, CHARLES NELSON, ed., *Hamline University* (1939).

PETERSON, CONRAD, *Remember Thy Past: A History of Gustavus Adolphus College, 1862–1952* (1953). The author was a teacher of history at the college for many years. He surveys the first ninety years of this Swedish Lutheran institution.

* POATGIETER, A. H., and J. T. DUNN, *Gopher Reader*, pp. 102–7. Early growth of Minnesota's schools. Pioneer conditions.

* *Report of the Governor's Minnesota Tax Study Committee*, pp. 451–56. The growth and administration of the state's permanent trust funds.

SELLE, ERWIN S., *The Winona State Teachers College* (1936).

TALBOT, JEAN, *First State Normal School 1860, Winona State College 1960* (1960). Not a detailed history. Major trends through the school's first century are portrayed. This centennial history first appeared in four issues of the *Quarterly Bulletin of Winona State College*, parts one and two in August, 1959, and parts three and four in November, 1959.

TEGEDER, VINCENT, O.S.B., "The Benedictines in Frontier Minnesota," *Minnesota History*, 32:34–43 (March, 1951). How St. John's University came to be established.

——— "Pioneering Monks," *Minnesota History*, 33:53–60 (Summer, 1952). Carries the story of St. John's University to 1890, and shows how the work of these monks pushed westward into Dakota.

WHITNEY, HELEN, *Maria Sanford*, pp. 1–267 (1922). The story of an unusually forceful teacher.

[VII. MINNESOTA BUILDS CULTURAL, SOCIAL, AND RECREATIONAL INTERESTS]

26. *The Church in Minnesota Life*

A. The Establishment of Churches

The planting of churches in Minnesota: Presbyterian, Congregational, Catholic, Methodist, Baptist, Episcopal, Lutheran, and others. Interest of the East in fostering religion among western immigrants through the American Home Missionary Society, the American Bible Society, denominational home mission boards. Support of the Catholic Church from abroad: Leopoldinen Stiftung, Society for the Propagation of the Faith. Attitude of the Lutheran churches in Europe toward the emigrants. Solicitation of funds. Dearth of pastors and priests. Laymen preachers. Circuit riders. End of outside support.

B. The Immigrant Church

The church as a link between the immigrant and his old home. Foreign-born elements in the Catholic and Lutheran churches, and in the synagogue. Effects of freedom from state-church control. Controversy and division among the Scandinavian Lutherans. The church as a factor in promoting settlement. Use of foreign languages in religious services and church schools. The transition to English. Decline of the foreign-language church.

C. The Church and Education

The role of pastor and priest in pioneer education. Training a ministry. Seminaries and academies. Establishment of colleges. Parochial high schools. The rise of women's finishing schools. Preparatory schools. The development of a church press. The tie between the denominational college and the supporting synod — is it a growing or a weakening one? The problem of finance; endowment funds; aid from large private corporations.

D. The Church as a Social Institution

Churches as pioneer social centers: picnics, fairs, suppers, bazaars; the camp meeting and revivals; ladies' aid societies; young people's clubs; benevolent societies; other organizations. Their charitable organizations: hospitals, orphanages, old people's homes, correctional institutions, welfare agencies. Fraternal organizations. The church and the farmer. The church and labor. Church attitudes toward liquor, cards, dancing, motion pictures. The church and the Indian problem. The institutionalized city church. Forces inimical to churchgoing in pioneer times and at present. Church art and architecture. Church music; the choir.

E. The Church and Finances

The change from financial dependency to self-sufficiency in Minnesota. Sources of church income. Amount. Church property. Debt. Church expenditure: amount and purpose.

F. Controversy, Union, and Interdenominationalism

The church and the state: position of Catholics, Lutherans, other groups. Proliferation of sects: effect of language differences and of doctrinal controversies. Strife and change among Lutheran synods. The move toward unity; the Norwegian Lutherans unite, 1918; the national drive for Lutheran unity of the mid-twentieth century. The growth of interdenominational activity: W.C.T.U., Federal Council of Churches of Christ in America, American Sunday School Union, Church Peace Union, Church League for Industrial Democracy, Lord's Day Alliance, National Conference of Christians and Jews, American Lutheran Con-

136

ference, and other organizations. The present-day church situation in a typical Minnesota village. The rural church.

G. The Church in a Changing World

Transition from the pioneer to the modern setting of the church. Outstanding pioneer and modern Minnesota church leaders. Characteristic problems, old and new, and the attitude of the churches toward them: the slavery controversy, war and peace, scientific theory and the issue between fundamentalism and modernism, the question of an anti-evolution teaching law, the adjustment of education in church-controlled schools to changing needs and conditions, the distribution of wealth and political theories, poverty and social problems, sex, marriage, divorce, integration with the Negro and the Indian.

QUESTIONS AND SUGGESTIONS

1. Describe the beginnings of your church in Minnesota with particular attention to the help it received from outside sources, if any; the difficulties it encountered, such as scarcity of pastors and of church members; measures taken to meet these difficulties; activities other than purely religious ones.
2. Were frontier conditions favorable for religion or not? Were the pioneers religious?
3. In the opinion of one writer, "more than was the case in any other sphere of life, religion bound Minnesota to the older areas of the country and to Europe." Challenge or defend this view.
4. What are "immigrant churches"? What were some of the special problems that they had to meet?
5. Why were the Scandinavian Lutheran churches in the homelands rather indifferent to the religious welfare of the Scandinavian immigrants in America?
6. Make some study of the importance of the church as an educational institution; as a social institution; as an economic institution.
7. Has strict denominationalism tended to decline or to increase?
8. What reasons can you advance for the apparent decline of doctrinal controversy among the churches?
9. Investigate the attitude of your church toward war.
10. What serious problems is the church facing today in the rural areas of the state?
11. What is revivalism? evangelism? fundamentalism? modernism? a synod?
12. What contributions has the church made to the artistic life of Minnesota in architecture, sculpture, painting, music? Is there a modern trend in any of these areas?

13. Topics: The history of a particular denomination in Minnesota; inter-denominational organization; the extra-religious activities of one de-nomination; the story of some church founder or later leader.
14. Project: Make a report on the church records preserved by the various churches in your community.
15. There are many accounts and histories of individual churches or par-ishes in Minnesota. Typical of them are Gustavus A. Hagstrom, *History of the First Swedish Baptist Church, Minneapolis, Minnesota* (1921); Christian A. Rasmussen, *An Historical Sketch of Christ Church Parish, Red Wing, Minnesota* (1922); James M. Reardon, *The Church of St. Mary of St. Paul* (1935); Frederick Wiechmann, *History of St. Wende-lin's Parish* (1935); H. Meyer, *History of St. Paul Evangelical Lutheran Church of Rost, Jackson County, Minnesota* (1935); Emeroy Johnson, *Scandia Grove: A History of the Scandia Grove Lutheran Church, St. Peter, Minnesota, 1858–1958* (1958).

REFERENCES

ANDERS, JOHN O., *The Origin and History of Swedish Religious Organiza-tions in Minnesota, 1853–1885* (1932).

BACKLUND, JONAS O., *Swedish Baptists in America*, pp. 49–54 (1933). The Swedish Baptists in Minnesota.

*† BLEGEN, THEODORE C., *Building Minnesota*, pp. 348–52.

——— *Norwegian Migration to America: The American Transition*, pp. 131–74 (1940). A portrayal of the development of the immigrant church.

BRECK, CHARLES, comp., *The Life of James Lloyd Breck, D.D.*, pp. 334–423 (1883). Episcopal schools, missions, and other activities, 1857–65.

* BRINGS, LAWRENCE M., ed., *Minnesota Heritage*: Daniel J. Halfrey, "The Church in Minnesota," pp. 139–47.

CARLSEN, CLARENCE J., *The Years of Our Church* (1942). The establishment and development of the Lutheran Free Church of America.

EDWARDS, MAURICE D., *History of the Synod of Minnesota, Presbyterian Church* (1927).

FRUTH, ALBAN, *A Century of Missionary Work among the Red Lake Chip-pewa Indians* (1958).

GILBERT, MAHLON N., "Beginnings of the Episcopal Church in Minnesota," Minnesota Historical Collections, 9:181–96 (1901). The mission of Park Place, St. Paul.

JARCHOW, MERRILL E., "Red Rock Frontier Methodist Camp Meeting," *Minnesota History*, 31:79–92 (June, 1950). An aspect of Methodism in early Minnesota.

JOHNSON, EMEROY, *A Church Is Planted: The Story of the Lutheran Min-nesota Conference, 1851–1876* (1948). Establishment and early growth of the Lutheran Minnesota Conference of the Augustana Evangelical Lutheran Church.

—— *God Gave the Growth: The Story of the Lutheran Minnesota Conference, 1876–1958* (1958). A companion volume to the one above. Carries the story to mid-twentieth century.

—— *Eric Norelius: Pioneer Midwest Pastor and Churchman* (1954). Biography of a prominent Swedish Lutheran pastor who first came to Minnesota in 1854. He was editor, church administrator, founder of institutions.

KREY, AUGUST C., "Monte Cassino, Metten, and Minnesota," *Minnesota History*, 8:217–31 (Sept., 1927). The Benedictine community in Minnesota.

MEYER, H., *The Planting Time of the Minnesota District of the Evangelical Lutheran Synod of Missouri, Ohio, and Other States* (1932).

MOYNIHAN, HUMPHREY, "Archbishop Ireland," *Acta et Dicta*, 6:12–34 (Oct., 1933).

MOYNIHAN, JAMES H., *The Life of Archbishop John Ireland*. The first archbishop of St. Paul was a dominant religious leader, not only in Minnesota, but in the nation as well.

NELSON, E. CLIFFORD, and EUGENE L. FEVOLD, *The Lutheran Church among Norwegian-Americans* (1960). Minnesota occupies a central position in this story. Volume I covers the years 1825 to 1890; Volume II 1890–1960. An extensive and able treatment.

*NELSON, LOWRY, *The Minnesota Community*, pp. 114–25. A sociologist's discussion of religious trends. While some attention is given to beginnings, the main stress is on twentieth-century developments.

Our Fathers Built: A Century of Minnesota Methodism (1952). Prepared by the Historical Society of the Minnesota Methodist Conference, Charles Nelson Page, ed. A collection of articles by numerous authors; not an integrated or carefully worked out history.

PREUS, JOHAN C. K., *Norsemen Found a Church: An Old Heritage in a New Land* (1953).

REARDON, JAMES MICHAEL, P.A., *The Catholic Church in the Diocese of St. Paul from Earliest Origin to Centennial Achievement* (1952).

* SELKE, ESTHER A., "Pioneers of German Lutheranism in Minnesota," *Minnesota History*, 14:45–58 (March, 1933).

STEPHENSON, GEORGE M., *The Founding of the Augustana Synod, 1850–1860*, pp. 88–104 (1927). The Minnesota synod.

—— *The Religious Aspects of Swedish Immigration*, pp. 1–396.

STRAND, ALGOT E., ed., *A History of the Swedish-Americans of Minnesota*, 1:137–270 (1910). The Swedish Lutheran, Methodist, Mission, Baptist, and Episcopal churches in Minnesota.

TANNER, GEORGE C., *Fifty Years of Church Work*, pp. 88–516 (1909). The Protestant Episcopal Church in Minnesota.

[VII. MINNESOTA BUILDS CULTURAL, SOCIAL, AND RECREATIONAL INTERESTS]

27. *Changes in the Social Order*

A. Cultural Diffusion and Agencies of Uniformity

"Bridges Facing East": the lyceum, the chautauqua, lectures, the theater, music, newspapers, and others. Social and intellectual effects of improvements in transportation. The spread of news: growth of the press, improvement of the postal service, advent of the telephone. Impact of the transportation and communications revolution: the automobile and an improved highway system, the motion picture, radio, and television.

B. Some Changing Customs

Gradual elimination of isolation for the farmer through such agencies as farmers' organizations, rural free delivery of mail, the automobile and good roads, rural electrification. Growing complexity of city life: multiplicity of organizations, traffic and parking problems. City and town life contrasted.

C. City Parks

The first parks in St. Paul and Minneapolis. Development of parks in St. Paul. Charles M. Loring and the Minneapolis park system. Other city parks. Social value of parks.

D. Women's Clubs

Social activities of the pioneer woman. The sewing circle. Examples of early women's clubs. The Ladies Floral Club of Austin, 1869: floriculture, beautification of the village, establishment of libraries. The Grecian Study Club of Minneapolis, 1873. The Schubert Club of St. Paul, 1882. Minnesota Federation of Women's Clubs, 1894. Expansion of the club movement. Emancipation of women.

E. Woman Suffrage

Jane Grey Swisshelm. State Suffrage Association, 1869. Activities. Women gain the right to vote on school questions, 1875; to serve on library boards and vote for library board members, 1898. Admitted to law practice, 1877. The Populist and Prohibition parties declare for woman suffrage, 1892. Agitation for the Nineteenth Amendment; its ratification, 1920. Political activity of women since ratification; the League of Women Voters.

F. Libraries

Early lyceums and reading circles. Local libraries; the Mercantile and

Y.M.C.A. libraries of St. Paul. The Athenaeum library of Minneapolis. The state law of 1879 authorizing tax support for public libraries and the resultant growth of public libraries; encouragement from Andrew Carnegie gifts. Impressive libraries: St. Paul Public, 1883; Minneapolis Public, 1889; University of Minnesota; James J. Hill Reference; the several state and liberal arts colleges. The county library movement: WPA beginnings; growth through the 1940's and 1950's; use of mobile units.

G. Historical Societies and Museums

Unique character of the Minnesota Historical Society; its manuscripts and research; its museum activities. Rise of county historical societies; their museums and libraries.

H. Adult Education

QUESTIONS AND SUGGESTIONS

1. Suggest some notable changes affecting the dissemination of news that have occurred since pioneer times.
2. What are some of the forces in modern life that tend to promote uniformity in thought and action? Did these forces exist under pioneer conditions?
3. Do you feel that standardization tends to promote or retard cultural development?
4. Compare the ways of popular instruction, amusement, and sociability in rural communities of the 1880's or 1890's with those of today.
5. Picture the revolution which has occurred in "life on the farm" between 1858 and 1958.
6. There are those who hold that the movement for public parks and playgrounds is an effort to preserve the primitive aspect of pioneer life. Does this seem reasonable?
7. Charles M. Loring made a singular contribution to the development of Minneapolis, and in an indirect way, perhaps, to many another Minnesota city. What was this contribution?
8. Contrast the role of "pioneer woman" with that of "modern woman," giving special attention to such things as household tasks, contributions to the economic life of the family, kitchen furnishings and devices, availability of leisure time, and family relationships.
9. How strong a hold did the view that "woman's place is in the home" have in pioneer days? at the turn of the century? at mid-twentieth century?
10. In what ways, legal as well as customary, have women greater freedom of action now than they had in 1850?
11. An annual report of club activities in Minnesota appears in the December issue of the *Minnesota Clubwoman*, the official publication of the

Minnesota Federation of Women's Clubs. List activities and spheres of interest of the Minnesota Federation of Women's Clubs.

12. The League of Women Voters has shown an active interest in a number of public issues or movements within the state. Name some of these.

13. How effective has the League of Women Voters been in achieving some of its goals?

14. Publication activities of the League of Women Voters include the following: *Minneapolis Is Your Business, ABC's of City Government* (1955), *Ninety Days of Lawmaking* (1939), *Reapportionment in Minnesota: Democracy Denied* (1954), *St. Paul at Your Service* (1955), *The State You're In* (1957), *You Are the Government* (1949, 1958).

15. Note the relationship between the women's clubs and the rise of public libraries.

16. The *Historical Sketch of the Minneapolis Athenaeum with Its Charter, By-Laws, and Other Matters Relating Thereto*, published in 1876, states that the library grew from 273 volumes in 1860 to 5,714 in 1876. A list showing what books were available to the reading public of Minneapolis is found in the *Catalogue of the Library of the Minneapolis Athenaeum* (1877).

17. Interesting topics for reports: The establishment of a city park, a woman's club, a local library, the career of Charles M. Loring and its meaning to Minneapolis.

REFERENCES

ANTHONY, SUSAN B., and IDA H. HARPER, eds., *The History of Woman Suffrage*, 4:772–82 (1902). The woman suffrage movement in Minnesota.

* BERTHEL, MARY W., and HAROLD D. CATER, "The Minnesota Historical Society: Highlights of a Century," *Minnesota History*, 30:293–330 (Dec., 1949). A splendid sketch; based on annual reports of the society, minutes of the executive council, letters, documents, and newspaper accounts.

* † BLEGEN, THEODORE C., *Building Minnesota*, pp. 352–57.

* ———— "A Century of Manuscript Collecting," *Minnesota History*, 34: 337–40 (Winter, 1955). A report of the work of the state's historical society in gathering and organizing manuscripts and in making them readily available to scholars.

———— *The Land Lies Open*, pp. 220–25. Horace W. S. Cleveland, planner of playgrounds and parks for the Twin Cities in the 1870's and 1880's.

———— "The Minnesota Historical Society and the University of Minnesota," *Minnesota History*, 23:1–10 (March, 1942). Tells of the close ties and the work of these two cultural institutions.

* BRINGS, LAWRENCE M., ed., *Minnesota Heritage:* Russell W. Fridley, "The

Minnesota Historical Society," pp. 241–43. A very brief history; then activities at the time the article was written (1959). Glen Lewis, "Minnesota's First Public Libraries," pp. 244–49.

CASTLE, HENRY A., *Minnesota: Its Story and Biography*, 1:332–52 (1915). The activities and influence of Minnesota women.

CHASE, RAY P., *Statement to the Nineteen Hundred Twenty-Three Legislature*, pp. 23–83 (1923). The state park system.

CHRISTIANSON, THEODORE, *Minnesota*, 2:261–63. The library movement.

ENGEBRETSON, BETTY L., "Books for Pioneers: The Minneapolis Athenaeum," *Minnesota History*, 35:222–32 (March, 1957). How a private subscription library developed into a city public library.

*FOLWELL, WILLIAM W., *History*, 4:425–34. Charles M. Loring as an apostle of parks and playgrounds.

FOSTER, MARY D., *Who's Who among Minnesota Women* (1924). Biographies of Minnesota women and sketches of some of the women's organizations.

*† FRIDLEY, RUSSELL W., "The Minnesota Historical Society," *Gopher Historian*, 12:2–4 (Winter, 1957–58).

GRAY, JAMES, "The University and the Historical Society," *Minnesota History*, 32:1–11 (March, 1951). Recognizes the brilliant contributions of many university leaders to the work of the state historical society through the years.

JERABEK, ESTHER, "Library of the Minnesota Historical Society," *Minnesota Libraries*, 18:204–7 (Sept., 1956). A brief description of its holdings and activities.

LEONARD, MARGARET, "The Blue Earth County Library," *Minnesota Libraries*, 14:166–70 (June, 1944). An account of the establishment of Minnesota's first county library. Similar accounts of the Waseca and Stearns county libraries may be found in the same issue of this magazine, a publication of the state Department of Education.

LORING, CHARLES M., "History of Parks and Public Grounds of Minneapolis," Minnesota Historical Collections, 15:599–608 (1915). Loring was father of the Minneapolis park system.

MAYNE, EMILY L., "County Libraries, 1956," *Minnesota Libraries*, 18:275–76 (March, 1957). A report of the county libraries of the state for 1956.

MITAU, G. THEODORE, *Politics in Minnesota*, pp. 83–85. Activities of the League of Women Voters.

Parks, Parkways and Playgrounds of Minneapolis (1931). This little pamphlet, issued by the Board of Park Commissioners, has a short history of the parks.

PEABODY, LLOYD, "History of the Parks and Public Playgrounds of St. Paul," Minnesota Historical Collections, 15:609–30 (1915).

SMITH, HANNIS S., "Public Library Statistics," *Minnesota Libraries*, 19:119–31 (March, 1959). Data on volumes, circulation, and finances for public libraries of city, town, and county.

[VII. MINNESOTA BUILDS CULTURAL, SOCIAL, AND RECREATIONAL INTERESTS]

28. *The Development of Sports, Vacationing, and Tourism*

A. Pioneer and Immigrant Sports

Characteristics of pioneer sports: individualistic, incidental, amateur. Pioneer display of skill and prowess: individual pitted against individual in running, jumping, wrestling, husking bees, shooting matches, log rolling. *Turnverein* and *Sokol* societies, variants on this pattern, with both individual and group activity. Hunting and fishing in pioneer Minnesota.

B. The Rise of Organized Sports

The "safety-valve" theory applied to sports: relief from confining tendencies of industrialization to be found in sports. A westward movement in sport fads; Minnesota participation by the 1870's and on. Promotion by individuals, clubs, county and state fairs. Early areas of interest: horse racing, bicycling, hiking, croquet, golf, tennis, baseball, boating, skating, skiing, curling, and others. Early clubs of note: Minnesota Boating Club, 1870; Flour City Cyclists' Club, 1880's; Red Wing Ski Club, 1883; St. Paul's Town and Country Club, 1888, and Minneapolis' Minikahda Club, 1898 — forerunners of many later country clubs. School-sponsored sports. In the University of Minnesota: the Big Ten; the "Golden Gophers" in football; other sports; intramural emphasis. In state and liberal arts colleges: the state college conference and the two liberal arts college conferences; trends in intercollegiate and intramural competition. In secondary schools: rise of interscholastic competition; state meet in track, 1909; in basketball, 1913; the Minnesota High School League, 1916; the state basketball tournament and other promotional activities. The coming of commercialism. In baseball: Minneapolis and St. Paul baseball clubs, 1877 and on; state-wide mushrooming of baseball leagues. In boxing and wrestling. In winter sports: St. Paul Ice Carnival, 1886; Shipstead and Johnson Ice Follies, 1936. In basketball: the Lakers, 1947. In summer sports: the Minneapolis Aquatennial, 1940. Notable rise in sports participation despite spectator emphasis of commercial and school-sponsored sports: growth of corner lot baseball and Little Leaguers; of golf; of tennis; of swimming. Newspapers and sports.

144

c. A Vacationland and the Movement for Public Parks and Playgrounds

Post-Civil War enthusiasm for Minnesota's outdoors: popularity of the climate as being healthful for invalids; the ten thousand lakes attract thousands of fishermen; a steady boom in lake resorts, primarily for residents of the state but also for out-of-staters. State park system beginnings: Camp Release Wayside Memorial, 1889; Jacob V. Brower and Itasca State Park, 1891. Steady increase in the number of parks; WPA activities of the 1930's and expanded facilities; 1959 totals, 38 state parks, 4 state reserves, 16 state waysides, 9 state monuments; their recreational, scenic, and historic attraction to the tourist. Broadening of city park systems to incorporate the playground idea; leadership of Minneapolis nationally recognized. Rise of public golf courses.

D. Tourism

Growth of an important new frontier of business: supplying the fisherman, hunter, canoeist, and photographer. State promotion: equipping state parks with cabins and camp sites, some with modern facilities; road construction; advertising. Private promotion: Ten Thousand Lakes of Minnesota Association, 1916, and Minnesota Arrowhead Association, 1923. The Quetico-Superior Wilderness Area; a problem and a challenge: preserving the wilderness aspect of certain parts of the state. Size of the annual tourist influx; meaning to the state.

QUESTIONS AND SUGGESTIONS

1. Professor Paxson believes that there is a relation between the disappearance of the frontier and the organization of sports, the latter supplying the American people with a social safety valve that takes the place of the one furnished by the frontier in an earlier day. Read his article for the national picture that it gives and note how the development of sports in Minnesota is correlated with the broader movement.

2. Contrast the point of view of the early Minnesota sportsman with that of the present day. Consult the article by Mary W. Berthel for a good account of pioneer Minnesota hunting.

3. What are some characteristic immigrant contributions to Minnesota sports?

4. It is interesting to observe that in the same period in which country people were being drawn toward the city, city people were more and more being drawn into the country. List the sports, inventions, and other factors that have tended to take city folk into the country.

5. Is it possible that activities which in present-day Minnesota are called sports would not have been regarded as sports in pioneer days? Might the reverse be true?

6. Consult *The Thirty-Sixth Annual Official Handbook of the Minnesota*

State High School League, 1958, for a report of its activities. A skeleton history may be found on pp. 17–19. Sports sponsored are baseball, basketball, cross country racing, football, golf, gymnastics, hockey, skiing, swimming, tennis, wrestling.

7. Discuss the intercollegiate conferences which now serve the athletic needs of Minnesota's institutions of higher education.
8. Defend or condemn the increase of spectator participation in sports that came with school-sponsored and commercial sports.
9. In recent decades, charges that intercollegiate and university athletics have become "big business" have been made. Are these justified?
10. Why has the term "amateur" grown in importance in twentieth-century athletics? How is the twentieth-century use of the term different from that of the nineteenth century?
11. Account for Twin City sponsorship of the Ice Carnival and the Aquatennial.
12. As the state developed its public park system what attention did it give to recreation? to historical interests?
13. Account for the early fame of Lake Minnetonka as a resort area. You will note several references to Lake Minnetonka in the citations which follow.
14. Apropos of the "family lake cottage movement": (a) How was it related to the economic status of the families which participated? (b) How was it related to transportation development? (c) How do you explain the changing popularity of different parts of the state in its development?
15. A worthwhile study: The development of the Minneapolis public playground system.
16. Make a survey of the facilities and equipment for sports in your home town, listing the public and private golf courses, tennis courts, baseball parks, football fields, gymnasiums, etc. Then compare this with the situation in the cities of the first class.
17. Describe the activities of the Ten Thousand Lakes of Minnesota Association or the Minnesota Arrowhead Association.
18. With respect to the Quetico-Superior Wilderness Area: (a) Show how the two governments of Canada and the United States cooperated to bring it into being. (b) What role did the public play? (c) In what sense is this a unique area? (d) What is its present status?
19. Can you secure figures to show the amounts spent by the government of Minnesota in advertising its vacationland? other figures to show whether this advertising has been profitable?
20. If a satisfactory newspaper file is available, compare the space and treatment given sports in a newspaper of the seventies and eighties with the sports section of a present-day paper.

146

21. Topics worthy of individual study: The history of any one sport in Minnesota; the growth of intercollegiate conferences; the story of the *Turnvereins* or *Sokols* in Minnesota; the story of one of Minnesota's state parks (its origin, special features, extent of public use); the rise and work of the Minnesota State High School League; Minnesota's sponsorship of tourism; tourism as a business.

REFERENCES

* BERTHEL, MARY W., "Hunting in Minnesota in the Seventies," *Minnesota History*, 16:259–71 (Sept., 1935).

* † BLEGEN, THEODORE C., *Building Minnesota*, pp. 338–47.

*——— "The Saga of Saga Hill," *Minnesota History*, 29:289–99 (Dec., 1948). Reminiscences of Lake Minnetonka as a summer resort area.

BRINGS, LAWRENCE M., ed., *Minneapolis, City of Opportunity*, pp. 70–73, 134–43, 214–15. Minneapolis' park system, the Aquatennial, and Lake Minnetonka.

BROOKS, PAUL, "Roadless Area," *Atlantic Monthly*, 193:47–50 (June, 1954). A description of the vacationland in northern Minnesota known as "canoe country."

CARLSON, STAN W., *Dr. Henry L. Williams: a Football Biography* (1938).

CONNELLY, BRENDAN J., "The State Parks Story," *Conservation Volunteer*, 18:1–18 (May–June, 1955). Descriptions of forty-four of Minnesota's sixty-four state parks.

DEWDNEY, SELWYN, "Hunting the Heartless Moose," *Naturalist*, 9:9–15 (Fall, 1958). The nature and significance of the Indian pictographs found on rocks in the north border country. There is an excellent map and fine illustrations.

DOBIE, JOHN, *The Itasca Story* (1959). An account of the formation and many-sided development of this popular state park.

DRURY, NEWTON B., "A State Park Guide and Philosophy," *Conservation Volunteer*, 21:52–55 (July–Aug., 1958). A statement on how a state park system should be built and run, written by one experienced in the field.

* HEILBRON, BERTHA L., *The Thirty-Second State*, pp. 246–62.

HOLMQUIST, JUNE D., "Fishing in the Land of 10,000 Lakes," *Minnesota History*, 33:252–59 (Summer, 1953). Gives brief mention of efforts of the state to regulate fishing, but is essentially a nostalgic report of the excellent fishing of the 1880's and 1890's.

JAQUES, FLORENCE PAGE, "Cherished Wilderness," *Natural History*, 59:254–58 (June, 1950). Written shortly after the creation of the airplane reserve known as Quetico-Superior, this article is an exciting description of this wilderness area. Illustrations by Francis Lee Jaques are fascinating. Two slim but attractive books on the same theme by the same author and illustrator are *Canoe Country* (1938) and *Snowshoe Country* (1945).

JOHNSON, H. NAT, "Minnesota State Parks," *Conservation Volunteer*, 21: 42–43 (July–Aug., 1958).

* KANE, DOROTHY, "Frontier Vacation Land," *Gopher Historian*, 5:12–13 (March, 1951). Comments on the fame of Minnesota as a resort area before 1880.

* LATHROP, HAROLD W., "Minnesota — A Pioneer in State Parks," *Conservation Volunteer*, 21:16–19 (July–Aug., 1958). Brief, but an excellent survey of the rise of state parks in Minnesota.

——— "Minnesota State Parks," *Minnesota Conservationist*, 33:13–14, 17 (Feb., 1936); 34:4–6, 20–21 (March, 1936).

* *Legislative Manual, State of Minnesota, 1957–1958*, pp. 310–23. A description of the state park system.

MONROE, CECIL O., "The Rise of Baseball in Minnesota," *Minnesota History*, 19:162–81 (June, 1938). A report of beginnings.

NUTE, GRACE LEE, "The Picture Rock of Crooked Lake," *Minnesota History*, 29:130–36 (June, 1948). An account of a symbol of the historically romantic past, of Indians and the fur traders in canoe country.

OLSON, SIGURD F., *The Singing Wilderness* (1956). Illustrations by Francis Lee Jaques. Lovers of Minnesota's northern canoe wilderness will appreciate this volume. Written in a poetically beautiful style, it is not a history, but rather a report of personal experiences.

*——— "Winning a Wilderness," *Naturalist*, 9:2–5 (Fall, 1958). The fight to secure the wilderness area of Quetico-Superior.

* PAXSON, FREDERIC L., "The Rise of Sport," *Mississippi Valley Historical Review*, 4:143–60 (Sept., 1917).

RIIS, PAUL B., "The Birth of an International Wilderness Park," *Parks and Recreation*, 18:138–45 (Dec., 1934). The Quetico-Superior Park.

SCHEFTEL, ZANE S., "Fishing Is Fun — And Big Business," *Conservation Volunteer*, 20:7–9 (May–June, 1957). Some evidence of the role played by tourism.

UNIVERSITY OF MINNESOTA GENERAL ALUMNI ASSOCIATION, *The Golden Gophers* (1935).

WILSON, BLANCHE NICHOLS, *Minnetonka Story: A Series of Stories Covering Lake Minnetonka's Years from Canoe to Cruiser* (1950). This is not the product of intensive reading or research, but it deals with one of Minnesota's most famous resort lakes.

ZIMMERMAN, CHARLES A., "Hunters' Paradise: The Kandiyohi Country in the 1870's," *Minnesota History*, 33:141–54 (Winter, 1952). A reprint from *Scribner's Monthly*.

VIII. THE STATE PROMOTES THE PUBLIC WELFARE

29. Programs of Correction, Protection, Relief, and Security

A. Social Views Prevailing circa 1850 — and Then in 1950

Pioneer view: care of the aged, sick, poor, or defective the duty of family or church; the insane not treated as criminals, yet not generally considered ill; handling of law violators an acknowledged function of the state; emphasis on individual responsibility for employment and labor conditions. Growing transfer of responsibility for socially handicapped from home and church to state; some exceptions. The beginnings of local relief. Influence of the New Deal of the 1930's. Today's views.

B. The Minnesota Record: Penal Institutions

State prison, 1851; prison policy, old and new; prison industries and educational system; the parole system (Board of Pardons, 1897, and Board of Parole, 1911). Training school for boys at Red Wing, 1867; reformatory for men at St. Cloud, 1889; training school for girls at Sauk Center, 1911; women's reformatory at Shakopee, 1915. Dominant policy in these four institutions: reform and uplift. Youth Conservation Commission, 1947; its services. Minnesota's penal program compared with that of other states.

C. The Minnesota Record: Care of the Physically Handicapped

Establishment of schools for the deaf and mute, Faribault, 1858; the blind, Faribault, 1866; the feeble-minded and epileptic, Faribault, 1879, and Cambridge, 1925. Hospitals for the insane at St. Peter, 1866; Rochester, 1875; Fergus Falls, 1887; Anoka, 1899; Hastings, 1899; Willmar, 1907; Moose Lake, 1935; their programs of medical care, diversional and occupational therapy; expanding services; Governor Youngdahl's crusade of the 1940's. School for dependent neglected children at Owatonna, 1866, the first such school in the United States; a similar school at Owasso, 1955. Establishment of a hospital for crippled and deformed children in 1897 (another case of Minnesota pioneering in the nation), which later became Gillette Hospital. Treatment for inebriates at Willmar, 1907. Treatment of tuberculosis: Minnesota State Sanatorium at Walker, 1903; district sanatoria; notable accomplishments. Centralizing administration of welfare services: state Board of Corrections and Charities, 1883, and Hastings Hornell Hart; Board of Control, 1901; Department of Public Welfare, 1953. Scope of the program: numbers treated, buildings and equipment, cost to the state.

D. The Minnesota Record: Aid for the Aged, Unemployed, and Minority Groups

Establishment of the Soldiers' Home, 1887. City and county welfare work: mothers' aid, child welfare boards, and county homes; support of

149

local efforts by state through Mothers' Pension Act, 1913, and Old Age Pension Act, 1929. Response of Minnesota to federal matching of funds in the New Deal program of the 1930's. The Unemployment Compensation Law, 1936, and its benefit payment services and employment agency activities; administration of the law by the Department of Employment Security since 1953. Program of aid for Indians, Negroes, migrant workers, and other such groups: Governor's Commission on Human Rights, 1943, an interracial program of education, investigation, and assistance; Fair Employment Practices Commission, 1955, which seeks to ensure equal employment opportunities to all.

E. Some Private Welfare Agencies

The Red Cross. Public health nurses. Infant and family welfare associations. Hospitals, orphanages, schools, homes for the aged. Medical and dental clinics. Community houses. Salvation Army and Goodwill Industries. Volunteers of America. Gospel missions. Leagues for the blind and hard of hearing. Community fund campaigns.

QUESTIONS AND SUGGESTIONS

1. Contrast generally the pioneer and the present-day attitude toward the shouldering of social responsibility. What are some of the basic changes in the conditions of American life that help explain the adoption of new social viewpoints?

2. Compare the pioneer and the modern prison policy.

3. Make a study of the powers and activities of the Department of Public Welfare. Its activities are multifarious. The state *Legislative Manual* gives some information, which may be supplemented by writing to the department for copies of recent reports.

4. What is the nature of the corrective program which the Youth Commission of the state seeks to carry out?

5. What were the circumstances that prompted Governor Luther Youngdahl to embark upon his crusade to better the state's services to the mentally ill? How did the legislature react to his program? Did his crusade bear fruit?

6. Has Minnesota lagged behind or led other states in legislation for the care of the unfortunate, sick, and dependent, and for the protection of women, children, and workers? A comparison of Minnesota's social legislation with that of other states may be found in Paullin, *Atlas*, Plate 132.

7. Many of the state institutions have their own publications. These are valuable reflections of the institutions and their inmates. Look up the *Prison Mirror* at Stillwater, the *Reformatory Pillar* at St. Cloud, the *Companion* of the school for the deaf, and the *Riverside* of the training school for boys.

8. Select for special study some private or semiprivate welfare agency, pay-
   ing particular attention to its origins, organization, finances, achievements, and relation to the state and to other welfare agencies. In St.
   Paul there are upwards of a hundred organizations, institutions, boards,
   bureaus, and committees that function in one way or another as welfare
   agencies. A few are listed here merely to indicate their diversity: Community Chest, Neighborhood House, Lyngblomsten Home, Twin City
   Linnea Society, St. Paul Council of Parents and Teachers, Urban League,
   Council of Jewish Women, Home of the Good Shepherd, Goodwill Industries, Child Guidance Clinic, Children's Preventorium, Guild of
   Catholic Women, Salvation Army, Y.M.C.A., Y.W.C.A., Boy Scouts,
   Girl Scouts, Campfire Girls.
9. If you live in a small town or village, study its welfare work and interview
   the persons in charge of it.
10. Is it possible for a person to secure training for social work in Minnesota's
    institutions of higher learning?
11. If your city has a United (Community) Fund Drive, list the various wel-
    fare agencies supported by it, and study the campaign methods used.
    Is it accomplishing its intended purpose?
12. Topics: Hastings Hornell Hart, social pioneer; the career of Mrs. Blanche
    La Due; the history of one state institution; the New Deal and welfare
    work in Minnesota.

REFERENCES

BARTLETT, GEORGE L., *Through the Mill by "4342": A Prison Story That's
Different* (1915). Life in the state prison at Stillwater.

* † BLEGEN, THEODORE C., *Building Minnesota*, pp. 319–27.

BLEGEN, THEODORE C., and PHILIP D. JORDAN, *With Various Voices*, pp.
324–28. An excerpt from the first biennial report of the Minnesota Board
of Corrections and Charities. Written by Hastings H. Hart, it reflects
the miserable conditions of jails at the time, as well as offers recommendations for reform.

BRINGS, LAWRENCE M., *Minnesota Heritage*: John C. Kidneigh, "In the Interests of Humanity," pp. 344–70.

CHRISTIANSON, THEODORE, *Minnesota*, 2:99–100, 135–39, 306–7, 362–63.
Phases of the state welfare activities.

COMMISSIONER OF MENTAL HEALTH, *The Minnesota Mental Health Program* (1951).

ESBJORNSON, ROBERT, *A Christian in Politics: Luther W. Youngdahl*, pp.
169–96 (1955). Governor Youngdahl's successful drive for a new approach in the treatment of the mentally ill.

FOLWELL, WILLIAM W., *History*, 4:407–13. Hastings H. Hart.

HOLCOMBE, RETURN I., *Minnesota in Three Centuries*, 3:481–97. Correctional and charitable institutions.

KISE, JOSEPH, *Minnesota's Government*, pp. 147–54. Care of dependent and disabled persons.

Legislative Manual, State of Minnesota, 1957–1958, pp. 180–83, 201–4, 215, 295–309. A brief description of present-day functions of state institutions, boards, and commissions dealing with welfare.

MCEWEN, WILLIAM E., "Social Legislation in Minnesota," Papers and Proceedings of the Minnesota Academy of Social Science, vol. 2, no. 2, pp. 214–25 (1909).

NOYES, DANIEL R., "Charities in Minnesota," Minnesota Historical Collections, 12:167–82 (1908). Noyes was the founder of the St. Paul Relief Society.

Public Welfare in Minnesota, Services and Programs of State and County Agencies (1958). A publication of the state Department of Public Welfare.

RIGG, DOUGLAS C., "Minnesota's 'Big House,'" *Gopher Historian*, 13:22–25 (Spring, 1959). The state prison, its administration and program. Mr. Rigg is warden of the prison.

RITTER, L. B., "Man and Resource Rehabilitation," *Conservation Volunteer*, 20:1–5 (March–April, 1957). Use of inmates of penal institutions in forestry projects.

WAITE, EDWARD F., *The Origin and Development of the Minnesota Juvenile Court* (1920).

[VIII. THE STATE PROMOTES THE PUBLIC WELFARE]

30. *Conservation*

A. Developing Interest in Conservation

Pioneer belief in inexhaustible abundance of natural resources; easy transfer of priceless resources from public to private hands; quick profits; careless methods of exploitation and waste. Pioneer abuses: stripping land of trees for farming; wholesale cutting of forests, with "poverty woods" left; lack of forest fire defense; drainage of bogs, swamps, and shallow lakes; impoverishment of wild life; soil erosion; exhaustion of minerals. Forces working for a changed attitude: preaching of farsighted prophets of conservation; observance of Arbor Day since 1872; catastrophic forest fires. State conservation movement influenced by the national movement. Gradual growth of concern for conservation. Important reorganization in the Conservation Act of 1931 when all activities were brought under one head, the Department of Conservation.

B. Forestry

The Minnesota Horticultural Society, 1866, and its continued interest in forests; the Tree Bounty Act, 1873; Leonard B. Hodges and the state Forestry Association, 1876, the first such organization in the United States. Christopher C. Andrews and forty-four years of conservation leadership. Populist advocacy of conservation, 1892. The Hinckley holocaust, 1894: the damage done; the need for reform driven home. Act for the preservation of forests, 1895, providing for fire commissioner, chief fire warden, and fire wardens; a campaign of education; state Forestry Board, 1899; beginnings of state forests. Other fires and more action: Chisholm fire, 1908, and appointment of fire rangers, 1909; Baudette-Spooner fire, 1910, and state Forest Service, 1911; Moose Lake-Cloquet fire, 1918, and abandonment of state drainage and ditching activities in forest areas. The constitutional amendment of 1926 authorizes the legislature to enact laws to promote reforestation of public and private land. Regulation of Christmas tree cutting — laws of 1927, 1935, 1947. Reorganization of state conservation offices by the acts of 1931 and 1937 putting the five divisions under one commissioner. Cutting practices law, 1943, applying to both private concerns and the state. The first two state forests, Pillsbury, 1899, and Burntside, 1903. Extension and development of state forests, 34 by 1956. Establishment of the first tree nursery, 1903, three by 1958; tree planting program on state and private lands; forestry camps of the Youth Conservation Commission. The first state park, Itasca, 1891, placed under the Department of Conservation for supervision, 1907; grant of land use in Itasca to University of Minnesota School of Forestry, 1907. Growth of state parks: 38 by 1959. National forests: Chippewa, 1908; Superior, 1909. Civilian Conservation Corps camps of the 1930's; Keep Minnesota Green Association, 1944. Establishment of monument sites.

c. Game and Fish

Tardiness in imposing vigorous regulation: approximately half-year hunting season for quail, grouse, deer, and elk, 1858; first game warden, 1873; first hunting license requirement, 1897; first fishing license requirement, 1927. Cycles of scarcity and abundance; instances of extinction. Growth of concern: office of fish commissioner, 1874; Board of Game and Fish Commissioners, 1889; department, 1915; division, 1931. The work of Frank D. Blair. Some trends: protection and propagation of game and fish (game farms, game refuges, fish hatcheries); introduction of carp and ring-necked pheasants (a nuisance and a prized game bird); halt in interstate shipment of game. Promotional activity of private organizations: Izaak Walton League, 1923; the Minnesota Conservation Federation, 1936. Present-day functions of the Game and Fish Division.

d. Water

Unfortunate policy of the first half century: to increase farm areas by getting rid of wetlands, especially in the North; drainage instead of conservation. Laws of early decades authorizing drainage; establishment of the Commission for Drainage, 1893; catastrophic consequences, with three fourths of the bog areas drained by 1914. Hint of policy change: the law of 1919 establishing the Department of Drainage and Waters. Factors influencing reversal of policy: E. V. Willard's drive to discredit drainage; drouth years of the 1920's and 1930's, with a drop in lake levels, silt-clogged streams, run-off erosion; sewage pollution of rivers. Reorganization effected by the act of 1931. Halt in state ditching operations. Water conservation acts, 1937, 1947, 1957, to "save the wetlands," maintain lake levels, control and protect waters both above and below ground. Pollution control. Watershed District Act, 1955. Industrial expansion and water supply.

E. Lands and Minerals

Tragic loss of topsoil in early decades. Early efforts to alert and educate. The work of the College of Agriculture, University of Minnesota. Aid from the federal government: the Smith-Lever Act of 1914 and the growing services of county agents; United States Soil Conservation Service in the 1930's. State and county support of these agencies. Conservation districts and watershed districts. Contour, terrace, and strip farming practices. Volunteer aspect of soil conservation. State auditor acts as commissioner of lands, timber, and minerals, 1858–1931. Reorganization in 1931. Policies on state-owned lands since 1931: wetlands preservation, tree planting, research in low-grade iron ore.

F. Natural Resources of Minnesota at Mid-Twentieth Century

QUESTIONS AND SUGGESTIONS

1. Study the relation of the national conservation movement to Minnesota, particularly with reference to forest reserves. Did the activities of President Theodore Roosevelt in any way touch Minnesota?
2. What was the purpose of the Tree Bounty Act of 1873?
3. How did Christopher C. Andrews first become interested in forestry? What forestry principles did he enunciate? What benefits did he feel would accrue to the state if it followed a good program of forest conservation?
4. Under what circumstances did Minnesota get her first forest conservation law? Give the provisions of this law. Picture later developments in the expansion of the state's forestry conservation program.
5. How successful has the Division of Forestry been in reducing public indifference to its forestry program? What is its program?
6. How many national forests does Minnesota have? How were these secured?

7. What contribution to forest conservation did the CCC camps of the 1930's make?

8. A chart giving the amount and dollar value of forest products of Minnesota may be found in *Conservation Volunteer*, 21:42 (March–April, 1958).

9. How successful has the Game and Fish Division been in maintaining the kind of wild life supply which would receive the approval of sportsmen?

10. How do you explain the early Minnesota policy of draining its wetlands? What factors led to a reversal of this policy of drainage?

11. Give the meteorological explanation of Minnesota's relatively abundant water supply.

12. Are you aware of any recent changes of water table levels or lake levels over the state? How has the Water Resources and Engineering Division attempted to maintain levels? Explain why it is impossible for the division to have complete control of this.

13. Explain industry's interest in an abundant and steady supply of water. In attracting new industries to the state, how does Minnesota measure up on this point?

14. Discuss recent efforts of the state to eliminate pollution of its rivers. Has your home town in its sewage disposal activities felt the influence of the Water Resources and Engineering Division of the state?

15. What are some of the responsibilities of the Water Resources and Engineering Division?

16. If you would like an explanation of the meaning of the term "watershed," which the modern conservationist commonly uses, consult an excellent article by Alfred L. Nelson entitled "What Is a Watershed?" in *Conservation Volunteer*, 19:28–32 (Jan.–Feb., 1956).

17. The purposes of the Watershed Act of 1955 are clearly set forth in a half-page statement in *Conservation Volunteer*, 21:15 (Sept.–Oct., 1958) under the title "Water Control Starts on the Watershed." It tells of benefits accruing to farmers of Fillmore County who cooperated in the establishment of a watershed control area.

18. Water control programs of different units of government have at times conflicted. Give an example and explain.

19. Consider the role played by the federal government in promoting soil conservation.

20. The county agent is an important official in any program of soil conservation. How and when did the office come into being? What units of government give him his financial support? How is he connected with the College of Agriculture of the University of Minnesota? What activities of his relate to soil conservation?

21. With respect to contour, terrace, and strip farm practices: (a) How much

of this activity depends upon state initiative and how much on individual initiative? (b) What relationship prevails between these practices and education? (c) What progress has been evident in the use of these practices in the last decade or two?

22. Through the years, Minnesota's Department of Conservation has published three magazines: *Fins, Feathers, and Furs* (1915–28); *Minnesota Conservationist* (1933–40); and *Conservation Volunteer* (1940–   ). Articles in these magazines will reflect the policies and activities of the department and furnish a wealth of material.

23. Map exercise: On an outline map of Minnesota locate (a) state forests, (b) state parks, (c) national forests, (d) game reserves. To avoid cluttering, these might best be shown on four separate maps. An official highway map of the state, issued annually by the Department of Highways, contains all the above features. This map may be obtained free by writing to the department in St. Paul.

24. Special topics: (a) Christopher C. Andrews, Apostle of Forestry; (b) the work of the forest rangers; (c) the Hinckley fire and its consequences; (d) present restrictions upon the taking of game and fish; (e) the work of any one of the divisions of the Department of Conservation; (f) Itasca State Park, its history and characteristics; (g) the Superior National Forest and its relationship to Quetico; (h) the story of any one of Minnesota's parks; (i) Minnesota as a vacation and tourist playground.

REFERENCES

AHERN, GEORGE P., *Forest Bankruptcy in America*, pp. 120–25 (1933). An attack on forest policy in Minnesota.

* ANDREWS, CHRISTOPHER C., *Recollections*, edited by Alice E. Andrews, pp. 271–99 (1928). Andrews' work for forestry and conservation.

BABCOCK, WILLOUGHBY M., "Highways and History," *Minnesota History*, 13:377–84 (Dec., 1932). Historical highway markers in Minnesota.

* BLAIR, FRANK D., "A Century of Wildlife Administration," *Conservation Volunteer*, 21:34–46 (May–June, 1958). A detailed account of state and private efforts to build the game and fish resources of Minnesota.

*† BLEGEN, THEODORE C., *Building Minnesota*, pp. 381–88.

BRECKENRIDGE, W. J., "A Century of Minnesota Wild Life," *Minnesota History*, 30:123–34, 220–31 (June, Sept., 1949). Answers the question of how our wild life has fared against the hunting pressure of a century.

*† BUCKMAN, CLARENCE B., "Lumbering and the Pine Forests in East-Central Minnesota," *Gopher Historian*, pp. 9–13 (Spring, 1959). Historical background for conservation attitudes and action of the present day.

CHENEY, EDWARD G., and ALFRED L. NELSON, *Forestry in Minnesota* (1932).

An account of the activities of the Division of Forestry of the Department of Conservation.

*CHRISTIANSON, THEODORE, *Minnesota*, 2:92–93, 207–17, 298–303, 464–68, 495–96. The raid on the state's resources and measures to stop it.

DAVENPORT, F. GARVIN, "Newton H. Winchell, Pioneer of Science," *Minnesota History*, 32:214–25 (Dec., 1951). An acknowledgment of the prodigious work of Winchell as director of the geological survey of the state for twenty-eight years.

DOBIE, JOHN, "Commercial Fishing on Lake of the Woods," *Minnesota History*, 35:272–77 (June, 1957). From the beginnings in the 1890's to the present. Changes in catch through the years as earlier species were fished out, changes in regulatory laws, and changes in methods of marketing. Fine illustrations and map.

——— "Itasca Park — Pride of Minnesota," *Conservation Volunteer*, 19:35–38 (Nov.–Dec., 1955).

——— "The Natural Resources of a State," *Conservation Volunteer*, 21:44–48 (July–Aug., 1958). A rambling survey of what has happened to Minnesota game through a hundred years.

EGAN, JOHN M., "How Many Lakes? How Much Water?" *Conservation Volunteer*, 20:41–44 (Jan.–Feb., 1957). At its birth Minnesota had a wealth of water. A century later there was a growing crisis over water.

† "The First Geologist of the State," *Gopher Historian*, 6:9 (Sept., 1951). The career of Newton H. Winchell in brief.

*FOLWELL, WILLIAM W., *History*, 4:386–402. Christopher C. Andrews.

FRELLSEN, SIDNEY A., *Hydrological Atlas of Minnesota* (1959). A publication of the state Division of Waters. Gives detailed information on thirty-nine watershed units of Minnesota. A condensation of the introduction of this volume may be found in two issues of *Conservation Volunteer*. For part one, see 22:34–41 (July–Aug., 1959) and for part two, see 22:34–41 (Sept.–Oct., 1959).

HOLBROOK, STEWART H., "Death at Hinckley," *Gopher Historian*, 5:4, 5, 24 (March, 1951). A graphic description of the 1894 forest fire.

HOLCOMBE, RETURN I., *Minnesota in Three Centuries*, 3:498–501. State parks.

HOLMES, FRANK R., *Minnesota in Three Centuries*, 4:223–29. The forest fires of 1894.

HOLMQUIST, JUNE D., "Commercial Fishing on Lake Superior in the 1890's," *Minnesota History*, 34:243–49 (Summer, 1955). Has fine photographic reproductions.

†——— "State Parks in Southwestern Minnesota," *Gopher Historian*, 14:11–14 (Winter, 1959–60).

† JOHNSON, H. NAT, *Minnesota Panorama*, pp. 37–44.

† KANE, LUCILE, "Christopher Columbus Andrews," *Gopher Historian*, 6:11 (Sept., 1951). Andrews' work in the forest service of the state.

Legislative Manual, State of Minnesota, 1957–1958, pp. 172–76. Functions and services of the five divisions of the Department of Conservation.

* MINNESOTA REFORESTATION COMMISSION, *Report to House and Senate*, November, 1928, pp. 44–55 (1928). A concise history of forestry in the United States and in Minnesota. Elsewhere in the report is to be found much valuable material on forestry in Minnesota, the United States, and in Europe.

NELSON, ALFRED L., "The CCC and Minnesota's Resources," *Conservation Volunteer*, 19:1–6 (March–April, 1956). An estimate of the work of the CCC in forest conservation.

——— "Water Is Our Future Wealth," *Conservation Volunteer*, 20:32–35 (Jan.–Feb., 1957). The author, editor of the magazine, pleads that the title be the state's theme for its second century.

OBERHOLTZER, ERNEST C., "Conservation and the Economic Situation in Minnesota," *Minnesota Municipalities*, 16:472–76 (Dec., 1931).

ORFIELD, MATTHIAS N., *Federal Land Grants to the States, with Special Reference to Minnesota*, pp. 179–88. Discusses the prevention of forest fires.

† "Parks and Preserves," *Gopher Historian*, 14:7–10 (Fall, 1959). A brief portrayal of state and federal parks in northwestern Minnesota.

PETERSON, MELVIN J., "The Laws of the Watershed," *Conservation Volunteer*, 22:1–8 (Jan.–Feb., 1959). Sketches the story of state drainage laws and describes the Watershed Act of 1955.

* PROUT, CLARENCE, "Building Minnesota — Early-Day Forestry," "Building Minnesota — Modern-Day Forestry," "Building Minnesota — Forestry for Tomorrow," *Conservation Volunteer*, 18:21–26, 26–35; 19:37–42 (Sept.–Oct., Nov.–Dec., 1955, and Jan.–Feb., 1956). A brief but excellent history of forest conservation efforts in the state.

RIENOW, L. T., "Lament for Minnesota: One Hundred Years of Pillage," *Harper's*, 216:57–59 (May, 1958). A resident of Minnesota decries the waste in forest and mineral resources.

ROGERS, HARVEY, "The Pollution of Sky-Blue Waters," *Conservation Volunteer*, 20:50–55 (Jan.–Feb., 1957). Pictures the problem and offers measures for solution.

RYAN, FLOYD T., "Keep Minnesota Green Inc. — 1959," *Conservation Volunteer*, 23:42–46 (Nov.–Dec., 1959). A short account of the progress and accomplishments of this voluntary conservation organization.

SCOTT, WILLIAM E., "Fishing in Lake Superior," *Minnesota Conservationist*, no. 37, pp. 10, 11, 21 (June, 1936).

SPRECKER, STANLEY A., "Stamps for Ducks Makes Hunting," *Conservation*

Volunteer, 21:34–43 (Sept.–Oct., 1958). How the Migratory Bird Hunting Stamp Act works.

STENLUND, MILTON, "A History of Itasca County Deer," *Conservation Volunteer*, 2:19–24 (Sept.–Oct., 1958). An eye-opening account of the fluctuation of deer or other game as a consequence of lumbering, fires, changing plant growth.

TAYLOR, LYTTON, "A Prairie Lake Is Lost," *Conservation Volunteer*, 21:46–51 (Sept.–Oct., 1958). Heron Lake and how man's practices, including drainage, have changed it into a marsh.

THIEL, GEORGE A., "The Land of a Watershed," *Conservation Volunteer*, 22:34–38 (Jan.–Feb., 1959). Minnesota's water resources and characteristics as seen by a geologist.

* TRYGG, WILLIAM, and OTHERS, "A History of Natural Resources. The Centennial Story," *Conservation Volunteer*, 20:17–22 (Jan.–Feb., 1957), 20:7–13 (March–April, 1957), 20:10–17 (May–June, 1957), 20:11–15 (July–Aug., 1957), 20:13–21 (Sept.–Oct., 1957), 20:12–18 (Nov.–Dec., 1957). In this series of six articles, Minnesota is divided into six areas, and the resources of each area are assessed after a century of utilization.

UHLIG, HANS G., "Wildlife Can Live Modern," *Conservation Volunteer*, 21:29–31 (Sept.–Oct., 1958). An optimistic view of the outlook for game.

WEITZMAN, SIDNEY, "Problems of Watershed Management," *Conservation Volunteer*, 20:8–12 (Jan.–Feb., 1957). The importance of water in conservation.

* WOLFF, JULIUS F., JR., "A 2nd-Century Water Policy Needed," *Conservation Volunteer*, 21:1–5 (Sept.–Oct., 1958). A hundred years of water conservation in Minnesota. An excellent brief survey.

*———— "A State Division of Forestry Is Built," *Conservation Volunteer*, 21:34–38 (Nov.–Dec., 1958). A brief history of forest conservation in Minnesota. Excellent.

[VIII. THE STATE PROMOTES THE PUBLIC WELFARE]

31. *Public Health and the Advance of Medicine*

A. Medicine and Dentistry

Prevalence of sickness and epidemics in pioneer times; primitive medical knowledge; reliance upon home remedies, quack nostrums, and "the community grandmother"; inadequacy of medical and dental training; "diploma mills" and practice by quacks or irregulars; impure water; ignorance of sanitation fundamentals. Organization of the Minnesota Medical Association in 1853, with eleven doctors in attendance; irregularity of early meetings; the new constitution of 1870 and annual meetings thereafter; the contributions of Millard, Hewitt, and Folwell; the first state examining board, 1883, and its effort to weed out irregulars; the revised Board of Medical Examiners, 1887, independent of any medical school, the first of its kind in the United States. Earliest medical schools: St. Paul, 1871; Winona, 1872; Minneapolis, 1881 and 1883. Fusion of these schools in the organization of the College of Medicine and Surgery at the University of Minnesota, 1888. Erection of Millard Hall, 1912, and continuing expansion of facilities of the medical campus. The raising of requirements for both entrance and length of training. Giant strides of medicine from roughly 1890: progress in surgery with anesthesia and Listerian methods; Pasteur and Koch and the germ theory of disease; the use of X rays; development of glandular medicine; emphasis on observation and research. The leadership of Dr. W. W. Mayo and his famous sons; the Rochester Center and growth of the clinic form of organization. Dr. Justus Ohage of St. Paul, and others. The Mayo Foundation and its affiliation with the University of Minnesota. Rise of the medical specialist. Organization of the School of Dentistry, University of Minnesota; Dr. Alfred Owre; raising the standards of the dental profession, of dental education, and of dental research. Medical journals: *Journal Lancet* and *Minnesota Medicine*.

B. Growth of Hospitals

Dual sponsorship of hospitals: private agencies (generally religious groups) and the state. Earliest hospitals, few and privately sponsored. Impressive construction in post-Civil War years: a Minneapolis city hospital, 1871; a St. Paul city hospital, 1873; St. Barnabas, 1873; eight new hospitals during the 1880's, including the famed St. Mary's at Rochester; establishment of the Gillette State Hospital for Crippled Children, 1897; continuing hospital construction to a total of 267 in the state by 1940. Changing methods in hospital care; the effort to improve and enforce standards; the state Board of Health authorized to license hospitals by an act of 1941. A continuing shortage of beds; federal aid and the Hospital Survey and Construction Act of 1946; the building program of the 1940's and 1950's. Growing need for care of the aged and efforts to meet it; the Code of Standards Act of 1941 authorizing licensing of rest homes and nursing homes in addition to hospitals. The Old Age Assistance Act of 1937 modified in 1945 to include medical, dental, surgical, hospital, and nursing care. The issue of socialized medicine. Rise of voluntary health insurance plans such as Blue Cross and Blue Shield.

C. Concept of State Responsibility for Disease Prevention and Health Promotion

Pioneer individualism: health a family matter. Problems of the young state: disease influx with population influx, including those attracted

160

by advertisement of the state as a health resort; epidemics; medical ignorance. Leadership of Charles N. Hewitt; support from the state Medical Society; legislative backing in the law of 1872, establishing the state Board of Health, and the law of 1873, authorizing establishment of boards of health by local governments. Secretaries of the board: Charles N. Hewitt, 1872–97; Henry M. Bracken, 1897–1919; Charles E. Smith, 1919–21; Albert J. Chesley, 1921–55; Robert N. Barr, 1955–. Growth of city, town, and county boards of health; their cooperation with the state board. Division of the state into eight health districts. Impressive growth of activities of state and local boards under dominant leadership of the state board: combating contagious diseases; fighting for a pure water supply, pure food, and sanitary sewage disposal; attacking the "white plague"; battling river and lake pollution; caring for the mentally ill; promoting health education, nursing, and hospital growth; safeguarding the health of the worker, the mother and her child, the aged.

D. Evolution of the Public Health Program

Hewitt's twenty-five-year regime: Smallpox and the question of vaccination. Typhoid fever and tuberculosis — pure water and milk. Vital statistics. Sanitary investigations; laboratory work. Establishment of the Board of Medical Examiners to license physicians; aid in the establishment of the medical college at the University of Minnesota. Educational activities: pamphlets, public health, schools. Beginnings of improved water and sewage systems in St. Paul, Minneapolis, Duluth, Fergus Falls, Redwood Falls, and a few other towns. *Bracken's twenty-three-year regime:* Increased laboratory service with the cooperation of the University of Minnesota; diphtheria immunization program; the question of quarantine. Continued improvement of Twin City water systems with filtration and chlorination. Early efforts at inspection of meat, milk, and other foods; support from the federal pure food acts. The battle against tuberculosis: compulsory reporting of cases (1906); the work of Dr. H. L. Taylor; Walker Sanatorium (1907); the first county sanatorium (St. Louis, 1912); tag days (1911 and on). Lessons from the flu epidemic of 1918. *Chesley's thirty-four-year regime:* Victory over smallpox, typhoid, and diphtheria; great gains over tuberculosis with fourteen county sanatoria by 1946, portable X-ray units, and free examinations (1946 and since); increased attention to heart disease, cancer, and accidents. Financial aid from the federal Sheppard-Towner Act, 1921; preparation and distribution of vaccines and serums; Mantoux testing; establishment of trachoma clinics; promotion of maternity aid and infant hygiene, hotel inspection, rural health service, public health education, nursing, industrial health, dental health; coordination (matching) with federal Social Security program (1936 and since). At long last, effective drives against river and stream pollution with the survey and report of the Metropolitan Drainage Commission (1927–33) and the resultant erection of the Sewage Disposal Plant for the Twin Cities (1938); the Water Pollution Control Act of 1945, and pressure upon towns and cities to conform. A vigorous drive for improved care of the mentally ill; Governor Youngdahl and legislative support. The seven divisions of the Department of Health.

E. Nursing

The pioneer mother as nurse; midwives; the practical nurse. The slow march of professional nursing: the first graduate nurse in the United States, 1873; the first graduate nurse west of the Mississippi River, 1883; the first nursing class to be graduated west of the Mississippi River, 1889; Minnesota's first nursing school, St. Joseph's in St. Paul, 1894; establishment of the University School of Nursing, 1908. Nursing sisterhoods. Other schools. Beginning of public health nursing: Minneapolis, 1902; St. Paul, 1906. Beginning of school nursing: St. Paul, 1909; Minneapolis, 1910. Minnesota leads in bringing public health nursing to nonmetropolitan centers. Protection for the nursing profession through a law providing for state registration of nurses, 1907. The state organization for public health nursing; activities of the public health nurse in cities, towns, counties, schools.

QUESTIONS AND SUGGESTIONS

1. When Minnesota was young many people were attracted to the state because of its "health-restoring properties." This is beautifully portrayed in Helen Clapesattle's article "When Minnesota Was Florida's Rival." Other accounts may be found in Philip Jordan's *The People's Health*, pp. 1–16; J. Arthur Myers' *Invited and Conquered*, pp. 15–33; and Ralph H. Brown's "Fact and Fancy in Early Accounts of Minnesota's Climate," *Minnesota History*, 17:243–61.

2. For a graphic presentation of the conquest of certain contagious diseases consult the charts which appear in Jordan, *The People's Health*, pp. 432, 464.

3. Tract No. 1 of the state Board of Health is *Infectious Diseases. What Are They? How Are They Spread? How to Prevent Them: by Cleanliness, Ventilation and Disinfection* (1881). Tract No. 2 is *Smallpox (Variola). What Is It? Where Does It Come From? Who Are Liable to It? How to Avoid It. How to Deal with a Person or Persons Affected with It. How to Prevent Its Occurrence. A Guide to Heads of Families, Clergymen and Others Dealing with This Disgusting and Dangerous Disease* (1881).

162

4. A typhoid epidemic in a large city is now viewed as a municipal disgrace. Why?
5. Define "public health." What are some diseases that have been successfully fought through public health measures?
6. Observe the advance of state control in the field of public health and medicine. Make a list of the various state boards whose functions have to do with public health.
7. What were the main steps in the advance of nursing as a profession in Minnesota?
8. Special topics: (a) Dr. Charles N. Hewitt, "Apostle of Public Health"; (b) the work of either Henry M. Bracken or Albert J. Chesley; (c) Dr. William W. Mayo; (d) the Mayo brothers — Charles H. and William J.; (e) the Mayo Foundation; (f) Dr. Alfred Owre; (g) the history of the Mayo Clinic.
9. For an analysis of the present organization of the state Board of Health and its functions and services see *Legislative Manual, 1957–1958*, pp. 184–87.
10. Tell the story of the long and uphill fight to secure a pure water supply in the cities, towns, and farms of Minnesota. Do the same for sanitary sewage disposal.
11. In the history of immigration one speaks of the old and the new immigration, with the year 1890 as a kind of dividing line between them. That same year may, in a general way, be said to be a division point between what could be called "the old" and "the new" medicine. Explain. Would you agree with the statement that the progress which medicine has made since 1890 is greater than in all the previous years of the world's history?
12. What contributions to Minnesota medicine were made by William H. Eustis? by Michael H. Dowling?
13. Why did frontier folk tend to be their own doctors? Describe some of their remedies.
14. The diphtheria epidemic described by LeRoy Davis in the article cited below emphasizes the feeling of inadequacy of the doctors in pioneer times, the absence of nurses, the high mortality rate, and the readiness of frontier folk to try almost anything.
15. With respect to the Mayos of Rochester: (a) What role was played by the elder Mayo, Dr. William Worrall Mayo, in the establishment of the Mayo Clinic? (b) How did St. Mary's Hospital come to be established and of what importance was it to the work of the Mayos? (c) What did the medical partnership of the two sons of the elder Dr. Mayo mean to the growth of Mayo Clinic? (d) What principles and practices stressed by the Mayos of Rochester help to explain the growth of public confidence in their activities? (e) How did the Mayo Foundation come into

163

being? the Mayo Properties Association? (f) What is necessary before a medical student may qualify as a fellow of the Mayo Foundation? Contrast the training of a fellow with that of a doctor of the 1850's or 1860's.

16. The accompanying table appeared in *Minnesota Medicine*, 36:479 (Jan., Dec., 1936). These figures, and perhaps others somewhat similar, might

Population and Physicians in Minnesota and the Twin Cities

	1890	1950
Population		
Minnesota	1,301,826	2,982,483
Minneapolis	164,738	521,718
St. Paul	133,156	311,349
Physicians		
Minnesota	1,191	3,886
Minneapolis	280	1,141
St. Paul	201	511

be used as a basis for some questioning: (a) Has the number of physicians kept pace with population growth? (b) Has rural Minnesota seen the same relative increase of physicians as urban Minnesota? (c) How does Minnesota compare with other states in the matter of the number of people per physician? (d) Is the number of physicians in the state subject to regulation by any authority?

REFERENCES

BALFOUR, DONALD C., "One Hundred Years of Surgical Progress," *Minnesota Medicine*, 36:356–59 (April, 1953).

*† BLEGEN, THEODORE C., *Building Minnesota*, pp. 328–37.

BROWN, RALPH H., "Fact and Fancy in Early Accounts of Minnesota's Climate," *Minnesota History*, 17:243–61 (Sept., 1936).

BURNQUIST, JOSEPH A. A., *Minnesota and Its People*, 2:107–30 (1924). Medicine and dentistry in Minnesota.

CHATTERTON, CARL C., "Early Orthopedic Surgery in Minnesota," *Minnesota Medicine*, 36:360–63 (April, 1953).

CHRISTIANSON, THEODORE, *Minnesota*, 2:134–35, 141–42. Health legislation. The Mayo brothers.

* CLAPESATTLE, HELEN, *The Doctors Mayo* (1941 and 1954). The world fame of Rochester, Minnesota, and of the doctors who made it famous is witnessed by the fact that the 1941 edition of this book also appeared in ten languages besides English. The 1954 edition is an abridgment of the first. The book is more than a story of the Mayos; it is a history of medicine since 1860.

*——— "Health and Medicine in Rochester, 1855–70," *Minnesota History*, 20:221–42 (Sept., 1939). An interesting account of the backward state of medicine in pioneer days — even in Rochester.

†———— "The Mayo Brothers," *Gopher Historian*, 5:2–4, 21 (Dec., 1950). An excellent brief survey. The same article may be found in Poatgieter and Dunn, *Gopher Reader*, pp. 126–29.

*———— "When Minnesota Was Florida's Rival," *Minnesota History*, 35: 214–21 (March, 1957).

DAVIS, LeROY G., "A Diphtheria Epidemic in the Early Eighties," *Minnesota History*, 15:434–38 (Dec., 1934).

* DIEHL, HAROLD S., "Medical Schools and Medical Education over the Past Century," *Minnesota Medicine*, 36:332–36 (April, 1953). A brief but excellent description of the rise of medical education in Minnesota.

DRAKE, CARL B., "Medical Journalism in Minnesota," *Minnesota Medicine*, 36:344–48 (April, 1953).

* FOLWELL, WILLIAM W., *History*, 4:108–26, 413–25. The Mayo Foundation, the Eustis trust, Charles N. Hewitt.

GRAY, JAMES, *Education for Nursing: A History of the University of Minnesota School* (1960).

HAMILTON, ARTHUR S., "The Early History of Medicine in Minneapolis," *Journal Lancet*, new series, 37:123–31, 163–67, 192–201 (March 1, 15, April 1, 1918).

HANSEN, ERLING W., "Ophthalmology in the Past Century," *Minnesota Medicine*, 36:371–74 (April, 1953).

* HARTLEY, EVERETT C., *The Minnesota Department of Health: A Brief Review of Its Early Days and Its Subsequent Growth* (1930).

* JORDAN, PHILIP D., *The People's Health: A History of Public Health in Minnesota to 1948*. The most authoritative volume on the subject. Actually, the first history of public health to be written for any state.

LOVELACE, MAUD and DELOS, "Minnesota as a Health Resort in the Early Days," *Everybody's Health*, 20:1–3 (Jan., 1935).

MAGNEY, F. H., "History of the Minnesota State Board of Medical Examiners, 1851–1952," *Minnesota Medicine*, 36:341–43, 363 (April, 1953).

* MYERS, ARTHUR J., *Invited and Conquered: Historical Sketch of Tuberculosis in Minnesota*, pp. 1–33, 95–108, 592–624. The title is explained in the fact that many victims of consumption were attracted to the state because of its reputed health-restoring climate. The state was then saddled with the care of these people.

———— "Invited and Conquered," *Gopher Historian*, 5:18–19 (Jan., 1951). Excerpts from the book cited above. Note the graph on the declining mortality rate.

RIGGS, C. EUGENE, "Minnesota Medicine in the Making," *Minnesota Medicine*, 4:579–87 (Oct., 1921).

* ROSENTHAL, ROBERT, "One Hundred Years of Organized Medicine in Min-

nesota," *Minnesota Medicine*, 36:323–31, 370 (April, 1953). A centennial history of the Minnesota State Medical Association, 1853–1953.

Rowe, O. W., "Progress in Pediatrics in Minnesota," *Minnesota Medicine*, 36:364–67 (April, 1953).

Sadler, William P., "Minnesota Obstetrics, 1853–1953," *Minnesota Medicine*, 36:381–83 (April, 1953).

Wilson, Netta, and Albert J. Chesley, "Eighty Years of Public Health," *Minnesota Medicine*, 36:337–40 (April, 1953). The writers suggest Minnesota had three periods of public health growth: one of discovery, one of development, and one of consolidation.

IX. THE CALM OF THE EARLY TWENTIETH CENTURY ENDS WITH WORLD WAR I

32. *Material Well-Being in the Wake of a Panic and a War*

A. Minnesota in the Spanish-American War and the Philippine Insurrection
The outbreak of the war; labors for peace of Archbishop Ireland; labors in war of Senator Cushman K. Davis. The federal call for troops and Minnesota's response. Active participation of the Minnesota regiments in the Philippines; typhoid scourge in Georgia. Home activities. Governor Lind and the return of the troops. Cushman K. Davis as peace commissioner. Reaction in Minnesota to the issue of imperialism; the election of 1900.

B. Entering the Twentieth Century
Contemporary retrospect and forecast on entering the new century. The realization of national power after the defeat of Spain. Exit the day of the pioneer: death of Donnelly, 1901, Ramsey and Pillsbury, 1903; election of the last governor with Civil War service, Samuel R. Van Sant, 1900; election of the first native-born governor, John A. Johnson, 1904. Styles and amusements. Some 1900 statistics: total population, 1,750,-000; urban population, 600,000; foreign born, 500,000; number of farms, 150,000. Comparison with 1850 figures; with 1920 figures. Continuing dominance of flour milling and lumbering in industry, with 48 per cent of the total value of products, 24 per cent of the labor force, 26 per cent of wages and salaries paid — and yet 90 per cent of proprietors and 91 per cent of industrial establishments are to be found in fields other than these two.

C. Good Times, 1896 through World War I
Rise of the price index after 1896 with slight fluctuations, as in 1907; the similar pattern of other economic indices. Erection of a new state capitol, a symbol of well-being: acceptance of Cass Gilbert's plan, 1895; cornerstone laying, 1898; occupancy, 1905; the total cost, $4,500,000. Ever-

widening use of new inventions: telephone, electric light, typewriter, automobile, motion picture; their spread to rural areas. Quiet expansion of industrial plant. World War I boom.

D. Expansion of Banking Facilities

Background history: banking provisions in the state constitution; the banking act of 1858; early state banks; appearance of national banks with the passage of the National Bank acts of 1863 and 1865; elimination of state bank currency by the act of 1865; high interest rates; growth of both state and national banks in the late nineteenth century. Growth of the Twin Cities as a financial center: early dependence upon the East for capital; growing independence of New York and Chicago finance on the part of Twin City banks; financing demands of the Northwest; the Federal Reserve Act of 1913 and the establishment of Minneapolis as the capital for the Ninth Reserve District; the vast size of the Ninth Federal Reserve District. Twentieth-century trends: the tendency toward consolidation since 1890; bank chains and branch banking.

E. The First Serious Attempt at Tax Reform

Historical background: a general property tax the "backbone of the state tax system" for the first seventy-five years; fairly early taxation of corporations (a gross earnings tax on railroads, then later on telephone, telegraph, sleeping car, express, and freight companies); low tax rates; the third parties and taxation. A drive for tax reform under Governors Nelson, Lind, Van Sant, Johnson, and Eberhart; early reluctance of legislatures to follow recommendations of governors; influence of pressure groups; recommendations of the Special Tax Commission of 1902 unheeded by a special session of the legislature; the "wide open amendment" ratified by voters, 1906, opening the way for revision. The Permanent Tax Commission, 1907; classification of property for tax purposes; an inheritance tax; influence of the automobile in adoption of a one-fourth mill road tax, raised to one mill by a 1912 amendment. The problem of taxation of the mining industry. Attempts and failure to obtain an income tax.

QUESTIONS AND SUGGESTIONS

1. How vital a role did Minnesota troops play in the war with Spain?
2. The activities of the various Minnesota regiments are described in Franklin F. Holbrook's book, which devotes one chapter to each regiment. Note especially the story of the "Thirteenth Minnesota." A mutiny in the Fifteenth is dealt with in Folwell, *History*, 3:521–28.
3. What did the election of 1900 reveal about the attitude of Minnesotans toward the issue of imperialism? about unfulfilled aspects of the Populist program?

4. Justify the statement that when Minnesota entered the twentieth century it had left the pioneer period behind.
5. Characterize the years 1900 to 1918 in terms of price changes, technological advance, and employment opportunities.
6. An excellent introduction to the story of banking and taxation in Minnesota may be found in the references listed below by Patchin and Blakey.
7. Was the location of a Federal Reserve Bank in Minneapolis merited?
8. Examine the attitude of the Grange toward tax reform; of the Populists.
9. Were the charges of inequity levied against Minnesota's tax system in 1900 justified? What groups in the population worked for change? What groups were satisfied with the status quo?
10. Why was the "wide open" tax amendment of 1906 regarded as so important?
11. Special topics: The peace activities of Archbishop Ireland; the service of Cushman K. Davis on the peace commission at the end of the Spanish-American War; the history of mining taxation in this state.
12. Perhaps the best source for current information on public finance, taxation, and kindred subjects is the *Minnesota Year Book*, issued by the League of Minnesota Municipalities. Here will be found statistics on assessed valuations, tax rates, tax levies, indebtedness, and receipts and disbursements for school, township, village, county, and state governments.

REFERENCES

ANDERSON, WILLIAM, *Intergovernmental Relations in Review*, pp. 40–44. This survey of federal-state relations uses Minnesota for many illustrations. The "wide-open" tax amendment is a case in point.
——— *Local Government and Finance in Minnesota* (1935).
* BLAKEY, GLADYS C., *A History of Taxation in Minnesota* (1934).
*† BLEGEN, THEODORE C., *Building Minnesota*, pp. 415–22.
CHRISTIANSON, THEODORE, *Minnesota*. 2:191–206, 231–41, 251–65, Governors Nelson, Clough, and Lind. 2:241–46, 255–56, 273–74, 282–84, 292–95, 324, the war with Spain and tax legislation.
DONOVAN, FRANK P., JR., and CUSHING F. WRIGHT, *The First through a Century, 1853–1953* (1954). Centering on the story of the First National Bank, this comes close to being a history of banking in St. Paul.
* FOLWELL, WILLIAM W., *History*, 3:231–59, 286–90. The war with Spain and efforts at tax reform.
HELMES, WINIFRED G., *John A. Johnson, the People's Governor: A Political Biography* (1949). Pp. 169–70, 209–10, 290–93, taxation. Pp. 99–100, the Spanish-American War.

HOLMES, FRANK R., *Minnesota in Three Centuries*, 4:189–209, 231–67. Political history, 1893–1900, and the war with Spain.

* KUNZ, VIRGINIA BRAINARD, *Muskets to Missiles: A Military History of Minnesota*, pp. 113–31 (1958). The Spanish-American War.

ODLAND, MARTIN W., *The Life of Knute Nelson*, pp. 159–223. Nelson as governor; his campaign for the senatorship.

* PATCHIN, SIDNEY A., "The Development of Banking in Minnesota," *Minnesota History Bulletin*, 2:111–68 (Aug., 1917).

PREUS, JACOB A. O., "Knute Nelson," *Minnesota History Bulletin*, 5:329–47 (Feb., 1924). Governor Preus's political career began as Nelson's secretary.

* STEPHENSON, GEORGE M., *John Lind of Minnesota*, pp. 105–91. The war with Spain; politics, 1896 to 1902.

[IX. THE CALM OF THE EARLY TWENTIETH CENTURY ENDS WITH WORLD WAR I]

33. *The Progressive Movement*

A. Key Political Trends, 1896 to 1917: An Overview

In the nation: early Republican control; rise of the Progressive Movement; split in the Republican party over progressivism in 1912 and election of a Democratic president, also a "progressive." In Minnesota: rifts in both major parties, explaining in part the election of three Democratic governors, the first since the Civil War; successive legislatures essentially in control of the Republicans; support of progressivism by both parties; the choice of Republican presidential candidates in all elections, except in 1912; evidences of a new wave of independent political action in 1916 and 1918. Characteristics of the Progressive Movement: lack of a definite organization; leaders, found in both major parties, largely from the middle class; reforms rooted in earlier third-party planks; interest in Minnesota lively, but legislative accomplishment greater at Washington, D.C.

B. State Politics from 1896 to 1910

Defeat of Bryan and victory of Clough over Lind in 1896; election of Lind in 1898. Lind's statesmanlike proposals to the legislature; a cold reception by the legislature. Achievements of the agrarian reform movement to 1900; a lull in militant agrarian discontent. The national election of 1900 and the narrow victory of Samuel R. Van Sant. The direct primary law, 1901; pioneering of Wisconsin and Minnesota; coverage of all state and national offices by 1912. Re-election of Knute Nelson and election of Moses E. Clapp to the United States Senate. The muckrakers; the Ames regime in Minneapolis and exposure by Lincoln

Steffens in *The Shame of the Cities*. The pure food campaign. Theodore Roosevelt's conservation drive, and two national forests for Minnesota, Chippewa and Superior. Van Sant's battle against the Northern Securities Company; Theodore Roosevelt and the Supreme Court's order for dissolution of the Northern Securities Company; state railroad legislation. Other legislation: adoption of the Torrens system for property titles; creation of the game and fish commission. John A. Johnson, Democrat, thrice elected governor. Aided in 1904 election by Republican rift; the Collins-Dunn campaign for the Republican nomination. Progressive nature of Johnson's legislative program; hesitant response of the legislature. Legislation: inheritance tax; increased rate-fixing powers for the Railroad and Warehouse Commission; banning of free railroad passes; authorization for cities to own public utilities; a code for timber sales on state-owned land; a new code for life, fire, and marine insurance; banking reform; the creation of a state Highway Commission. Conservation and public welfare advanced: reforestation measures; repeal of the mineral release law; swampland drainage (this of questionable value); improved care for consumptives, inebriates, and the criminally insane. Challenge by railroads of the right of the state to fix passenger and freight rates; the Minnesota Rate Cases, with the decision of the United States Supreme Court favorable to the state, 1913. Johnson's personal triumph in the elections of 1906 and 1908; Johnson a national figure; a presidential possibility; death.

c. The Progressive Movement at High Tide

Republican Adolph O. Eberhart succeeds Democrat John A. Johnson. The progressive mood of both governor and legislature: school consolidation law, 1911; Putnam Act to stimulate vocational education; Dunn good roads amendment, 1912; a new primary law, 1912; ratification of the Sixteenth and Seventeenth amendments to the federal Constitution. The 1913 legislature evenly divided between "progressives" and "standpatters": reapportionment bill; adoption of presidential preference primary; the bill that made Minnesota's legislature "nonpartisan"; workmen's compensation act; failure of initiative, referendum, and recall amendments in 1914 and again in 1916. The "wet-dry" issue in the election of 1914; county option. The primary contest of 1914 and the election of a Democratic governor; administration and legislation under Winfield S. Hammond; Hammond's death. Succession of Joseph A. A. Burnquist, 1915; re-elected in 1916 and 1918; the shadow of World War I over his administration. Signs of political independency in the 1916 election. Repeal of the presidential preference law, 1917. Mrs. Andreas Ueland and growing sentiment for woman suffrage. Submission of a state prohibition amendment, 1917; failure of ratification. National attention to the

170

issues of prohibition and woman suffrage; ratification of the Eighteenth and Nineteenth amendments; the Volstead Act; the state Prohibition Enforcement Act, 1919.

QUESTIONS AND SUGGESTIONS

1. How important a part did Civil War veterans play in Minnesota politics?
2. What reasons can you advance for there being no active, militant, politically minded farmers' organization in Minnesota in the 1900's as there had been in the 1870's, 1880's, 1890's and was to be in the period after 1915?
3. What type of legislative program came to be promoted by progressives in Congress? by progressives in Minnesota's state legislature?
4. Show how a direct primary law would help fulfill a prime aim of the progressives.
5. Justify the claim that Senators Knute Nelson and Moses E. Clapp were progressives.
6. Did the muckraking of Lincoln Steffens bring about any change in the government of American cities?
7. What legal ground did Governor Van Sant have for his move against the Northern Securities Company?
8. What advantages led to the adoption of the Torrens title system?
9. Explain how John A. Johnson, a Democrat, came to be elected and twice re-elected governor of Minnesota.
10. A change in the process of amending the state constitution came in 1897, a change still in effect in 1960. What is that amending process?
11. Governor Johnson's drive for better regulation of insurance companies was especially significant; it even had national overtones. What led to his interest in this area? What was the character of the new code adopted? Was it effective? See Winifred O. Helmes's biography of the governor, pp. 177–84.
12. For the first time since the Civil War, the Republican party in 1912 failed to win Minnesota's electoral vote. Discuss the factors that allowed Theodore Roosevelt to carry the state.
13. Of what importance was the Supreme Court decision of 1913 in the Minnesota Rate Cases? See Christianson, *Minnesota*, 2:297–98.
14. The reapportionment bill of 1913 was destined to remain on the books for almost a half century. Why?
15. How would you explain Minnesota's failure to approve of initiative, referendum, and recall?
16. Special topic: Minnesota's participation in the Progressive Movement on both the local and the national scene.

REFERENCES

ADRIAN, CHARLES R., "The Origin of Minnesota's Nonpartisan Legislature," *Minnesota History*, 33:155–63 (Winter, 1952).

ANDERSON, WILLIAM, *Intergovernmental Fiscal Relations*, pp. 33–35, 51–53. Trends in Minnesota tax policy, 1913–53.

*† BLEGEN, THEODORE C., *Building Minnesota*, pp. 415–22.

* CHRISTIANSON, THEODORE, *Minnesota*, 2:251–354. Politics, 1898–1914.

DAY, FRANK A., and THEODORE M. KNAPPEN, *Life of John Albert Johnson*, pp. 104–88, 227–38. The political career of Governor Johnson.

* FOLWELL, WILLIAM W., *History*, 3:256–98. Politics, 1901–14.

HAINES, LYNN and DORA B., *The Lindberghs*, pp. 88–234 (1931). The political career and philosophy of the elder Lindbergh.

* HEIN, CLARENCE J., "The Adoption of Minnesota's Direct Primary Law," *Minnesota History*, 35:341–51 (Dec., 1957).

HELMES, WINIFRED G., *John A. Johnson, The People's Governor*. An able biography of a three-term governor who was considered a potential candidate for the presidency of the United States.

HOLMES, FRANK R., *Minnesota in Three Centuries*, 4:269–306. The administrations of Van Sant and Johnson.

* MITAU, G. THEODORE, *Politics in Minnesota*, pp. 8–11. Political trends from 1904 to 1918 — a Democratic interlude of six years followed by Progressive Republicanism.

* SALOUTOS, THEODORE, and JOHN D. HICKS, *Agricultural Discontent in the Middle West, 1900–1939*, pp. 31–55 (1951). Minnesota is one of the states dealt with, and even where the treatment is general, the analysis is pertinent. The chapter cited is "Populism to Insurgency." Insurgency is, of course, another name for the Progressive Movement. Perhaps the finest treatment available.

STEFFENS, LINCOLN, *The Shame of the Cities*, pp. 63–97. "The Shame of Minneapolis."

STEPHENSON, GEORGE M., *John Lind of Minnesota*, pp. 191–207. Minnesota politics, 1902–13.

YOUNG, JEREMIAH S., "Administrative Reorganization in Minnesota," *American Political Science Review*, 9:273–86 (May, 1915). The recommendations of the Efficiency and Economy Commission appointed by Governor Eberhart.

[IX. THE CALM OF THE EARLY TWENTIETH CENTURY ENDS WITH WORLD WAR I]

34. *Minnesota and World War I*

A. Entering the War

President Wilson's neutrality plea; impossibility of remaining neutral "in thought." Attitude of the people during the period of neutrality as revealed by the Minnesota press, racial groups, labor, and churches. The Minnesota Peace Society, the Woman's Peace Party, and the American School Peace League. Statements and actions of Minnesota's representatives in Congress. Support for Woodrow Wilson ("He kept us out of the war") in the election of 1916. Ernest Lundeen's postcard "peace poll" of his Minneapolis congressional district. The defeat of Moses E. Clapp and Charles A. Lindbergh and the election of Frank B. Kellogg to the United States Senate, 1916. The split vote of Minnesota's representatives on the war resolution of Congress, April, 1917. The National Defense Act, 1916; greater federal support to and control of Minnesota National Guard. A prelude: intervention in Mexico, 1916, and service by Minnesotans on the border. Growth of a war spirit upon entry into the European war.

B. Minnesotans in Camp and at the Front

Entry into the war. Raising troops: military camps and training schools; the Selective Service Act and the work of draft boards; Minnesota's manpower contribution — volunteers, draftees, nurses — a total of 118,-000. Obliteration of state lines in building army units; the consequent difficulty of speaking of a particular "Minnesota contribution" in military engagements, but large Minnesota representation in the 89th "Sunflower" Division and in the 42nd "Rainbow" Division, especially the 151st Field Artillery. Overseas action: halting the last German offensive and pushing the Germans out of France. Casualties. The Armistice celebrations.

C. Civilian War Efforts

Building civilian support: the governmental approach in World War I fevered, fraught with pressures, emotional — a contrast with World War II. Establishment of the Minnesota Commission of Public Safety in 1917: its members; its grant of dictatorial powers; its exercise of these powers. Examples of its orders: creation of a Home Guard to enforce its decisions if necessary, registrations of aliens, prohibition of strikes, suppression of disloyal talks, establishment of a public opinion program (propaganda), regulation of saloons and pool halls, inauguration of fisheries at Red Lake. Multiplicity of "drives." Food production and conservation: home and school gardens, food substitutes, meatless and wheatless days, punishment of violators. The coal shortage, 1917, and fuel conservation: regulation of prices and distribution; heatless days; instances of discrimination and violations; conservation of gasoline and electricity; daylight saving. Financing the war: the Liberty Loans; Thrift Stamps; bond selling drives. Propaganda to raise funds (posters, pulpit, press); Four Minute Men. Amounts subscribed to the loans by

Minnesota people. Organization of Minnesota industry for war: government contracts; Minnesota iron and flour vital to the war effort; shipbuilding at Duluth; prohibition of strikes with compulsory arbitration of disputes. Drives for relief agencies such as the Red Cross and the Salvation Army. The work of these agencies.

D. Some Products and By-Products of the War

Economic conditions. Widening scope of women's activities: work in factory and field, war work, the Twentieth Amendment. Extent and scope of propaganda, perfecting techniques, application in the postwar period. Local acts of patriotic terrorism; the attitude toward dissent; the "100 per cent" idea and intensification of nationalism and of intolerance; pressure toward uniformity; suspension of constitutional rights; use of yellow paint for "slackers." Postwar emphasis on education in Americanization. The "conscientious objector." The return to peace: the discharged soldier, the bonus, and veteran organizations.

QUESTIONS AND SUGGESTIONS

1. The position taken by Minnesota's senators and representatives at Washington on matters of neutrality, defense, and entrance into the war would make an interesting study. In general, did they side with the rank and file of Congress, or did they show a spirit of independence?

2. It is interesting to note that Moses E. Clapp, who worked hard for the Seventeenth Amendment that gave the country direct election of senators, failed of re-election to the Senate in Minnesota's first use of the amendment. In what way was this development related to the coming of World War I?

3. List some of the French battlefields which are linked with Minnesota's participation in the war.

4. How important a role did Minnesota's iron play in winning the war?

5. An interesting article appeared in the *New Republic*, April 15, 1937, in which senators who voted against the April, 1917, war resolution were asked to give their impressions of that vote twenty years after.

6. When the United States declared war against Germany on April 6, 1917, the Minnesota legislature was about to adjourn, not to meet again for two years. It was thought advisable to create a special body with power to take care of any situation that might arise in the meantime. This body was the Minnesota Commission of Public Safety. It was armed with extraordinary powers to the end that trouble might be prevented instead of punished after it had developed. And it exercised these powers in a wide range of activities. It is interesting to compare the iron-fisted state control thus set up during World War I with the situation in Minnesota in the Civil War and in World War II.

174

7. John Lind, governor of Minnesota from 1899 to 1901, served for a time on the Minnesota Commission of Public Safety. His withdrawal from the commission was, in a sense, a reflection of the spirit of the times. Explain.
8. In what way did World War I hasten the coming of woman suffrage?
9. The composition of Minnesota's population at the time of the outbreak of World War I was thought to have had a bearing upon the question of "entry into and support for the war." Is there a sound basis for this viewpoint? Consult Christianson, *Minnesota*, 2:395–96. Note the figures for foreign born as reported by the federal census of 1910. These figures may also be found in the pamphlet by Nelson, Ramsey, and Toews, *A Century of Population Growth in Minnesota*, p. 13, Table 3.
10. With the passage of time, Minnesotans regarded as intolerant many of the actions of the "excessive patriots" in 1917 and 1918. Describe some of these actions and reactions.
11. Special topics: (a) Public reaction to the activities of the Minnesota Commission of Public Safety; (b) effects of the war upon Minnesota's economy.

REFERENCES

* † BLEGEN, THEODORE C., *Building Minnesota*, pp. 423–34.

CHRISTIANSON, THEODORE, *Minnesota*, 2:384–403. World War I.

COLLINS, LOUIS L., *History of the 151st Field Artillery, Rainbow Division* (1924).

* FOLWELL, WILLIAM W., *History*, 3:312–19, 528–38, 556–75. Minnesota in World War I.

HEILBRON, BERTHA L., *The Thirty-Second State*, pp. 276–85.

HILTON, O. A., "The Minnesota Commission of Public Safety in World War I," *Bulletins*, 48:1–44 (1951). A publication of the Oklahoma Agricultural and Mechanical College.

HOLBROOK, FRANKLIN F., ed., *St. Paul and Ramsey County in the War of 1917–1918* (1929).

HOLBROOK, FRANKLIN F., and LIVIA APPEL, *Minnesota in the War with Germany*, 2 vols. (1928–32).

* KUNZ, VIRGINIA BRAINARD, *Muskets to Missiles*, pp. 132–58. World War I.

LEACH, GEORGE E., *War Diary* (1923).

LINDBERGH, CHARLES A., *Why Is Your Country at War and What Happens to You after the War and Related Subjects* (1917). A courageous publication in which the elder Lindbergh spoke his mind on the causes and consequences of war.

* STEPHENSON, GEORGE M., *John Lind of Minnesota*, pp. 207–329, 330–32, 333–36. Lind's career as United States diplomat, his attitude toward

World War I, his connection with the Minnesota Commission of Public Safety.

X. INDUSTRIAL ADVANCE, AGRICULTURAL ADJUSTMENT, AND POLITICAL EXPERIMENTATION ARE IMPORTANT FEATURES OF MINNESOTA'S DEVELOPMENT

35. *Modern Transportation and Industrial Growth*

A. The Automobile and the Good Roads Movement

Advent of horseless carriages; power sources (steam, electricity, gasoline); early hesitancy to welcome the automobile; the state law of 1907. First state registry of motor vehicles, 1909. Increase in number of automobiles gradual before and phenomenal after World War I. Factors in the good roads movement before the automobile: the bad roads of the 1890's; farmer interest in trips to local creameries, better access to markets, and rural mail delivery; town and city interest in extension of trade areas and in bicycle riding; state-wide good roads convention in St. Paul, 1893; State Fair good roads day, 1894; the Good Roads Association of Minnesota, 1895. Quickened tempo of the good roads movement with increased ownership of automobiles: the state Highway Commission authorized, 1898; established, 1906; replaced by state Highway Department, 1921. Road building and financing before the good roads movement a function of township, county, and city; then state aid to local units; finally direct state construction and financing. Revenue sources: at first, property taxes only and by all units of government; later, road user taxes, bond issues, federal aid. Agitation for a unified system of roads with a single highway commissioner. The important Babcock amendment, ratified in 1920. Aims of the Babcock amendment: a trunk highway system, new revenues (tax on motor vehicle registry and gasoline, bond issues authorized, reimbursing counties for past improvements). Later increases in gasoline taxes. Extension of trunk highway system in 1933, an addition of 4,574 miles to the original 6,877. Progress in the hard surfacing of roads; the mid-twentieth-century four-lane super highway with cloverleaf intersections. Mileage of Minnesota roads at mid-century. Highway amendment of 1956. Federal Aid Highway Act of 1956 — a "National System of Interstate and Defense Highways." Social consequences of the automobile age: increase in tempo of social and economic life; a new independence for women drivers; the summer hegira; the two- and three-car family; effect on the home, church, and the farm; juvenile delinquency; commuting for education and other worthy purposes; the parking problem; trailer cities; automobile accidents and safety campaigns.

B. Motor Vehicles and the Rise of Ancillary Industries

Concomitants of the automobile: gas stations and garages; tourist camps, cabin camps, and motels. Bus transportation: Carl E. Wickman and Andrew G. Anderson and the beginning of passenger transportation at Hibbing, 1914; expansion into the national Greyhound system; competition for Minnesota's intercity and intracity transportation; consolidation; the present bus system. Truck transportation: the development of intrastate and interstate freight hauling; efforts at regulation by state and national governments; competition among truck lines; the trend toward consolidation; growing importance of motor carrier systems; the number of trucks licensed to operate in Minnesota in 1936, 114,516; in 1957, 241, 170. The growth of automobile accident insurance.

c. Older Modes of Transportation: Competition and Modernization

The railroad system: Trunk lines virtually completed by 1900; new construction, 1900–20, chiefly feeder and cross lines. The consolidation trend and the Northern Securities case. Government management of railroads during World War I. Reasons for the serious plight of the railroads in the 1920's: competition from the automobile, bus, and truck; banker control and overcapitalization; trackage saturation; inadequate services; government regulation and fixed rates. Efforts at readjustment, with some bankruptcies and reorganizations; changed attitude of government on consolidation; reduced costs and rates; cooperation with trucks; streamlined trains, diesel motors, and more passenger accommodations. Improved conditions, 1935 through World War II. Renewal of financial difficulty for railroads at mid-century. *Urban and interurban transportation:* Street railway companies, Minneapolis, St. Paul, Duluth; electrification; spread of the electric street railway to the smaller cities. Decline of the streetcar with increased use of the automobile. The move to bus transportation in place of electric streetcars. *Reviving Mississippi river traffic:* Practical disappearance of river traffic by the end of the nineteenth century. The Upper Mississippi River Improvement Association and authorization of a six-foot channel, 1907. The upper Mississippi as a part of the Great Lakes to the Gulf development. The Upper Mississippi Barge Line Company. The Inland Waterways Corporation enters the upper Mississippi, 1927. Authorization of a nine-foot channel, 1930; the dam and lock system; progress under the New Deal; the nine-foot channel a reality, 1940. Development of barge traffic, although under difficulties of low water, bad channel conditions, seasonal character of shipping, limited docking space at Minneapolis. Incoming traffic largely fuels. Outgoing shipments largely grains. The Upper Harbor Project.

D. The Airplane and International Contacts

Appearance of the airplane in Minnesota; the barnstormer. The epochal flight of Charles A. Lindbergh, 1927. Air mail service beginnings, 1920; regular service, 1926 and on. Passenger service inaugurated by Northwest Airlines, 1927. Establishment of Wold-Chamberlain Airport at Minneapolis, 1923, and Holman Memorial Airport at St. Paul, 1927; 437 airports in the state by 1958. Interest of the federal government in airports for defense. State Aeronautics Commission, 1933; Department of Aeronautics, 1943. Expansion of air services: six commercial airlines by 1958; nation-wide and world-wide contacts; spectacular growth of passenger carriage; significant increase in freight carriage. As with railroads, the Twin Cities a hub. Growth in multifarious uses of the plane: travel of big firm executives, state conservation activities, air mapping and air prospecting, spraying trees and farm crops, traffic control, recreation, others. Financing airport construction and maintenance by local, state, and federal governments; the issue of an equitable tax program — gasoline, airport facilities, or what? Comparatively slow growth of private plane ownership.

E. Shipping on Lake Superior

Some nineteenth- and early twentieth-century developments: building the ship canal at Sault Ste. Marie and its effects; the Northern Pacific connects Duluth with the wheat country; Duluth becomes the largest grain-shipping port in the United States; Duluth as a lumber-shipping port; iron ore tonnage since 1890; the return cargo of coal; development of the Duluth-Superior harbor; other Lake Superior ports; loading facilities. The Great Lakes–St. Lawrence Seaway, an all-water route to the world for large ocean-going vessels, opened in 1959 after decades of battle for the deepened channel in both Canada and the United States. The Duluth Port Authority, 1954; the Arthur M. Clure Municipal Terminal and the International Duluth Seaport Corporation's private terminal; other improved docking facilities. Meaning of the seaway to Duluth; to Minnesota; to areas beyond Minnesota.

F. Manufacturing Development

Key characteristics for the first half of the twentieth century: healthy but uneven advance; peak and decline for early leaders, such as sawmilling and flour milling; spurt during World War I; rise of many new types of manufacture in years between the two world wars; modest growth, but also regression; lively forward surge, 1939 and on; heavy emphasis on manufacturing in the Twin Cities; the significant rise of manufacturing in the smaller cities; industry abreast of, and ready to move ahead of, agriculture by 1950. The rate of industrial advance in Minnesota compared with the United States as a whole in general slower

178

to 1939, faster from 1939 to 1950, as shown by population trends, production data, employment patterns, and per capita wealth statistics. Variety in Minnesota manufactures: processed foods, machines and machine tools, printing and publishing, precision instruments, apparel, electric machinery, electronics, forest products, textiles, furniture, and many others. Leading firms: Minneapolis-Honeywell, Minnesota Mining and Manufacturing, General Mills, Minnesota and Ontario Paper, Munsingwear, Brown and Bigelow, Josten Manufacturing, Fairmont Motors, First Bank Stock, Gamble-Skogmo, Great Northern Railway, Halvorsen Tree, Northern States Power, Northwest Banco, Pillsbury, others. Growth and development of wholesale and retail trade.

QUESTIONS AND SUGGESTIONS

1. Obtain figures by decades which will show (a) the growth in number of registered cars in the state, (b) the same for trucks, (c) the growth in miles of hard surface roads, (d) the growth in annual miles of travel of commercial trucks, (e) the growth in passenger traffic of buses, (f) the growth in passenger miles of airplanes.

2. What factors help explain why the trunk highway system of Minnesota was created by constitutional amendment (Babock amendment) rather than by act of the state legislature? Why was the Babcock amendment spelled out at such great length?

3. Explain the use of the terms township roads, county-aid roads, rural state trunk highways, state trunk highways within cities, county roads within cities.

4. What sources of revenue have been used in the construction and maintenance of the state's roads? Give some indication of the extent of use of each source.

5. In 1956 the people of Minnesota ratified a highway amendment to the state constitution. How did this amendment alter the distribution of highway user revenue? What lay back of the drive for this amendment?

6. What part has the federal government played in the development of Minnesota's highways?

7. Railroads experienced serious financial difficulty first in the 1920's and 1930's, and then again in the 1950's. How are these difficulties to be explained? What measures did the railroads employ to meet the straitened circumstances of the first period? Has the attitude of the public toward railroad consolidation undergone any change since 1920? Explain.

8. To what extent is federal control exercised over railroads? over buses and trucks? over airplanes? Is there any state control?

9. Why have businessmen and the federal government attempted to revive Mississippi River traffic?

179

10. Trace the development of Lake Superior shipping and indicate its importance to Minnesota.
11. Trace the diplomatic negotiations between the United States and Canada which led to the Great Lakes–St. Lawrence Seaway.
12. What harbor and dock improvements were undertaken by Duluth to prepare for better exploitation of the Seaway?
13. How extensive is Minnesota's use of pipelines as a means of transportation?
14. Map exercises: (a) On an outline map of Minnesota draw Minnesota's trunk highway system as originally called for by the Babcock amendment. (b) Draw a map of your county showing its railroads and roads.
15. Railroads in the nation, and in Minnesota, seemed to have reached what sometimes is called the "saturation point" at about 1920. Explain.
16. Topics for special reports: (a) The work of Charles M. Babcock in the establishment of Minnesota's highway system; (b) early years of the Greyhound bus system; (c) developing facilities and services of the Wold-Chamberlain Airport; (d) the rise of any one of Minnesota's leading manufacturing firms; (e) the career of Charles A. Lindbergh.
17. Population trends are a kind of measure of industrial activity. For the periods 1900–19, 1919–39, and 1939–50, take note of Minnesota trends in the following areas: (a) rate of population growth in Minnesota compared with that of the United States as a whole, (b) net migration in or out of state, (c) rate of increase of nonagricultural employment in Minnesota compared with that in the United States. Interpret the data which you gather.

REFERENCES

*† A series of articles on transportation in the *Gopher Historian*, 11:1–2, 18–28 (Spring, 1957): Theodore C. Blegen, "Paddles, Wheels, and Wings," pp. 1–2. An overview. "Minnesota Roadways Today," pp. 18–20. Changing responsibilities of government units before and after 1900. Excellent. "Pipeline Transportation," p. 24. Bob Murphy, "Minnesota and the Great Lakes–St. Lawrence Seaway," pp. 25–27. A good brief account; fine maps.

BALD, F. CLEVER, *The Sault Canal through 100 Years* (1954). A booklet of thirty-six pages which traces the history of the Sault gateway.

BAUM, ARTHUR W., "How to Run a Sticky Business," *Saturday Evening Post*, 232:36–37, 100–102 (July 18, 1959). An account of the singular rise of the Minnesota Mining and Manufacturing Company.

* BLANK, JOSEPH P., "How to Please 210 Million People," *Gopher Historian*, 5:8–9 (May, 1951). Describes the Hibbing origin of the Greyhound Bus

Company. The article first appeared in the *Travel Magazine* and *Reader's Digest*.

*† BLEGEN, THEODORE C., *Building Minnesota*, pp. 401–12.

BOWEN, DANA THOMAS, "Great Lakes Ships and Shipping," *Minnesota History*, 34:9–16 (Spring, 1954). A brief and very general account, but well told.

* CHAMBERLIN, THOMAS W., "Transportation of the Area: The Great Lakes Seaway and Its Meaning," *Minnesota's Tomorrow*, pp. 83–90. Roads, railroads, pipelines, airlines, waterways, and the St. Lawrence Seaway.

* CHRISTIANSON, THEODORE, *Minnesota*, 2:303–5, 324, 374–78, 421–22, 453, 484,509. Minnesota roads.

Economic Analysis of the State of Minnesota, Report to the Minnesota Resources Commission, 1945, 4 vols. (1945). Prepared by the J. G. White Engineering Corporation. For their analysis of manufacturing trends consult Vol. II.

GRAY, JAMES, *Business without Boundary*, pp. 90–325. General Mills in the years after World War I — consolidation, centralization, the great depression, research, and expanded activities.

HARTSOUGH, MILDRED L., *From Canoe to Steel Barge on the Upper Mississippi*, pp. 212–78. Can the river come back as a factor in transportation?

HEILBRON, BERTHA L., *The Thirty-Second State*, pp. 190–200.

Highway Transportation in Minnesota: An Engineering Analysis, pp. 73–93 (1954). A brief history of the development of the state's highways. Excellent maps and charts.

HOLLOWAY, ROBERT J., *A City Is More Than People*. The fifteen Minnesota communities studied are the middle-sized towns in Minnesota, after the three cities of the first class and their suburbs. The pamphlet describes economic trends.

———— "The Trade and Industries of Our Small Cities,"*Minnesota Trends* (1954), pp. 26–34. A condensation of the preceding article.

HOLMES, FRANK R., *Minnesota in Three Centuries*, 4:334–36. Navigation on Lake Superior.

HORN, ARTHUR G., "The Modern Forest Industry," *Conservation Volunteer*, 20:45–51 (May–June, 1957). Pictures the importance of the forest products industries of the state.

HUCK, VIRGINIA, *Brand of the Tartan: The 3M Story* (1955). The story of Minnesota Mining and Manufacturing Company from the beginning to 1954, told in straightforward, lively fashion.

LINDBERGH, CHARLES A., *The Spirit of St. Louis* (1953). Lindbergh's own account of his epochal flight. A classic.

Minneapolis, Its People, History, Resources, and Government, pp. 41–62. While the economic trends here portrayed refer especially to the city of

Minneapolis, much applies to the state as a whole. Also, a large fraction of state manufacturing is in the Twin Cities area.

Minnesota at Midpoint, pp. 36–56. Public service enterprises and manufacturing. A report of the state's Department of Business Research and Development.

"Minnesota in the World of Aviation," *Minnesota History*, 33:236–46 (Summer, 1953). A symposium on aviation's first half century in the state. Three reports: Leslie L. Schroeder, "Fifty Years of Flight"; Harold R. Harris, "Commercial Aviation"; and Ralph H. Upson, "Aeronautical Science." These were given as talks at the 1953 annual meeting of the Minnesota Historical Society.

† POATGIETER, A. H., "In the Red River Valley Sugar Beets Mean Big Business," *Gopher Historian*, 14:17, 18 (Fall, 1959).

† ——— "Industry in St. Paul Today," *Gopher Historian*, 14:30–37 (Spring, 1960).

† ——— "Varied Industries in Southwestern Minnesota," *Gopher Historian*, 14:33–35 (Winter, 1959–60). The three articles by Poatgieter appeared in a ten-issue series of the *Gopher Historian*, each issue of which dealt with a certain section of the state. The series began with the issue of winter, 1958–59. For accounts of industries in any part of the state consult the several issues of this magazine. See also the citations under Poatgieter in topic 41.

POUND, ARTHUR, "Up from the Grass Roots," *Atlantic Monthly*, 156:249–56 (Aug., 1935). How General Mills came to be organized and some report of its side activities.

SMITH, HARLAN M., and ROBERT J. HOLLOWAY, "Minnesota Manufacturers Export to the World," *Business News Notes*, no. 10 (Nov., 1953).

WALTERS, DOROTHY V., "Pioneering with the Automobile in Minnesota," *Minnesota History*, 26:19–28 (March, 1945).

[X. INDUSTRIAL ADVANCE, AGRICULTURAL ADJUSTMENT, AND POLITICAL EXPERIMENTATION ARE IMPORTANT FEATURES OF MINNESOTA'S DEVELOPMENT]

36. *Agricultural Trends — Diversification, Cooperation, Mechanization, Scientific Application — and Depression*

A. Key Trends in the First Half of the Twentieth Century: An Overview
Spread of diversification; growth of cooperatives; increased mechanization; development of crops resistant to disease and cold; development of high-yield crops such as hybrid corn; use of scientific methods in livestock feeding, dairying, poultry raising, and others; insect control and control of animal diseases; use of commercial fertilizers; improved use

of grasslands; contour farming; artificial breeding; increase in size of farms; decrease of farm population with a rural to urban migration; growth in similarity of "life on the farm" to that in the city.

B. Diversification

Roots of diversification set about 1880 in southeastern Minnesota; spread to west, central, and northwest parts of state; both crop and livestock production involved; a continuous development through the first half of twentieth century. Early emphases: raising of cattle and hogs; butter and cheese making; some sheep raising; increased production of oats, barley, rye, corn, and potatoes; rise of a hardy alfalfa; some attention to fruits and vegetables. A half century of variation in crop production: wheat hits peak in 1898, then steady decline; oats surpass wheat by 1902, high production since 1920, peak in 1942; corn surpasses wheat by 1905, steady increase, surpasses oats by 1941, continued climb to present; rye shows a slow increase to 1922, then a decline; flax shows slight variations from 1890 to World War II, then an increase, with high production from 1939 to 1956; soybeans first introduced 1934, phenomenal rise to present; potato production sizable in 1895 and after, with many ups and downs; sugar beets show fluctuations from 1924 to 1945, then a steady climb. Rank in crop production in nation as shown by state-federal statistics of 1957: Minnesota fifth in value of total production; among top ten in eleven important crops (second in oats and sweet corn; third in corn, flax, and soybeans; fourth in hay and green peas; sixth in barley; eighth in rye and sugar beets; ninth in potatoes — but in wheat, seventeenth). Continuing emphasis on livestock production, including chickens and turkeys; packing plants at South St. Paul, Austin, and Albert Lea. Readiness of Minnesota's farmers to change to new crop emphases; economic and other factors prompting this adaptability. Agencies active in promoting state's agricultural welfare: state Dairyman's Association; University of Minnesota College of Agriculture; Agricultural Experiment Station; the Minnesota Farm Bureau Federation and the county agent; Minnesota Farmers Union; farm periodicals; boys' and girls' clubs; state Department of Agriculture, Dairy, and Food.

c. Cooperation

Growth of farmer cooperatives in Minnesota — a higher number of cooperatives than in any other state. The total number by 1956: 1,321. More producer cooperatives than consumer cooperatives, with creameries dominating. Factors explaining interest in cooperatives: Granger and Alliance movements; acquaintance of immigrant Danes and Finns with European cooperatives; state Agricultural Experiment Station; the work of Theophilus Haecker and Arthur J. McGuire; state Department of Agriculture (created in 1919); state laws legalizing cooperatives, especially those of 1919 and 1923; the Capper-Volstead Act of 1922, the Magna Carta of marketing for farmer cooperatives. Beginnings of the dairying cooperative movement in 1889: the influence of Clark's Grove Creamery; Haecker's promotion of a Danish style cooperative; the rise of small, local cooperatives, 4 or 5 in 1890, about 450 by 1899, over 500 by 1909. John Brandt and expansion of the Meeker County Creamery Association to Land O'Lakes, Inc., 1926. Achievements of Land O'Lakes and its marked influence upon creameries, cooperatives, and dairying. Dairying in the early period of the cooperative development: the Babcock test, scientific feeding, rise and fall of the centrifugal cream separator, sanitation standards, increase in number and size of herds, blooded stock (Holsteins, Guernseys, and others), the milking machine. "Dairying comes of age" in 1935 and on: centralization as large creamery plants replace many small local plants; creamery diversification with the manufacture of dry milk and concentrated milk; increased cheese manufacture; distribution of fluid milk in paper cartons and to grocer rather than to consumer; marketing of chickens, turkeys, and eggs; increase in size of herds, but decrease in total number of cows; increase in output per cow, due to better feeding, breeding, and management; milking parlors; artificial insemination 1 per cent in 1941, 36 per cent in 1955; sale by farmer to creamery of whole milk instead of farm-separated cream; exit the ten-gallon cream can, enter the five-hundred-gallon bulk tank truck. Cooperatives in other areas: producers — grain elevators, livestock shipping associations, potato marketing associations, egg shipping associations, turkey shipping associations, breeding associations; consumer — telephone, insurance, oil and gas, farm machinery, credit unions, power plants, groceries.

D. Mechanization

The new power sources and their spread: petroleum and electricity; growing availability of gasoline with the better roads movement; Rural Electrification Administration, 1935 and on. A mechanical revolution on the farm since 1920: retirement of the horse by the tractor; decline of manpower needs with greater use of the milking machine, corn picker, potato picker, and many other machines; increased output per agricultural worker. Concomitants of mechanization: increase in size of farm for more efficient use of machinery; decrease in number of farms; decline of farm population.

E. Depression

The grievous 1920's and 1930's: regression for the farmer. Failure of agriculture to recover from the recession of 1921; continued depression for farmers during the Coolidge prosperity years (1923–29); deepening of agricultural depression with the economic collapse of 1929. Factors in

184

the coming of the depression: acreage expansion of the war years; over-production; land speculation; foreign competition; the tariff; failures of country banks. Features of the depression: collapse of prices on farm commodities; increase of prices on goods purchased by the farmer; increase of farm mortgages and mortgage foreclosures; increase of farm tenancy; increase of tax delinquency.

QUESTIONS AND SUGGESTIONS

1. Explain the readiness of the Minnesota farmer to engage in a program of diversification in the twentieth century. Did all of the state engage in diversification with equal intensity? Did diversification mean the elimination of all emphasis on cash crops?
2. If possible, describe changing crop emphases in your county for the first half of the twentieth century; changing livestock emphases.
3. "Beginning in about 1900, cooperatives in the United States took a new lease on life." After making this statement, Saloutos and Hicks go on to give reasons for this growth (p. 57).
4. What agencies in Minnesota help to keep the farmer abreast of modern agricultural methods and teach him their utility?
5. From pioneer days in Minnesota there has been an effort by the farmer and farm leaders to improve farming methods and crops and to develop a more accurate body of knowledge about agricultural practices. Many volumes record these efforts. The reports of the Minnesota Agricultural Society, 1888–, which are the reports of the State Fair, include in the "Proceedings" much information on the movement for crop and livestock improvement, diversification, cooperation, and similar subjects. The annual reports of the Minnesota Crop Improvement Association, 1905–24, contain many papers on crop improvement read before that organization. The biennial reports of the state Department of Agriculture record the activities of the department in grading wheat, inspecting nurseries, eradicating weeds, and so forth. The *Minnesota Farmers' Institutes* (1888–1926) begins its record with the third annual institute. The annual reports of the state Horticultural Society begin in 1873. The records of similar organizations are available, in addition to the numerous farm journals and magazines published in Minnesota.
6. Trace the development of cooperation in the dairy industry.
7. What factors help explain the decline in the number of small, local creameries after 1935?
8. In a sense, the term "creamery" ceased being an adequate name for many of the larger plants which were established in Minnesota after 1935. Explain.

185

9. How do tariffs affect the Minnesota farmer? Relate your answer to the developments of the decade 1920 to 1930.
10. The farmer has tried to better his condition by science and by politics. List five particular efforts or methods in each domain and evaluate their results.
11. The pioneer farmer has been described as a typical example of American individualism. Can his modern Minnesota descendant still be so described?
12. In what ways has rural life become "citified" since 1890?
13. The percentage of the state's total employment in agriculture, manufacturing, mining and quarrying, and other industries since 1900 is shown by decades in *Minnesota Trends*, p. 96. Examination of the table will show the declining importance of agriculture as against manufacturing in the total picture of the state's economy.
14. Topics for special study: (a) The work of the "county agent" in Minnesota; (b) the career of any one of the following: John Brandt, Arthur J. McGuire, E. C. Stakman, Fred E. Haralson, Theophilus Haecker; (c) the Farm Bureau Federation: origin, aims, organization, policies; (d) dry milk: factors in its rise, its importance to dairying, its place in the nation's diet; (e) "Dad" Erickson and the 4-H Clubs of Minnesota or Future Farmers of America; (f) one of Minnesota's stockyards — origin, organization and activity, meaning to the farmer; (g) Land O'Lakes Creamery.
15. Much information about the relative position of Minnesota in agriculture compared with other states may be gathered from Paullin, *Atlas*, Plates 143–47.

REFERENCES

*† BLEGEN, THEODORE C., *Building Minnesota*, pp. 389–400.

Boss, ANDREW, *Minnesota Agricultural Experiment Station, 1885–1935* (1935). A historical sketch.

* BRAND, CHARLES J., *Grimm Alfalfa and Its Utilization in the Northwest*, pp. 7–9 (1911). An account of Wendelin Grimm.

BRINGS, LAWRENCE M., ed., *Minnesota Heritage:* Theodore Fenske, "From Furs to Farming," pp. 164–75. Some aspects of farming from 1890 on.

CASTLE, HENRY A., *Minnesota*, 1:294–313. Agricultural education, fairs, schools.

Cooperative Marketing (Senate Document No. 95, 70 Congress, 1 session, serial 8859), pp. 7–9, 16–19, 38–40, 47–56, 61–62, 141–43. A history of cooperatives in Minnesota.

EDWARDS, EVERETT E., "T. L. Haecker, the Father of Dairying in Minnesota," *Minnesota History*, 19:148–61 (June, 1938).

EDWARDS, EVERETT E., and HORACE H. RUSSELL, "Wendelin Grimm and Alfalfa," *Minnesota History*, 19:21–33 (March, 1938).

ERICKSON, T. A., with the assistance of ANNA NORTH COIT, *My Sixty Years with Rural Youth* (1956). The autobiography of a man who for thirty years was a 4-H Club leader in Minnesota.

FILLEY, H. CLYDE, *Cooperation in Agriculture*, pp. 30–45, 48–66, 281–84, 314–15, 318–19, 349–53, 378–80 (1929). Successful Minnesota cooperatives.

* FOLWELL, WILLIAM W., *History*, 4:402–7. Theophilus L. Haecker.

HAMILTON, LAURA M., "Stem Rust in the Spring Wheat Area in 1878," *Minnesota History*, 20:156–64. Calls attention to the barberry bush as alternate host for stem rust.

LUNDEEN, ERNEST, "Minnesota Leads in Cooperatives," *Congressional Record*, 74 Congress, 2 session, vol. 80, part 6, pp. 6739–62 (1936). A mass of material on cooperation in Minnesota is printed.

* MITAU, G. THEODORE, *Politics in Minnesota*, pp. 90–97. The Minnesota Farm Bureau Federation and the Minnesota Farmers Union; their programs and organization.

MOSBOEK, LUDWIG, *A Brief Historical Outline of the Askov Community* (1936). The cooperative movement in one of its Minnesota strongholds.

MUELLER, AGNES HARRIGAN, *That Inspiring Past: The Future Farmers of America in Minnesota, 1930–1955* (1955). The record of an important farm youth organization.

NELSON, LOWRY, "Minnesota Is Becoming an Urban State," *Minnesota Farm and Home Science*, 10:12, 13 (Oct., 1952). Has two excellent graphs on rural-urban population changes.

*———*The Minnesota Community*. This analysis is by an eminent sociologist. The twentieth century is stressed, with special emphasis being given to conditions between 1930 and 1960. Pp. 7–38, trends in size of farms, tenancy, crops, and migration within the state. Pp. 70–82, changes in the material well-being of the Minnesota farmer.

* ROBINSON, EDWARD V., *Early Economic Conditions and the Development of Agriculture in Minnesota*, pp. 107–234. Diversification and other changes in Minnesota agriculture.

RUBLE, KENNETH D., *Men to Remember: How 100,000 Neighbors Made History* (1947). Formation of the nation's largest farmer cooperative, Land O'Lakes. Written at the invitation of the corporation. Well done, readable. Dairying of course is treated at length.

* SALOUTOS, THEODORE, and JOHN D. HICKS, *Agricultural Discontent in the Middle West, 1900–1939*, pp. 3–30, 56–110, 286–320. A general treatment of a region of which Minnesota is a part. There is also frequent mention of Minnesota. Discusses the cooperative movement, World War I and its

impact, and farm problems. An outstandingly fine analysis. For an explanation of the coming of the agrarian depression of the 1920's see pp. 98–110.

* SCHRIMPER, RICHARD J., *Minnesota Agriculture — Crops, 1858–1958*. Compiled by the Minnesota Department of Agriculture, Dairy, and Food, cooperating with the United States Department of Agriculture. Invaluable for its data on Minnesota's first century of agriculture. Besides statistics, charts, and maps, it has descriptive comment.

——— *Minnesota Corn, Production and Marketing* (1958). Similar to the pamphlet cited above, except that it deals only with corn, and in greater detail.

WEAVER, JOHN C., and LEVERETT P. HOAG, "The Changing Use of Minnesota Farm Land," *Minnesota Trends*, pp. 3–10 (1954). Emphasizes the period since 1920.

ZIMMERMAN, CARLE C., and JOHN D. BLACK, *The Marketing Attitude of Minnesota Farmers*, pp. 20–54 (1926). The farmers' attitude toward cooperatives.

——— "The Migration to Towns and Cities," *American Journal of Sociology*, 32:450–55; 33:105–9, 237–41; 36:41–51 (Nov., 1926; July, Sept., 1927; July, 1930). A study of 357 farm families of Minnesota.

[X. INDUSTRIAL ADVANCE, AGRICULTURAL ADJUSTMENT, AND POLITICAL EXPERIMENTATION ARE IMPORTANT FEATURES OF MINNESOTA'S DEVELOPMENT]

37. *Depression and New Political Currents*

A. The Coming of the Depression to Minnesota

Postwar emotional currents: disillusionment and reappraisal; the "jazz age"; the flapper; fashions; prohibition enforcement and evasion; the pacifist movement. Postwar economic change: desire for normalcy and the removal of war controls; a temporary boom and inflation; the depression of 1921; partial recovery for industry, but not for agriculture; the "Coolidge Prosperity Years," 1923–29. New methods, products, and inventions in industry; installment buying; business fluctuations; irregularities of employment; bank failures, mergers, and consolidations; mortality in business firms; speculation in stocks, bonds, and commodities. The stock market panic, 1929. Early impact of the depression on Minnesota; the Foshay receivership. Deepening of the depression, 1929–33; intensification of distress for the already depressed farmer; widespread industrial unemployment and business failures.

B. Postwar Political Trends: An Overview

Twenty years of flux, 1918–38: Republican party control in the period preceding the 1929 collapse; a new agrarian revolt and strong third-party activity; the Nonpartisan League and the Farmer-Labor party; the Farmer-Labor party in power, 1930–38. Three Republican governors: Burnquist to 1920; J. A. O. Preus, 1920–24; Theodore Christianson, 1924–30. Three Farmer-Labor governors: Floyd B. Olson, 1930–36; Hjalmar Petersen, 1936; Elmer A. Benson, 1936–38. Pattern and variations in elections to Congress, state legislature, and other state offices. Comparison of Minnesota's political picture with that of the nation.

c. Rise and Decline of the Nonpartisan League

The bases for agricultural discontent. Background of Arthur C. Townley; organization of the League in North Dakota, 1915; its objects and methods; success in the North Dakota election of 1916; spread to Minnesota. Leaders, organization, and methods in Minnesota; primary election strategy; the Republican primary campaign of 1918, Burnquist versus Charles A. Lindbergh, Sr.; tarring the League with charges of disloyalty. Union with labor; first use of the label "Farmer-Labor." Defeat for the League with re-election of Burnquist in 1918; Farmer-Labor strength in the legislature. Prosecution of Townley and other Nonpartisan leaders; role of the Minnesota Public Safety Commission in the hysteria of 1918. The fiercely contested election of 1920; Preus defeats Shipstead for the governorship; the Republicans triumph in other state and national offices. Decline of League strength and of Townley's influence; failure of the effort to join forces with the Democratic party in the election of 1922; decision of the anti-Townley faction to engage in third-party action; the Farmer-Labor party. Farmer-Labor strength in the election: Shipstead replaces Kellogg as senator; Kvale and Wefald become representatives. The Republicans maintain their hold on the state government by re-electing Preus. Forces contributing to the disintegration of the Nonpartisan League: internal dissension, the agricultural depression, bipartisan combinations against the League, growth of the Independent Voters' Association, rise of the more conservative Farm Bureau Federation, and the decision in favor of full-fledged third-party action.

d. Administrations of Governors Preus and Christianson

Death of Senator Knute Nelson, 1923; Magnus Johnson defeats Preus for the vacancy. The issue of socialism in the election of 1924; Republican victory with Christianson elected governor, Senator Magnus Johnson replaced by Thomas D. Schall. Re-election of Christianson as governor, 1926 and 1928. Attempts to appease the farmer: cooperative marketing laws; further regulation of the grain trade; the rural credit system. Legislation seeking the favor of labor: modification of workmen's compensation; the industrial commission. Failure to secure an income tax. Legislative approval for a single commissioner of highways rather than three; an iron ore occupation tax amendment and a royalty tax. The reorganization of state government under Christianson; the "Big Three." Notable efforts of farm groups to get relief from the federal government; the Farm Bloc, 1920–23; the McNary Haugen Plan; the Federal Farm Board.

F. The Farmer-Labor Regime

Early career and political aspirations of Floyd B. Olson; the building of a party machine. Re-election of Senator Shipstead, Farmer-Labor, 1928 and 1934. The Farmer-Labor victories of the 1930's; their relation to the depression, to the Upper Midwest farm movement, and to national victories of the Democratic party. The political revolution of 1932; Minnesota's electoral vote goes to a Democrat. The failure of congressional reapportionment. Problems for the Farmer-Labor party: conflicting interests of farmer and laborer; successive failures of the party to secure control of the state legislature; handling the spoils of office; communist infiltration. Olson's political strategy in maintaining support of his evolving program. Intensification of the depression and relief measures under Olson: moratorium on mortgage foreclosures, 1933; reduction of property taxes; introduction of income tax; appropriations for direct relief; a public works program with increased road building; strengthened powers for the bank commissioner and the insurance commissioner; a chain store tax; a tax on oleomargarine; cuts in appropriations for state activities and offices. Inability of the state to cope with the depression; cooperation with President Franklin D. Roosevelt and the New Deal; attitude of Governor Olson and that of the legislature. Application of New Deal measures in Minnesota: the bank holiday, 1933; A.A.A.; R.E.A.; F.E.R.A.; F.C.A.; C.C.C.; W.P.A.; Social Security. The matching of funds. Refusal of the state legislature to approve all aspects of the Farmer-Labor program. Other developments during the Farmer-Labor regime: establishment of the Metropolitan Sewage Disposal Commission, 1933; ratification of the Twenty-First Amendment; the Minneapolis truck drivers' strike of 1934 and Olson's proclamation of martial law; Olson's use of the veto power. Death of Governor Olson, 1936, and its impact; succession of Hjalmar Petersen to the governorship; leadership rivalries within the party. The campaign of 1936; last Farmer-Labor victory; Elmer Benson elected governor and Ernest Lundeen United States senator; popular endorsement of President Roosevelt and the New Deal. Factors in crushing Farmer-Labor defeat in the election of 1938: charges of administrative incompetence and of corruption; communist infiltration; quarreling of rival factions within the party; weak legislative leadership; the return of better times.

190

1. What were some of the causes for the persistence of the "agrarian crusade" into the twentieth century?
2. Consider the program of the Nonpartisan League; its methods.
3. The Minnesota election of 1918 had unsavory aspects. What were they?
4. Was the Nonpartisan League able to profit from the fact that Minnesota's legislature was required to be "nonpartisan" in make-up? Was the League able to make capital out of the Nineteenth Amendment, ratified in 1920?
5. The Farm Bureau Federation, with its all-important county agent, was one of those farm organizations which cut into the strength of the Non-partisan League. Its origin and growth are worth special study. Note sources of financial support, organizational setup, variety of activities engaged in, effectiveness.
6. How did Republicans under Governors Preus and Christianson seek to lighten the distressed conditions of the farmers? Did these efforts have any effect upon political trends?
7. Describe the birth of the Farmer-Labor party.
8. Account for the demise of the Nonpartisan League in Minnesota.
9. A comment frequently heard during the 1920's was that the farmer and the laborer could never work together in the same party because their interests often conflicted. Try to find conflicts between them during the Farmer-Labor regime. Suggested areas of such conflict: rural credits, spoils, highway code for laborers. How do you account for the fair amount of cooperation which did prevail?
10. You should understand what is meant by the "Farm Bloc," the McNary Haugen Plan, A.A.A. and R.E.A. and the other agencies established by the New Deal.
11. Worthy of special study and report are the careers of Arthur C. Townley, Charles A. Lindbergh, Sr., Knute Nelson, Frank B. Kellogg.
12. Was the rise of a third party, composed of farmers and laborers, peculiar to Minnesota or did the movement have sectional or national overtones?
13. When speaking of the special election of 1923, Saloutos and Hicks said: "Both wings of the Farmer-Labor party flapped together." What did they mean? See p. 354.
14. Arthur Naftalin has given four main reasons for the failure of the Farmer-Labor party to gain control of the state legislature during its regime of 1931 to 1939. What were these? See the article cited below.
15. When speaking of Governor Floyd B. Olson's program, George H. Mayer said, "He set out for a promised land halfway between Populism and socialism." Mayer also classified the governor as a "rebel," but not a "radical." Do you feel these expressions to be accurate?

16. Henrik Shipstead served three terms in the United States Senate. How important a role did he play in the politics of the Farmer-Labor party during this period? Describe his relationship with Governor Floyd B. Olson. Was this relationship symptomatic of a weakness within the Farmer-Labor party?

17. How do you explain the contrast between the socialistic pronouncements of the constitution of the Farmer Labor Association and the rather moderate platforms of the Farmer-Labor party in 1930 and 1932?

18. How did the Farmer-Labor platform of 1934 differ from the two previous ones? Why did the state central committee of the party see fit to publish a revised version of it in May, 1934?

19. One of the planks of the 1934 Farmer-Labor platform called for state printing of school textbooks. Account for the heated criticism leveled against this plank.

20. There was much talk in 1935 of a "three per cent assessment" upon state office holders' salaries. How did the conservatives react to this report?

REFERENCES

ADRIAN, CHARLES R., "The Origin of Minnesota's Nonpartisan Legislature," *Minnesota History*, 33:155–63 (Winter, 1952).

ANDERSON, WILLIAM, *Intergovernmental Fiscal Relations*, pp. 29–33, 35, 36, 68–84. Financial support for Minnesota from the federal government, 1913–53. Federal grants-in-aid.

ALLEN, FREDERICK L., *Only Yesterday* (1931). For general background, especially social aspects.

*† BLEGEN, THEODORE C., *Building Minnesota*, pp. 435–50.

BLOODWORTH, JESSIE A., *Social Consequences of Prolonged Unemployment* (1933). A Minnesota study.

BURNQUIST, JOSEPH A. A., *Minnesota and Its People*, 1:366–78. Governor Burnquist's account of the years 1916–23.

* CHRISTIANSON, THEODORE, *Minnesota*, 2:367–74, 400–3, 405–523. Politics, 1918–34.

CLEAVER, CHARLES G., "Frank B. Kellogg's View of History and Progress," *Minnesota History*, 35:157–66 (Dec., 1956). The author attempts to analyze the mental processes of Kellogg, his philosophical outlook, to show the bases for his foreign policies and his faith in the peace pact of 1928.

FOLWELL, WILLIAM W., *History*, 3:298–312, 319–22, 538–56. Politics, 1916–24.

* HAINES, LYNN and DORA B., *The Lindberghs*, pp. 234–307. See a review of this book by George M. Stephenson in *Minnesota History*, 13:188–90 (June, 1932).

192

HANSEN, ALVIN H., DRENG BJORNARAA, and TILLMAN M. SOGGE, *The Decline of Employment in the 1930–1931 Depression in St. Paul, Minneapolis, and Duluth* (1932).

HANSEN, ALVIN H., and TILLMAN M. SOGGE, *Occupational Trends in Minnesota* (1933).

HEILBRON, BERTHA L., *The Thirty-Second State*, pp. 266–69.

HICKS, JOHN D., "The Persistence of Populism," *Minnesota History*, 12:3–20 (March, 1931).

LUNDEEN, ERNEST, "Farmer-Labor Party — History, Platforms, and Programs," *Congressional Record*, 74 Congress, 2 session, vol. 80, part 9, pp. 9694–725 (1936). Contains a mass of information on the party.

McGRATH, JOHN S., and JAMES J. DELMONT, *Floyd Bjørnsterne Olson, 1891–1936: Minnesota's Greatest Liberal Governor, A Memorial Volume* (1937). In two parts. Part I is a biography of the governor, highly laudatory in tone. Part II is a collection of twenty-six of the governor's speeches.

MAYER, GEORGE H., *The Political Career of Floyd B. Olson* (1951). The best biography of this Farmer-Labor leader.

MINNESOTA WORKS PROGRESS ADMINISTRATION, *The Works Progress Administration in Minnesota* (1936). A description of the kinds of work provided.

* MITAU, G. THEODORE, *Politics in Minnesota*, pp. 10–18. A brief portrayal of political trends from 1910 to 1939 — progressive Republicanism followed by Farmer-Labor dominance. Excellent.

* MORLAN, ROBERT L., *Political Prairie Fire: The Nonpartisan League, 1915–1922* (1955). A thorough treatment of this agrarian protest movement and its attempt to take over the Republican party. With failure, the stage was set for the Farmer-Labor party.

——— "The Nonpartisan League and the Minnesota Campaign of 1918," *Minnesota History*, 34:221–32 (Summer, 1955). A chapter from the book cited above. Discusses the role of Charles A. Lindbergh in this important election.

* NAFTALIN, ARTHUR, "The Failure of the Farmer-Labor Party to Capture Control of the Minnesota Legislature," *American Political Science Review*, 38:71–78 (Feb., 1944). The lack of control of the legislature by the Liberals during the Farmer-Labor period of the 1930's and the reasons for it. Written by a leader of that party.

*——— "The Tradition of Protest and the Roots of the Farmer-Labor Party," *Minnesota History*, 35:53–63 (June, 1956). Pictures the origins of the Farmer-Labor party in the movements of agrarian discontent of the nineteenth and early twentieth centuries. Drawn from the author's unpublished "History of the Farmer-Labor Party of Minnesota," manu-

script copies of which may be found in the libraries of the Minnesota Historical Society and the University of Minnesota.

"Public Works Administration in Minnesota," League of Minnesota Municipalities, *Minnesota Year Book, 1936,* pp. 51–54 (1936).

RARIG, FRANK M., JR., "Division of Relief," Seventeenth Biennial Report of the State Board of Control, pp. 50–75 (1934). An account of relief administration during the period when it was the responsibility of the Board of Control.

———*A Report of the Minnesota State Board of Control as the State Emergency Relief Administration, September 29, 1932 to July 1, 1934* (1934). An important document.

"Relief in Minnesota," League of Minnesota Municipalities, *Minnesota Year Book, 1936,* pp. 55–59.

SALOUTOS, THEODORE, "The National Producers' Alliance," *Minnesota History,* 28:37–44 (March, 1947). An abortive farm organization of the 1920's, but having its connections with the Nonpartisan League and the Farmer-Labor party.

* SALOUTOS, THEODORE, and JOHN D. HICKS, *Agricultural Discontent in the Middle West, 1900–1939.* Note especially pp. 149–218, 255–85, 321–41, 342–71, 372–451, 452–537. The Nonpartisan League, Farm Bureau Federation, origins of the Farmer-Labor party, relief efforts through congressional action, the New Deal. Pages 538–62 contain a summary view of the farm protest movement. The volume deals with the Upper Midwest region, not just Minnesota, but the state comes in for much attention. Valuable.

* STEPHENSON, GEORGE M., *John Lind of Minnesota,* pp. 333–47. The election of 1918.

XI. THE ARTS FLOURISH IN MINNESOTA

38. *Minnesota Literature and Allied Interests*

A. Early Writings

Travelogues: Minnesota as it appeared to explorers and traders, including Hennepin, Carver, Pike, Long, Beltrami, and Schoolcraft. Reasons for these narratives; their varying quality; their veracity. Accounts by pioneers of their experiences and observations: Stephen R. Riggs, *Mary and I*; William J. Snelling, *Tales of the Northwest*; Mrs. Seth Eastman, *Dahcotah: or, Life and Legends of the Sioux around Fort Snelling*; Henry H. Sibley, *Unfinished Autobiography* and *Iron Face: The Adventures of Jack Frazer*; William W. Warren, *History of the Ojibways*; Harriet E. Bishop, *Floral Home: or, First Years in Minnesota*; Arthur J. Larsen, ed., *Crusader and Feminist: Letters of Jane Grey Swisshelm*; Charlotte

O. Van Cleve, *"Three Score Years and Ten"*; Augustin Ravoux, *Reminiscences*; Hans Mattson, *Reminiscences*; Henry B. Whipple, *Lights and Shadows of a Long Episcopate*; Charles E. Flandrau, *History of Minnesota and Tales of the Frontier*. Historic value of these accounts; their literary value.

B. Two Generations of Writers (to World War I): Sparse Production

Preoccupation with building typically a deterrent to writing in a frontier state; tardiness in the use of native themes. The first book written and published in Minnesota: Charles Hoag's *Henry Clay* (1857). The first novel written and published in Minnesota: Dillon O'Brien's *Daly's of Dalystown* (1866). Four well-known novelists: Edward Eggleston, Ignatius Donnelly, Knut Hamsun, and William Stearns Davis. Eggleston's *Mystery of Metropolisville* (1873) and *Hoosier Schoolmaster* (1883). Donnelly's *Caesar's Column* (1890), *Doctor Huguet* (1891), and *Golden Bottle* (1892). Knut Hamsun's *Hunger* (1890) and other writings. Davis's historical novels, *Friend of Caesar* (1900), *Victor of Salamis* (1907), and several others; Davis's serious historical writings. Prominence of essayists and social scientists: Donnelly's *Atlantis, Ragnarok*, and *The Great Cryptogram*; Thomas M. Newson's *Indian Legends of Minnesota Lakes* and *Pen Pictures of Saint Paul*; Charles M. Flandrau's *Viva Mexico!*; Cushman K. Davis; geological writings of Newton H. Winchell; economist Thorstein Veblen's *The Theory of the Leisure Class*; Edward D. Neill, pioneer Minnesota historian; Charles A. Eastman, interpreter of Sioux Indian life.

C. Four Decades of Rich Literary Production (1918 to the Centennial Year 1958): Emergence of a Native Literature

An eminent triumvirate of novelists, of national and international fame: Sinclair Lewis, the first American to win the Nobel prize in literature; F. Scott Fitzgerald, portrayer of the "roaring twenties"; and Ole E. Rölvaag, supreme artist of the pioneer story. Their better known works: Lewis, *Main Street* (1920) and *Babbitt* (1922); Fitzgerald, *This Side of Paradise* (1920) and *The Great Gatsby* (1925); Rölvaag, *Giants in the Earth* (1927). The foreign-language novel. Other, highly productive novelists: Darragh Aldrich, Margaret Culkin Banning, Grace Flandrau, Maud Hart Lovelace and Delos W. Lovelace, Martha Ostenso, Cornelia J. Cannon, James Gray, William J. McNally, Frederick F. Manfred, Robert Penn Warren. A great many less prolific novelists. Increasing use of native themes: pioneer life, immigrant experiences, industrial development, social conflicts, family sagas, tensions in the modern scene, and many others. Some writers of historical fiction: Ramsey Benson, Walter O'Meara, Neil Swanson, William Swanberg, and others. Mystery novelists: Mabel Seeley and Ruth S. Wallis. Writers of juvenile books

195

and short stories: Meridel LeSueur, Wanda Gág, Carol R. Brink, Emma L. Brock, Laura I. Wilder, Dietrich Lange, Frances R. Sterrett, and others. Minnesota poets: many, but relatively few with national renown. The serious poet and the dilettante. Newspaper poetry of the nineteenth century. An early twentieth-century poet with promise: Arthur Upson; his untimely death. Other twentieth-century poets: Allen Tate, Robert Penn Warren, John Berryman, Louis Coxe, James Wright, Reed Whittemore, Joseph W. Beach, Oscar W. Firkins, Betty Bridgman, Elaine V. Emans. The League of Minnesota Poets and its anthologies. Playwrights and literary critics: Oscar W. Firkins, Joseph W. Beach, Elmer E. Stoll, James Gray, William Van O'Connor, and others. Authors of natural history: Florence Jaques, *Canoe Country* and *Snowshoe Country*; Sigurd F. Olson, *Singing Wilderness* and *Listening Post*, artistic productions in prose that borders on poetry. Charles A. Lindbergh, *The Spirit of St. Louis*, Pulitzer prize winner. Journalistic productions: Harrison E. Salisbury, *Russia on the Way, American in Russia, Shook-up Generation*; (Arnold) Eric Sevareid, *Not So Wild a Dream* and *Small Sounds in the Night*; Arthur J. Russell, *The Other Side of the Street* and *Goodbye Newspaper Row*.

D. Newspapers in Minnesota

Pioneer papers: the *Minnesota Pioneer, St. Anthony Express*, and many others. Personal journalism: James M. Goodhue, Jane Grey Swisshelm, Earl S. Goodrich, Joseph Wheelock, David Blakely, Sam Whiting, Harlan P. Hall. Transition to modern journalism: Alvah Eastman, Clarence A. French, William E. Easton. Representative modern journalists and publishers: William J. Murphy, Herschel V. Jones, Henry Z. Mitchell, Benjamin E. Darby, Clarence M. Hillam, Harold Barker, Herman Roe, John Cowles, the Ridders, and others. The foreign-language press: T. Guldbrandsen, Joseph Mott, Swan Turnblad, Carl G. Hansen, Peer Strömme, and others. Decline of the foreign-language press. Growth of newspaper advertising and circulation. Changes in the gathering and sending of news: telegraph, telephone, teletype, wirephoto, and other inventions. Specialization: syndicated article, funny page and section, sports reporting, financial news, women's departments, the columnist. Improvement in printing methods: steam and electric presses, modern high-speed press; color printing, linotype, stereotype, and other developments. Trend toward dominance of one newspaper in city or town; the chain. Dailies, weeklies, and specialized newspapers in present-day Minnesota. The Minnesota Press Association. Radio and television and their relations with the press.

E. Magazines and Publishing

Beginnings. Development of magazine publishing in Minnesota. The

Bellman and other literary enterprises. The Augsburg Publishing House and other church publishers. The National Weeklies of Winona. The Webb Publishing Company. Bruce Publishing Company. Concentration of national legal publishing in the West Publishing Company. *Modern Medicine, Journal Lancet,* and other medical publications. Dental magazines. Trade journals. The Fawcett publications and their vogue. T. S. Denison and Company. The University of Minnesota Press. Other publishers. Housewives', foreign-language, fraternal, religious, learned, farm, labor, sports, and pulp magazines.

QUESTIONS AND SUGGESTIONS

1. How do you explain that Minnesota country had found a place in literature long before "Minnesota" existed either as name or entity?

2. Study critically one of the records of exploration or fur trading in Minnesota. Who wrote it? Does it describe personal experience or report hearsay? Appraise its accuracy and veracity. Did the author copy from other accounts or rely upon his own knowledge? or both? Was the account revised or rewritten before publication? How many editions or translations were printed? What is the value of the document as a historical record?

3. Minnesota's first sixty-five or seventy years were not productive of an extensive list of literary works. Why not?

4. Consider nineteenth-century writing in Minnesota, noting particularly the types emphasized, attention to native themes, variety and extent.

5. What did Donnelly's *Caesar's Column* have in common with Edward Bellamy's *Looking Backward?* How was it different? Has the attention which has been accorded to *Caesar's Column* been due to its literary merit or to its historical value? Present-day interest in this novel is to be observed in the fact that a reprint of *Caesar's Column* appeared in 1959 under the imprint of the John Harvard Library of the Belknap Press.

6. Much can be obtained from John T. Flanagan's several articles on midwestern fiction. Note, among other things, what he has to say about the tardiness of novelists in using agricultural themes.

7. Select a book dealing with pioneer times and evaluate its accuracy in reflecting pioneer conditions. Does the book reflect historical research? Is it based upon personal experience? or both? or neither?

8. What are some of the outstanding characteristics of small-town life in Minnesota as portrayed by Lewis in *Main Street?* The novel aroused much discussion about the typicalness and completeness of the picture it presented. What is your opinion on these two points?

9. Numerous articles and books on Sinclair Lewis have appeared, in addi-

tion to those given in the reading references. Among them are Bernard De Voto, "Sinclair Lewis," *Saturday Review of Literature*, 9:397–98 (Jan. 28, 1933); Christian Gauss, "Sinclair Lewis *vs*. His Education," *Saturday Evening Post*, 204:20 (Dec. 26, 1931); William J. McNally, "Mr. Babbitt, Meet Sinclair Lewis," *Nation*, 125:278–81 (Sept. 21, 1927); Stuart P. Sherman, *The Significance of Sinclair Lewis* (1922); and Carl Van Doren, "Sinclair Lewis and Sherwood Anderson," *Century*, 110:362–69 (July, 1925).

10. What is distinctive about Rölvaag's *Giants in the Earth*? Justify its use in the reading program of a high school history class.

11. Would it be correct to say that the novels of F. Scott Fitzgerald are historical novels?

12. How closely associated with the state were such writers as Ole E. Rölvaag, Sinclair Lewis, Thorstein Veblen, Edward Eggleston, Knut Hamsun?

13. Brief sketches of seven Minnesota authors, Margaret Culkin Banning, Maud Hart Lovelace, Sinclair Lewis, F. Scott Fitzgerald, Martha Ostenso, Frances R. Sterrett, and William J. McNally, written by various persons, were printed in the *Minnesota Journal of Education*, 13:48, 86, 124, 164, 236, 270, 302 (Sept., 1932–May, 1933).

14. To what extent does Minnesota verse portray reactions to the Minnesota environment? Newspaper and magazine files are valuable for the study of Minnesota poetry. In addition to the newspapers, consult files of such magazines as the *Frontier Monthly* (published at Hastings in 1859), the *Minnesota Monthly: A Northwestern Magazine* (published at St. Paul in 1869 and 1870), the *Literary Northwest* (published at St. Paul in the early nineties), and the *Bellman* (published at Minneapolis from 1906 to 1913). Files of these and other magazines of the Northwest are in the library of the Minnesota Historical Society. Some of the earlier books of Minnesota poetry are the following: Harriet N. Arnold, ed., *The Poets and Poetry of Minnesota* (1864), an early anthology in which twenty-five poets are represented; Thomas P. Beyer, ed., *Hamline Poems: A New Sheaf from the Bridgman Prize Poems, 1932, 1933, 1934* (1934); Harriet E. Bishop, *Minnesota: Then and Now* (1869); Hanford L. Gordon, *Indian Legends and Other Poems* (1910); Louise Leighton, ed., *Year Book of the League of Minnesota Poets, 1935*; Maude C. Schilplin, ed., *Minnesota Verse: An Anthology* (1934); and John Talman, *Minnesota in Panorama* (1923).

15. Newspapers of today are vastly different from those of the 1850's, 1860's, or 1870's. Indicate some of these differences. You might pay attention to such matters as editorial policy; manner of handling headlines; use of signed articles; size; use of illustrations, charts, maps; advertisements;

attention to local, national, and international news; use of syndicated articles; ownership; the number of newspapers in any one town.

16. How do Minnesota's publication activities compare with those of certain eastern states (for example: New York, Massachusetts, Pennsylvania)? Can you explain differences which you detect?

REFERENCES

BRIDGMAN, ELIZABETH (KLEIN), *This Is Minnesota* (1958). Twenty-four poems on Minnesota themes.

BRINGS, LAWRENCE M., ed., *Minnesota Heritage:* Edwin Emery, "Communications, the Mass Media Mature: Newspapers, Magazines, Graphic Arts, Radio and Television," pp. 313–28.

COLCORD, LINCOLN, Introduction to Rölvaag's *Giants in the Earth*, pp. xi–xxii (1927).

COMMAGER, HENRY, "The Literature of the Pioneer West," *Minnesota History*, 8:319–28 (Dec., 1927). An essay inspired by Rölvaag's *Giants in the Earth*.

DORFMAN, JOSEPH, *Thorstein Veblen and His America* (1934).

EGGLESTON, EDWARD, "The Kit Carson of the Northwest," with an introduction by William Peirce Randel, *Minnesota History*, 33:269–81 (Autumn, 1953). Reprint of an article which appeared in *Harper's New Monthly Magazine* (1894). The hero, George W. Northrup, was a well-known, almost legendary figure of the 1850's and 1860's. An example of Eggleston's fine prose.

EMCH, LUCILLE B., ed., "An Indian Tale by William J. Snelling," *Minnesota History*, 26:211–21 (Sept., 1945). A reprint of one of Snelling's stories not included in his *Tales of the Northwest*.

FLANAGAN, JOHN T., "Knut Hamsun's Early Years in the Northwest," *Minnesota History*, 20:397–412 (Dec., 1939).

———"The Middle Western Farm Novel," *Minnesota History*, 23:113–25 (June, 1942). Much attention is paid to Minnesota novels.

———"The Minnesota Backgrounds of Sinclair Lewis' Fiction," *Minnesota History*, 37:1–13 (March, 1960).

*———"Thirty Years of Minnesota Fiction," *Minnesota History*, 31:129–47 (Sept., 1950). An analysis of the state's novels for the period 1920–50 by one who gave years of study to the field.

"The Frontier Press: Two Communications," *Minnesota History*, 15:86–89 (March, 1934). Comments occasioned by Herman Roe's article.

GREBSTEIN, SHELDON, "Sinclair Lewis' Minnesota Boyhood," *Minnesota History*, 34:85–89 (Autumn, 1954). The writer holds that an unsatisfactory boyhood in Sauk Centre colored Sinclair Lewis's writing.

HAUGEN, EINAR, "O. E. Rölvaag: Norwegian-American," *Norwegian-Ameri-*

can Studies and Records, 7:53–73 (1933). Perhaps the best appraisal of the author of *Giants in the Earth.*

JOHNSTON, DANIEL S. B., "Minnesota Journalism from 1858 to 1865," Minnesota Historical Collections, 12:183–262 (1908).

——— "Minnesota Journalism in the Territorial Period," Minnesota Historical Collections, vol. 10, part 1, pp. 247–351 (1905).

JORGENSON, THEODORE, and NORA O. SOLUM, *Ole Edvart Rölvaag: A Biography* (1939).

* LARSON, LAURENCE M., "Tellef Grundysen and the Beginnings of Norwegian-American Fiction," *Norwegian-American Studies and Records,* 8:1–17 (1934).

LEWIS, GRACE HEGGER, *With Love From Gracie. Sinclair Lewis: 1912–1925* (1955). Memoirs of Sinclair Lewis's first wife.

McMURTRIE, DOUGLAS C., "The Printing Press Moves Westward," *Minnesota History,* 15:1–25 (March, 1934).

MIZENER, ARTHUR, *The Far Side of Paradise: A Biography of F. Scott Fitzgerald* (1951).

* O'CONNOR, WILLIAM VAN, ed., *A History of the Arts in Minnesota* (1958). The middle section is written by Grace Lee Nute and is on "Minnesota Books and Authors." Because of its brevity it sometimes resembles a catalogue, but it remains the best single treatment available. This section also appears as a separate pamphlet under the title *A History of Minnesota Books and Authors.*

PARRINGTON, VERNON L., *Main Currents in American Thought,* 3:360–69, 387–96 (1927). Sinclair Lewis and Ole E. Rölvaag.

RANDEL, WILLIAM PEIRCE, "Edward Eggleston's Minnesota Fiction," *Minnesota History,* 33:189–93 (Spring, 1953). Author Eggleston's Minnesota stay (1856 to 1866) and the writing that developed therefrom.

RICHARDS, CARMEN NELSON, ed., *Minnesota Skyline: Anthology of Poems about Minnesota* (1944). A publication of the League of Minnesota Poets.

* RICHARDS, CARMEN NELSON, and GENEVIEVE R. BREEN, *Minnesota Writes: A Collection of Autobiographical Stories by Minnesota Prose Writers* (1948).

RIESMAN, DAVID, *Thorstein Veblen: A Critical Interpretation* (1953). An interpretation of a prominent Minnesota philosopher whose economic theories were widely read. The author perhaps does not fully appreciate the influence Veblen exerted.

ROE, HERMAN, "The Frontier Press of Minnesota," *Minnesota History,* 14:393–410 (Dec., 1933).

ROTHFUSS, HERMANN E., "The Early German Theater in Minnesota," *Minnesota History,* 32:100–5, 164–73 (June, Sept., 1951). A report of German interest in light and serious drama, particularly in St. Paul, Minneapolis, and New Ulm.

———— "Plays for Pioneers: German Drama in Rural Minnesota," *Minnesota History*, 34:239–42 (Summer, 1955).

A Selected Bio-bibliography: Minnesota Authors, compiled by the Minnesota Centennial Literature Group (1958). Lists 700 authors and their publications. No annotations to speak of; essentially a catalogue of authors and their books.

STEPHENSON, GEORGE M., *The Religious Aspects of Swedish Immigration*, pp. 415, 419–24. Swedish-American literature.

STEVENS, JOHN H., "Recollections of James M. Goodhue," Minnesota Historical Collections, 6:492–502 (1894).

* TAEUBER, IRENE B., "Weekly Newspapers in Pioneer Minnesota," *Minnesota History*, 14:411–15 (Dec., 1933).

VAN DOREN, CARL, *Sinclair Lewis: A Biographical Sketch* (1933).

[XI. THE ARTS FLOURISH IN MINNESOTA]

39. *Music, Theater, Art, and Architecture*

A. Music: Foundations to 1900

Indian music: Frances Densmore's recordings; hymn singing at missions. Voyageurs' songs; the fiddler. Loggers' songs and ballads. The settler: immigrant songs and ballads; instruments — guitar, melodian, harpsichord, violin, and later the popular piano; church music (organ, solo voice, quartet, choir); singing societies (*Saengerfests*) of national groups, especially the Scandinavian, German, and Welsh. Advent of the concert and of locally organized performing groups: appearance of Ole Bull and Adelina Patti as early as 1856–57; local opera in St. Paul; the St. Paul Musical Society and George Seibert's Orchestra, 1858 and on; the Minneapolis Musical Society, 1872 and on; the Danz Orchestra concerts of the 1880's and 1890's, starting Minneapolis on the way to becoming an orchestra city; troupes of bell ringers, zither players, cornet bands, and singing families, including the Hutchinson and Andrews families. A wealth of concertizing in the 1880's and 1890's: opera companies and their leading lights; instrumental soloists, especially violinists and pianists; visiting orchestras from the East, especially Theodore Thomas's New York Philharmonic. Promotional activity of women's clubs: St. Paul's Schubert Club, the Thursday Musicale of Minneapolis, and Duluth's Matinee Musicale.

B. Music: Trends since 1900

The Minneapolis Symphony Orchestra: A most impressive contribution to the world of music. Its birth, 1903; founder and conductor (1903–21)

Emil Oberhoffer. Succeeding conductors: Henri Verbrugghen (1923–30), Eugene Ormandy (1931–35), Dimitri Mitropoulos (1937–48), Antal Dorati (1949–60), and guest conductors. Its regular Friday evening concerts, Sunday "Pops," since 1906, and Young People's Programs, since 1911. Its several homes, Northrop Auditorium since 1930. Its regular home audiences the largest any orchestra in the United States plays before. Financial underwriting by patrons, E. L. Carpenter and others. Its tours: "the world is their concert hall." Its influence in elevating and maintaining standards in music. Other orchestras: St. Paul Symphony, 1906–14; Rochester Symphony, 1920's to present; Hibbing Symphony, 1921 to present; Duluth Symphony, 1932 to present; St. Cloud Symphony, 1944–48; Mankato Symphony, 1957; Austin Symphony, 1957. Growth of concert courses in towns, cities, and schools throughout the state; instrumental and vocal soloists the leading attractions. *Opera:* Local efforts by civic operas of Minneapolis and St. Paul; visiting opera companies, San Carlo (early 1900's), Chicago Civic (1910–40), and the Metropolitan (1880–1910; 1945 and on). The University of Minnesota as a music center. *Choral music:* "Our singing state." Two significant organizations of the 1890's, the Philharmonic Club and the Apollo Club. Lengthy tenure and impressive record of the Apollo Club. Unique position of the St. Olaf Lutheran Choir; its founder and director (1903–44), F. Melius Christiansen, "patron saint of Minnesota choral singing"; emphasis on a cappella singing; annual tours since 1911, three to Europe; influence on the spread of a cappella singing, improved church and school choirs; Olaf C. Christiansen, director since 1944. Proliferation of choirs in colleges, public high schools, churches, and even business organizations. *Composers:* The state's claim to some of these questionable because of their migration into or out of the state. Some nineteenth-century composers: Willard Patton, E. O. Baldamus, William Rhys Herbert, Arthur Farwell. Greater creativity of the twentieth century in both the instrumental and vocal fields: Donald N. Ferguson, Thurlow Lieurance, Stanley R. Avery, J. Victor Berquist, Arthur Bergh, Hamlin Hunt, Orvis Ross, Clara Edwards, the several conductors of the Minneapolis Symphony Orchestra, F. Melius Christiansen, his two sons Olaf and Paul, C. Wesley Anderson, Peter Tkach, Leland B. Sateren, Ralph Williams, Paul Manz, and others. *Other significant aspects:* The rise of the private teacher of music and of music schools; the appearance of educators' promotional organizations, such as the Minnesota Federation of Music Clubs; the impact of jazz, particularly since 1920, and its meaning to the younger generation; radio and television as factors in music education; the growing importance of music in daily life.

202

c. The Theater through One Century

The one-hundred-year picture: flow of plays from the East rich during first 75 years, meager in last 25; home-produced plays meager in the nineteenth century, steadily increasing in number and quality in the twentieth century. *Beginnings:* Home talent plays at Fort Snelling and early St. Paul; traveling troupes up the Mississippi to St. Paul and other river towns in 1850's and 1860's during the summer months; small-cast plays, minstrel shows, and Uncle Tom shows presented in crude halls and tents; "parlor theatricals"; German, Scandinavian, and Irish dramatic presentations. *The 1870's and 1880's:* A steady increase of traveling companies and touring groups; development of a "Minnesota circuit" including Winona, Red Wing, Mankato, St. Cloud, Duluth, and other towns; improved theaters or opera houses; multiple role players. *The "Gay 90's":* Musical comedy, burlesque. *A "golden age of theater in Minnesota" in the late nineteenth and early twentieth centuries:* High quality plays from the East; improved acting (Frank Mayo, Joseph Jefferson, Edwin Booth, James O'Neill, Maggie Mitchell, Lotta Crabtree, and others); new playhouses; energetic promoters (L. N. Scott, the Shubert Brothers, Dick Ferris, "Buzz" Bainbridge); high public patronage. Rise of the resident stock company, particularly in the Twin Cities. The long life of the Bainbridge Players (1912–33); its stars: Lee Baker, Edith Evelyn, Florence Stone, Marie Gale, Victor Jory, and others. *Later trends:* Invasion by Hollywood and vaudeville; theaters to movie houses; near death of legitimate theatrical production. Growth of amateur theatricals in university, college, and high school; Frank M. Whiting and the University of Minnesota Theater; the "little theater" idea: the Duluth Playhouse, Theatre St. Paul, Excelsior's Old Log Theater, the Theater in the Round Players, others.

D. Art through One Century

On the frontier: Artist visitors, the painter reporters: Peter Rindisbacher, Samuel Seymour, James O. Lewis, George Catlin, Seth Eastman, Carl Wimar, Frank B. Mayer, John M. Stanley, Edwin Whitefield, Eastman Johnson; their style "surface naturalism." Scenic and historical panoramas: Leon de Pomarede, Henry Lewis, John C. Wild, Anton Gág. Daguerreotypes. Advertising Minnesota through art. *Foundations to 1900:* Meager financial support for resident creative artists. Rise of private collectors of world art: Henry M. Rice, E. S. Goodrich, Morris Lamprey, James J. Hill, Robert Mannheimer, others. Few painters native to Minnesota. Some resident painters: Carl Gutherz, J. D. Larpenteur, Charles Noel Flagg, A. F. Loemans, Peter G. Clausen, Stephen A. Douglas Volk, Alexis J. Fournier, Robert Koehler. Minor role of sculpture. Leading resident sculptor: Jakob H. F. Fjelde. His Hiawatha and

Minnehaha, Ole Bull, and Gettysburg monument to the First Minnesota Regiment. Establishment of Minneapolis Society of Fine Arts, 1883 (parent to the Minneapolis School of Art, 1886, and the Minneapolis Institute of Arts, 1915), and the St. Paul School of Fine Arts, 1894 (became the St. Paul Institute, 1910, and later the St. Paul Gallery and School of Art, 1918). Promotional work of William W. Folwell and Thomas B. Walker; the Walker Gallery opened to the public, 1894. *Trends since 1900:* Increase in galleries; growing richness of bequests and gifts and hence of art acquisitions by galleries. Opening of Minneapolis Institute of Arts; Walker Art Gallery and Walker Art Center; University of Minnesota Gallery; Tweed Gallery in Duluth; Rochester Art Center, others. Annual exhibits of Minneapolis Society of Fine Arts, 1900 and on. Varying style of painters, some native born, some resident: Adolf Dehn, Arnold Blanch, Wanda Gág, Elizabeth Olds, Harry Gottlieb, Dewey Albinson, William Saltzman, Elof Wedin. Modern art — its proponents, its critics. Sculptors whose works are to be seen in parks, public buildings, state capitol grounds, and elsewhere in the state: Daniel C. French, Andrew O'Connor, John K. Daniels, Carl Brioschi. Other sculptors associated with the state: Paul Manship, John B. Flannagan, John Rood, Alonzo Hauser, Evelyn Raymond. Photography as a serious, expressive art a twentieth-century development: John Szarkowski and his 1958 *The Face of Minnesota*, Allen Downs, Jerome Liebling, Earl E. Seubert and news photography. Art departments in public and private schools.

E. Architecture through One Century

Frontier architecture: Influenced by immediate needs and by Old World patterns. Log cabin, plain frame house, occasional stone structures, early church structures, the "grid system" of town lay-out (following the survey system). *Later nineteenth-century architects and their buildings:* A reflection of European and eastern American trends with little individuality or independence. Robert S. Alden, A. F. Knight, Franklin B. Long, Le Roy S. Buffington and the development of the skyscraper. The Minnesota capitol and Cass Gilbert; his national renown. *The twentieth century:* Some early twentieth-century architects of acknowledged talent: Louis Sullivan, the bank building at Owatonna; Purcell and Elmslie, the bank building at Winona; Marcel Breuer, the Abbey of St. John's University; Harry Jones, the Butler Brothers Building in Minneapolis. Features of a modern trend, circa 1930 and on: functionalism, straight line, individuality, break with the past. Influences leading to the new trend: a national movement, Frank Lloyd Wright, Roy Jones and Ralph Rapson of the University of Minnesota School of Architecture, financial well-being of the 1940's and 1950's. New designs for churches and business buildings; a new departure in home construction — the split-level

204

house, the rambler. Art in the interior decoration and furnishing of the
mid-twentieth-century home.

1. Is there any relationship between the cultural advance of a people and
the financial well-being of that people? In your response, give thought to
cultural development in Minnesota.
2. What attention was given to music by the pioneer Minnesotan? to painting? to architecture?
3. Give the meaning of the following: (a) a Scandinavian *Saengerfest*, (b) a
Welsh *Cymmanfa Ganu*, (c) the "singing families."
4. Topics for special reports: (a) Emil Oberhoffer and the birth of the Minneapolis Symphony Orchestra, (b) the Minneapolis orchestra and the
gaining of national and international renown, (c) F. Melius Christiansen
and the St. Olaf Choir, (d) the importance of music to the mid-twentieth-
century Minnesotan.
5. John K. Sherman, arts editor of the *Minneapolis Tribune*, has said:
"Without question the chief sound that Minnesota culture makes is the
music the Minneapolis Symphony plays. This sound in 55 years' time
has become world-famed. It has 'toured' the United States regularly for
a half century; it has conveyed the masterpieces of tonal art, classical
and modern, as molded by master interpreters; it has raised the orchestra
to the level of 'one of America's top-ranking ensembles,' in the words of
critic Jay Harrison of the *New York Herald Tribune*" (from the *Minneapolis Sunday Tribune*, Oct. 19, 1958).
6. Which has been more important to the average Minnesotan: the creation
of or the appreciation of music? Consider changes in each of these aspects
of music through Minnesota's first century.
7. What influences were at work to elevate musical taste in Minnesota's first
century?
8. What musical organizations exist in your community? When did they
begin?
9. Why does John K. Sherman refer to the late nineteenth and the early
twentieth centuries as the "golden age of theater in Minnesota"? Consult O'Connor's *A History of the Arts in Minnesota*, p. 43.
10. What period of Minnesota's history did John K. Sherman have in mind
when he said, "But a generation was being born that would grow up
without ever seeing, or only rarely seeing, a legitimate theatrical production"? Why did this situation develop? What type of play presentation tended to fill the gap left by the dearth of "legitimate plays"? See
O'Connor's *A History of the Arts in Minnesota*, p. 57.
11. It is difficult to know who should be included in any list of Minnesota

artists because of the freedom with which they moved into or out of the state. How do you explain this "restlessness"?

12. Select for special study one of the modern artists mentioned in the topic outline. Examples of the work of each can be found scattered through the art magazines. The *Minnesota Journal of Education*, 14:4–5, 46–47, 84–85, 116–17, 156–57, 188–89, 230–31, 278–79, 320–21 (Sept., 1933–May, 1934), has published brief sketches of Paul Manship, Wanda Gág, Dewey Albinson, Adolf Dehn, Edmund M. Kopietz, Gilbert Fletcher, André Boratko, Cameron Booth, and Glen Mitchell. An illustration of the work of each artist is given.

14. An interesting development in Minnesota education is the Owatonna Art Education Project, an investigation promoted by the University of Minnesota and the public schools of Owatonna. The first two of a series of unusual publications issued for the project by the University of Minnesota Press are Melvin E. Haggerty's *Art a Way of Life* (1935) and August C. Krey's *A City That Art Built* (1936).

15. What are some examples of art in your community—architecture, music, sculpture, painting, etc.?

16. Art pilgrimages: The Minneapolis Institute of Arts; the University Gallery at Northrop Auditorium; the annual art exhibit at the State Fair; the Walker Art Center in Minneapolis; the Tweed Gallery in Duluth; the Rochester Art Center; the Ramsey County Courthouse, where Milles's marble statue of the Indian stands; many another public building for the works of art it houses.

17. So-called "modern art" has its stanch supporters and its severe critics. Explain.

18. Topics for special reports: (a) The panorama, frontier motion picture; (b) the use of the daguerreotype in Minnesota; (c) the work of Jakob Fjelde, sculptor; (d) the modern trend in architecture.

19. At the campus of the University of Minnesota, take note of Burton Hall, Pillsbury Hall, Murphy Hall, any one of the buildings of the Mall, and the Mayo Memorial. What architectural periods do these buildings represent? What artistic influences do they reflect?

20. In any town or city of Minnesota, take note of certain of its buildings and seek answers for the same two questions found in no. 19.

REFERENCES

BENISOVICH, MICHEL, ed., "Peter Rindisbacher, Swiss Artist," *Minnesota History*, 33:155–62 (Autumn, 1951).

* BERGMANN, LEOLA NELSON, *Music Master of the Middle West: The Story of F. Melius Christiansen and the St. Olaf Choir* (1944).

* † BLEGEN, THEODORE C., *Building Minnesota*, pp. 359–68.

BRINK, CAROL RYRIE, *Harps in the Wind* (1947). The Hutchinson family singers.

BURRIS, EVADENE A., "Building the Frontier Home," *Minnesota History*, 15:43–55 (March, 1934). Well illustrated with examples of typical Minnesota residences.

BUSHNELL, DAVID I., JR., *Seth Eastman: The Master Painter of the North American Indian* (1932). Fifteen of Eastman's paintings are reproduced.

* BUTTS, PORTER, *The Art Experience of the Middle West Frontier: Art in Wisconsin* (1936). Excellent for its analysis of the relation of art to the frontier. Although the book deals with Wisconsin, the principles expounded apply to Minnesota as well. One chapter, "The Significance of the Frontier," is especially valuable.

CASTLE, HENRY A., *Minnesota*, 1:314–31. Minnesota art, art schools, and art collections.

CATLIN, GEORGE, *Letters and Notes on the Manners, Customs, and Condition of the North American Indians*, 2 vols. Besides the first edition of 1841, several other editions of Catlin's *Letters and Notes* contain his drawings. See that of 1842 and *North American Indians*, 1926.

CHRISTIANSON, THEODORE, *Minnesota*, 2:283–84. Cass Gilbert.

CHRISTISON, MURIEL B., "Le Roy S. Buffington and the Minneapolis Boom of the 1880's," *Minnesota History*, 23:219–32 (Sept., 1942).

CLARK, KEITH, "Adventures in Popularizing Art," *Minnesotan*, vol. 2, no. 4, pp. 15–19, 46 (Oct., 1916).

DUBOIS, CORNELIA ANDREWS, "Operatic Pioneers: The Story of the Andrews Family," *Minnesota History*, 33:317–25 (Winter, 1953). A well-written account of a southern Minnesota family famous for its musical presentations of the 1870's, 1880's, and 1890's.

† DUNN, JAMES T., "Cultural Activity in St. Paul," *Gopher Historian*, 14:17–21 (Spring, 1960). While emphasizing mid-twentieth-century activities, there is some review of earlier attention to music, drama, painting, and sculpturing.

EASTMAN, MARY H., *The American Aboriginal Portfolio, Illustrated by S. Eastman, U.S. Army* (1853).

EDGAR, RANDOLPH, "Early Minneapolis Theaters," *Minnesota History*, 9:31–44 (March, 1928).

FLANAGAN, JOHN T., "Oscar Wilde's Twin City Appearances," *Minnesota History*, 17:38–48 (March, 1936).

FOLWELL, WILLIAM W., "Douglas Volk," *Minnesotan*, vol. 1, no. 10, pp. 17–21 (May, 1916). The Minneapolis Society of Fine Arts and its first director.

—— *History*, 4:465–72. Thomas B. Walker, art patron.

HEILBRON, BERTHA L., "Edwin Whitefield's Minnesota Lakes," *Minnesota*

History, 33:247–51 (Summer, 1953). Note the several reprints of his paintings.

—— "Lewis' 'Mississippithal' in English," *Minnesota History*, 32:202–13 (Dec., 1951).

—— "A Pioneer Artist on Lake Superior," *Minnesota History*, 21:149–57 (June, 1940). The artist is Eastman Johnson. His frontier paintings were done in 1856 and 1857.

—— "Seth Eastman's Water Colors," *Minnesota History*, 19:419–23 (Dec., 1938).

—— ed., "Making a Motion Picture in 1848. Henry Lewis on the Upper Mississippi," *Minnesota History*, 17:131–49, 288–301 (June–Sept., 1936). Some of Lewis's sketches are reproduced.

—— ed., *With Pen and Pencil on the Frontier: The Diary and Sketches of Frank B. Mayer.*

HICKS, JOHN D., "The Development of Civilization in the Middle West, 1860–1900," *The Sources of Culture in the Middle West*, edited by Dixon R. Fox, pp. 73–101 (1934). The Midwest had completed its provincial period before 1900 and in some respects was by then instructing the East.

JAEGER, LUTH, "Two American Sculptors: Fjelde — Father and Son," *American-Scandinavian Review*, 10:467–72 (Aug., 1922).

JENSEN, ANDREW F., "Two Decades of Trouping in Minnesota, 1865–85," *Minnesota History*, 28:97–119 (June, 1947). A picture of professional dramatic entertainment.

JONES, ROBERT A., "Cass Gilbert: Forgotten Giant," *Northwest Architect*, 23:28–30, 33, 51, 52 (Nov.–Dec., 1959). A brief account of the impressive career of this architect who designed Minnesota's capitol, two other state capitols, the Woolworth building, and the Supreme Court building.

JORDAN, PHILIP, "The Hutchinson Family in the Story of American Music," *Minnesota History*, 22:113–32 (June, 1941).

—— *Singin' Yankees* (1946). A chronicle of a New Hampshire family (the Hutchinsons) which gained musical fame in Europe and America. They founded the town of Hutchinson, Minnesota, in 1855.

KEATING, WILLIAM H., *Narrative of an Expedition to the Source of the St. Peter's River*. Contains the drawings of Samuel Seymour.

LANDIS, PAUL H., "Social Change and Social Interaction as Factors in Culture Change," *American Journal of Sociology*, 41:52–58 (July, 1935). A study of cultural change in the mining towns of the Mesabi Range.

LEWIS, JAMES O., *The Aboriginal Portfolio* (1835). The 1844 edition has twelve additional plates. Most of the portraits were painted at the treaties of Prairie du Chien, Fort Wayne, Fond du Lac, and Green Bay.

"Minnesota Historical Society Notes," *Minnesota History*, 3:463–64 (Aug., 1920). Edwin Whitefield.

Newhall, Beaumont, "Minnesota Daguerreotypes," *Minnesota History*, 34:28–33 (Spring, 1954).

Nute, Grace Lee, "Peter Rindisbacher, Artist," *Minnesota History*, 14: 283–87 (Sept., 1933).

* O'Connor, William Van, ed., *A History of the Arts in Minnesota*. The first section, entitled "Music and Theater in Minnesota History," is written by John K. Sherman. The last section, entitled "A Century of Art and Architecture in Minnesota," is written by Donald R. Torbert. Despite their brevity, both of these surveys of a century of cultural development are the best available. Each section is reprinted in a separate pamphlet with titles as above.

Sackett, Leonard, "Two Minnesota Masters of Sculpture," *Bulletin of the Minnesota State Art Society*, vol. 2, no. 4, pp. 2–8 (May, 1925). Paul Manship and James E. Fraser.

Scott, Alma, *Wanda Gág: The Story of an Artist* (1949). A beautifully written biography of a nationally known artist and writer. Her specialty: children's books.

* Sherman, John K., *Music and Maestros: The Story of the Minneapolis Symphony Orchestra* (1952). The standard work; entertainingly written.

*——— "The Birth of a Symphony Orchestra," *Minnesota History*, 33:93–104 (Autumn, 1952). A chapter from the volume cited above, on the founding of the orchestra.

Simpson, Eugene E., *A History of St. Olaf Choir* (1921).

Szarkowski, John, *The Face of Minnesota* (1958). A collection of most attractive photographs, illustrative of Minnesota life in many phases. There is some textual comment. All photographs were taken by the author, an acknowledged artist in this field.

Woods, Donald Z., "Playhouse for Pioneers: The Story of Pence Opera House," *Minnesota History*, 33:169–78 (Winter, 1952). A famous theater of the nineteenth century and some of the artists who performed on its stage.

XII. MINNESOTA PARTICIPATES IN A SECOND WORLD WAR AND FACES POSTWAR PROBLEMS

40. *World War II and Its Aftermath*

A. The State's Contribution to the War Effort

Re-establishment of the Minnesota National Guard, 1920; support for the National Guard from the federal government with the National Defense Act of 1920. Peacetime uses of the National Guard: disaster rescue operations, guard duty during visits of the President of the United States, enforcement of martial law (Minneapolis truck drivers' strike,

1934). Construction of the new Camp Ripley on the site of the old Fort Ripley, 1931. Erection of armories throughout the state. Minnesota reaction to the overseas drift toward war: early support for isolationism and for neutrality laws of the United States; later growth of interventionist sentiment. Defense measures: the Selective Service Act, 1940; mustering of national guardsmen and reservists into service, 1940 and 1941. Pearl Harbor and solid support for the war effort. No state identity of units. Minnesotans in almost all theaters of action: Bataan and the "death march"; the southwest Pacific; the north African campaign; Sicily and the drive up the coast of Italy; the Normandy landings; the drive into Germany; final stages of the war in the Pacific. Casualties: comparison with previous wars; lowered losses because of improved medical care. The home front: absence of high-tension mobilization of public opinion; acceptance of rationing; role of Minnesota's iron; technological contributions of Minneapolis Honeywell (airplane controls, the proximity bomb). Postwar developments: demand for hasty demobilization; state National Guard units again restored; participation in the Korean War, 1950; enlargement of Camp Ripley, 1951.

B. The Veteran: Government Benefits, Population Upsurge, and Educational Expansion

National Veterans Administration; various benefits. Drive for a state bonus; ratification of World War II Bonus Amendment, 1948, and passage of the Bonus Bill, 1949; method of payment; the Korean Bonus Bill, 1957. Fooling the sociologists — increase of the birth rate during the war and after. Implications of the population upsurge: a "youthful" population; a boost to the economy; demands upon the educational system, elementary, secondary, higher. Education for the returned veteran: federal G.I. bills following both World War II and the Korean War. Effect of war upon university and college enrollments in the state: the trend between the two world wars (149 per cent enrollment increase); reversal of this trend during the war years; flood of veteran students at war's end (fall enrollments of 1946 showed five for every two students in the midwar years); the many college adjustments (jammed classrooms, lengthened teaching day, difficulty of securing well-trained college teachers). The record of the G.I. student a favorable one.

QUESTIONS AND SUGGESTIONS

1. Of what value to the national government was the existence of National Guard units when World War II broke out?
2. Why did Minnesota establish a Commission of Public Safety in World War I but not in World War II?
3. Records show that Minnesota men rated exceptionally high in army in-

telligence tests and in physical fitness examinations during World War II. Find supporting data for this statement.

4. During World War II, it was well-nigh impossible to refer to an action as having been performed by some Minnesota regiment or other unit. In the Civil War, however, one spoke of the exploits of the First Minnesota or the Second Minnesota, etc. Is there an explanation for this?

5. One of the few instances when a fairly large number of Minnesotans acted together in a military engagement came early in the war under Colonel Ernest B. Miller of Brainerd. Tell of the military record of his 34th Tank Company.

6. What effect did the war have upon iron mining in Minnesota?

7. How would you explain the error made by many sociologists when they predicted a decline in population with the coming of World War II?

8. Explain the ease with which the Bonus Amendment of 1948 was ratified. What method did Minnesota use to pay for the soldiers' bonus following World War II and the Korean War?

9. Describe the nature of educational benefits available to the G.I. Is it possible that the use of these benefits may have altered the pattern of college attendance?

10. What impact did the returned G.I. have upon college life? Note especially scholarship, marriage, housing, use of the automobile.

11. Research topic: A study of the effects which veterans had upon the life and organization of any one of Minnesota's colleges.

12. Contrast the methods used by the state and federal governments in World Wars I and II to solicit the wholehearted support of the public for the war effort.

13. Topic: The career of General Lauris Norstad, Supreme Allied Commander in Western Europe of the forces of NATO. General Norstad is a native Minnesotan.

REFERENCES

"Federal and State Aid to Veterans' Education," *School Review,* 54:441–44 (Oct., 1946). Special attention is paid to Minnesota efforts to assist the veteran in his use of G.I. benefits.

"The GI Student Is Good," *Newsweek,* 28:82 (July 8, 1946). A report from Kansas, but equally applicable to Minnesota.

"The Great Baby Boom," *Reader's Digest,* 63:95–96 (Dec., 1953). Significance of the population upsurge of the war and postwar period.

HAUSER, PHILIP M., "Population and Vital Phenomena," *American Journal of Sociology,* 48:309–22 (Nov., 1942). A sociologist predicts a war and postwar decline in population.

HAYES, WILLIAM E., "The Post-War Liberal Arts College and the GI Bill:

An Analysis," *Education*, 66:45–49 (Sept., 1945). Describes the "G.I. Bill of Rights" and then makes predictions, several of which were not fulfilled.

* Kunz, Virginia B., *Muskets to Missiles*, pp. 159–91. World War II and the Korean conflict.

Minnesota Commission on Higher Education, *Higher Education in Minnesota*, pp. 56–58, 349, 353–54. Effect of war on college enrollments.

Nelson, Lowry, and Hazel Clampitt, *Population Trends in Minnesota, 1940*, Bulletin 387, Agricultural Experiment Station, University of Minnesota (June, 1945).

"Preview of the Postwar Generation: It Will Be Smaller; But It Can Be 'Demographically' Sounder," *Fortune*, 27:116–17, 130–42 (March, 1943). Note the map on birth rate by states and the chart on birth rates of Germany and the United States between the two world wars.

Schweickhard, Dean M., "GI Bill for Education," *Minnesota Journal of Education*, 34:26 (Nov., 1952). Provisions of the Korean G.I. bill, known as Public Law 550, with some mention of the older G.I. bill.

[XII. MINNESOTA PARTICIPATES IN A SECOND WORLD WAR AND FACES POSTWAR PROBLEMS]

41. *War and Postwar Prosperity*

A. An Expanding Economy, 1939–59

An impressive industrial advance during the war and postwar years, when industry moved abreast of agriculture in Minnesota — agriculture ahead in certain indices, industry in others; but the rate of industrial advance modest when compared with that of the United States as a whole. The rate of Minnesota's industrial advance more rapid from 1939 to 1949 than from 1949 to 1959. Minnesota patterns which reveal trends: the urban population greater than the rural by 1950; the rate of population growth since 1940 only about one-half that of the United States as a whole; a greater out-migration from the state than in-migration since 1940; the increase in nonagricultural employment between 1940 and 1950 faster than in the United States as a whole, and about the same from 1950 to 1959; the percentage gain in per capita personal income in Minnesota between 1940 and 1950 slightly greater than in the United States as a whole; the percentage gain in manufacturing payrolls above the national average for the years 1940 to 1954; with respect to total personal income of Minnesotans between 1939 and 1954, a slight rise in that part of it derived from manufacturing payrolls and a slight drop in that part of it derived from agriculture. Continued fundamental role of agriculture in the state; extent of farm-related industries such as grain milling, meat packing, butter and cheese making, manufacture of farm machinery and implements.

B. Aspects of Industrial Growth

The important role played in manufacturing advance by a few firms, like Minneapolis-Honeywell and Minnesota Mining and Manufacturing. Impressive expansion of wholesale and retail trade. The remarkable growth of suburban Twin Cities metropolitan area. Agencies which endeavored to attract industries to Minnesota: the state government, chambers of commerce, private corporations, other business organizations; nature of their activities.

C. Determinants of Industrial Growth

Power, transportation, raw materials, markets, labor, capital. Minnesota weaknesses: relatively slow growth of population, distance to highly populated markets, cost of importing needed raw materials. Strengths: variety of raw materials, a skilled and reliable labor supply, demonstrated excellence of product, abundant water supply, managerial skill and business ability.

D. Minnesota Agriculture at Mid-Twentieth Century

Continuation of New Deal farm assistance programs; their successive modifications. World War II and an agricultural boom. The appearance of new farm problems in the 1950's. Some 1950 statistics: extent of land in farms, 49 per cent; number of farms, 179,101, a drop from 203,302 in 1935; average size of farm, 183.6 acres, an increase from 161.4 acres in 1935; farm population, 776,000, a drop from 915,000 in 1940. Of the state's total employed, the percentage engaged in agriculture in 1944 was 15.8, a drop from 34.9 in 1900; the percentage engaged in manufacturing was 24.4 in 1944, an increase from 22.2 in 1900. Science comes to the farm: a major trend through several decades; state and private agencies promote scientific application; readiness of the farmer to adapt to new trends. Sociological developments: migration to the city; larger church parishes; school consolidation; decline in number of weekly newspapers; continuing effectiveness of farm organizations; organizations for farm youth such as 4H and F.F.A.; breakdown of rural isolation effected by mail delivery, automobile, rural electrification, radio, and television.

QUESTIONS AND ANSWERS

1. Characterize Minnesota's manufacturing development during World War II; the period immediately following the war. Explain these trends. How did they compare with national trends?

2. Despite the advance made by industry in Minnesota during the first half of the twentieth century, agriculture continued to be a vital part of the state's economy. Some authorities claimed that Minnesota at mid-

century should still be classified as basically an agricultural state. Build a case in support of this view. Having done that, point to statistics or developments which might suggest that industry has overtaken agriculture.

3. In 1954 Minnesota Selective Service registrants had a lower percentage of disqualification as a result of mental tests than any other state in the Union. In 1957 her rating was second among the states. The precise figures are for 1954, 1.8 per cent of Minnesotans failed the Selective Service mental test while the United States median for such failures was 16.7 per cent; for 1957, 4.2 per cent as against 18.9 per cent. These figures are from the Research Department of the National Education Association. Promoters of industrial expansion have referred to this in their claims that Minnesota has a labor force of superior quality. What other features of Minnesota's labor force have been advertised to attract industry to the state?

4. What is meant by the term "net out-migration"? What has Minnesota's record been since 1940 with reference to this characteristic? See Charles E. Ramsey and others, *Migration in Minnesota, 1940–50,* and *Report of the Governor's Minnesota Tax Study Committee,* pp. 55–62.

5. Give reasons for the lively growth which suburbs around the Twin Cities enjoyed in the two decades following the beginning of World War II. Did this growth pattern have counterparts in smaller cities of the state? in other larger cities of the nation? What special problems did these suburbs have to contend with? What advantages have been claimed for suburban living?

6. The period since World War I has seen various agencies campaign to encourage manufacturing within the state. Account for this. If you were to prepare a brochure to advertise assets of interest to manufacturers, what characteristics of Minnesota would you stress?

7. At mid-twentieth century, Minnesota had a fair balance between agriculture and industry. Could a case be built in behalf of maintaining this balance?

8. The tabulation given below is from *Minnesota's Tomorrow,* p. 44, and shows land usage in Minnesota in 1950.

	Percentage
Cropland	40.8
Pasture and grazing land	8.2
Forest and woodland	37.5
Urban areas, roads, farmsteads, etc.	7.5
Marshes, wasteland, etc.	6.0

Some authorities combine the top three figures to show that 64.2 per cent of Minnesota's land is in farms. There is, of course, a growing practice of classifying trees as a crop, but the average person is likely to think

214

of farmland as being separate from forest and woodland. The land in Minnesota devoted to farming would then, according to this usual interpretation, be 49 per cent of the total.

9. Changes which have taken place on Minnesota's farms since 1939 have, at times, been characterized as a "farm revolution." List some of these changes.

10. Reference is made below to several articles by A. H. Poatgieter appearing in the *Gopher Historian*. They are a part of a special ten-issue series of that magazine on present-day Minnesota. Each issue in this series is devoted entirely to a given section of Minnesota, with much attention to agricultural and industrial conditions. The series began in winter, 1958–59. Anyone interested in a particular part of the state would do well to examine the issue of *Gopher Historian* devoted to that section.

REFERENCES

ANDERSON, WILLIAM, *Intergovernmental Relations in Review*, pp. 125–29. On problems of government for metropolitan areas. While the discussion is general, some attention is given specifically to the Twin Cities and Duluth.

* BODDY, FRANCIS M., "Manufacturing — Developments and Prospects," *Minnesota's Tomorrow*, pp. 74–82.

† BROOKINS, JEAN, "Ramsey County Villages," *Gopher Historian*, 14:28, 29 (Spring, 1960). St. Paul suburban development. Very brief. Note the map on p. 29.

* BUSINESS EXECUTIVES' RESEARCH COMMITTEE, *Industrial Location and the Minnesota Economy* (1954). A study and report by business executives of the state and members of the School of Business Administration of the University of Minnesota. Points out favorable and unfavorable factors for the location of businesses in Minnesota. An excellent analysis of industrial conditions at mid-century.

* † CLARK, JAMES W., "Making Metal Goods in Southeastern Minnesota," *Gopher Historian*, 13:16–19 (Winter, 1958–59). A description of industries as of 1958. Excellent photographs and drawings, as well as text.

* † DUNN, JAMES T., "The Towns of East-Central Minnesota," *Gopher Historian*, 13:4–18 (Spring, 1959). Stillwater, Anoka, Cambridge, Mora, and several other towns. Historical treatment, but the emphasis is on the prevailing economy in 1958.

* KOLLER, E. FRED, "Changes in Minnesota's Dairy Industry," *Minnesota's Tomorrow*, pp. 56–62. A brief but excellent account of trends since 1935.

KRZENSKI, EDWARD, and PAUL LAMPI, "St. Lawrence Seaway," *Gopher Historian*, 5:19–20 (May, 1951). A good survey up to 1951. Much has happened since.

Minnesota at Midpoint: An Economic Survey of Minnesota at the Turn of the Half-Century, 1950. A publication of the state Department of Business Research and Development. Pages 15–22 treat agriculture.

NELSON, LOWRY, "The Outlook for the Small Town," *Minnesota Trends,* pp. 19–25. To exist, the small town must meet competition.

―――― *The Minnesota Community.* Pp. 54–69, a sociological analysis of the family in Minnesota at mid-twentieth century — size, marriage patterns, divorce, rural and urban differences. Pp. 147–63, predictions of likely changes for farm and town in Minnesota.

*†POATGIETER, A. H., "Agriculture and Its Industries in Southeastern Minnesota," *Gopher Historian,* 13:8–14 (Winter, 1958–59).

*†――――"Agriculture and Its Industries in Northwestern Minnesota," *Gopher Historian,* 14:28–32 (Winter, 1959–60).

*†――――"Agriculture in Northwestern Minnesota," *Gopher Historian,* 14:11–16 (Fall, 1959). The emphasis in the above three articles is on the present-day economy.

*†――――"East-Central Minnesota Industries," *Gopher Historian,* 13:26–31 (Spring, 1959).

*†――――"Varied Industries in Northwestern Minnesota," *Gopher Historian,* 14:19, 20 (Fall, 1959).

*†――――"Varied Industries of Southeastern Minnesota," *Gopher Historian,* 13:15–26 (Winter, 1958–59). While some attention is given to earlier developments, the prime emphasis in this and the two preceding articles on industry is on the mid-twentieth century. Discussion of agriculture and industry for other sections of the state may be found in other issues of the *Gopher Historian.* See also citations under Poatgieter in topic 35.

* RAUP, PHILIP M., "Agricultural Land: Changing Patterns in Its Use," *Minnesota's Tomorrow,* pp. 43–62. A fine analysis of trends since about 1930.

―――― "Getting Started in Farming," *Minnesota Trends,* pp. 11–18. Seeks to answer the question "What are the possibilities for a man to break into farming in Minnesota at mid-twentieth century?"

Report of the Governor's Minnesota Tax Study Committee, 1956, pp. 14–64. A technical analysis of Minnesota's economy, especially for the years 1940–54. Many tables. Note also pp. 3–13 for a summary of the committee's findings.

*†SAARI, MATT, "Conservation in Southeastern Minnesota," *Gopher Historian,* 13:3–6 (Winter, 1958–59). Discusses efforts to encourage conservation of soil and wild life since 1935 by contour farming and other such techniques.

SELTZER, GEORGE, "The Future of Iron-Ore," *Conservation Volunteer,*

22:6–8 (July–Aug., 1959). Mining activities for the period 1948–57 and speculation about the future.

SMITH, HARLAN M., and ROBERT J. HOLLOWAY, "Minnesota Manufacturers Export to the World," *Business News Notes*, no. 10 (Nov., 1953).

"South St. Paul Livestock Market," *Gopher Historian*, 13:15 (Winter, 1958–59). A description of its functions and of the meaning of such a market to the farmer.

Summary: Report of the Governor's Study Commission on Agriculture (1958). A comprehensive study and report of agricultural developments and problems in the 1950's.

TURNBULL, JOHN G., "Personal Income in Minnesota, 1929–1958," *Business News Notes*, no. 46 (Jan., 1960).

* THE TWIN CITIES METROPOLITAN COMMISSION, *The Challenge of Metropolitan Growth*, Report No. 1 (1959). Portrays the rapid growth of the suburbs since 1940. Maps and charts are outstandingly good.

*WEAVER, JOHN C., "The Problems of Our Region in a National Perspective," *Minnesota's Tomorrow*, pp. 91–105. Agriculture is dealt with especially on pp. 96–103.

[XII. MINNESOTA PARTICIPATES IN A SECOND WORLD WAR AND FACES POSTWAR PROBLEMS]

42. *Politics: Conservatives and Liberals*

A. Key Political Trends, 1938–59: An Overview

Characteristic independence of the Minnesota voter often in evidence; a period of political fluidity. Decline of the Farmer-Labor party and reassertion of power by the Republican party, 1938–48; the fusion of the Farmer-Labor party with the Democratic party, 1944; growth in strength of the Democratic-Farmer-Labor party, 1948–59. Four Republican governors and one Democratic-Farmer-Labor governor: Harold E. Stassen (1938–43), Edward J. Thye (1943–46), Luther W. Youngdahl (1946–51), C. Elmer Anderson (1951–54), Republicans; Orville L. Freeman (1954–   ), Democrat-Farmer-Laborite. Control of United States Senate seats by Republicans Joseph H. Ball (1940–48) and Edward J. Thye (1946–58) lost to Democrat-Farmer-Laborites Hubert Humphrey (1948–   ) and Eugene J. McCarthy (1958–   ). Emergence of Hubert H. Humphrey as a key figure of the Democratic-Farmer-Labor party.

B. Developments under Republican Hegemony

Election of 1938: Stassen's background, his youth; organization of the Young Republican League; decisive victory over Benson. Stassen's advocacy of a new Republican liberalism; some opposition from the Old

Guard; legislature in essential political sympathy with the governor; the building of a political machine. Achievements: governmental clean-up; economy and a balanced budget; the Civil Service Law of 1939; the Labor Relations Act of 1939; reorganization of the state government in 1939; reduction of the state debt; stimulation of tourism. Some criticism of Stassen as a "fake liberal." Outbreak of World War II; Stassen's election pledge to enter the Navy, 1942; his selection of Thye as lieutenant governor to succeed him as governor. Stassen in the national limelight: keynoter at the Republican National Convention of 1940; on Admiral Halsey's staff in the Navy; participation in the San Francisco Convention which drafted the United Nations Charter; an unsuccessful bid for the presidency, 1948; presidency of the University of Pennsylvania; subsequent attempts to gain the nomination for the presidency. Thye, war governor: agricultural background; grooming by Stassen; continuation of Stassen policies; election to the United States Senate in 1946. Youngdahl, crusading governor: early legal training and decision to enter politics; ability to command strong support from the people of Minnesota; dynamic leadership qualities. Accomplishments: Anti-Slot Machine Bill, 1947; campaign for vigorous enforcement of all laws; labor legislation (banning of secondary boycotts and grant of right to sue unions for damages resulting from labor disputes); successes as labor conciliator; establishment of the Youth Conservation Commission, 1947; adoption of a thoroughly revised mental health program in 1949; efforts to assist Minnesota Indians; Commission on Resettlement of Displaced Persons. Growth of opposition to Youngdahl's hard-driving tactics; the uncooperative 1951 legislature, which failed to approve several Youngdahl recommendations: a fair employment practices bill, a family court bill, revision of the state constitution, legislative reapportionment, adoption of party designation for legislators. Youngdahl's resignation to accept appointment as a federal district judge at Washington, D.C.; political repercussions following this appointment. Succession of C. Elmer Anderson to the governorship; his career.

c. Democratic-Farmer-Labor Party Achievements

Reasons for Democratic-Farmer-Labor alliance. Birth pangs: the purging of left-wing elements in the schism of 1948; effective organizational work of Humphrey and Freeman. Humphrey's academic and political background; his election in 1948 to the United States Senate; re-election, 1954; increasing stature in the Senate; national prominence; aspirations for the presidency. Freeman's entry into politics; legal and other background; election to the governorship, 1954; re-elections, 1956 and 1958. His record as governor. Lack of solid support from the legislature; a conservative Senate. The reapportionment bill of 1959.

218

D. Attention to Two Issues of Long Standing

Reorganization of state government: Beginnings in 1899; first state Board of Control, 1901; work of Governor Eberhart's commission, 1913 to 1915; the establishment of the Commission of Administration and Finance, 1925; difficulties of the Big Three; loss of certain powers during the Farmer-Labor regime; the far-reaching Reorganization Act of 1939; creation of the Efficiency in Government Commission in 1949 (the Little Hoover Commission) and its report in 1950; modification of the 1939 Reorganization Act in 1951; Governor Freeman's recommendations for extensive reorganization. *Tax reform:* No significant changes in state tax structure from 1858 to 1920. Key changes since 1920: highway user taxes and iron ore occupation and royalty taxes of the early 1920's; personal and corporation income taxes, 1933; the "homestead" reduction of property taxes, 1933; excise taxes on liquors, 1933; increase of income taxes, 1937 and later; the special taxes to finance the veterans' bonus, 1949; the omnibus tax bill, 1955. Expansion of state and governmental services and corresponding increase in need for revenue. Recommendations of the Governor's Tax Study Committee, 1956. Failure of legislatures of 1957 and 1959 to follow recommendations. Conflict over withholding as a means of collecting income taxes and the sales tax. The "marathon special session" of 1959 and failure to adopt either withholding or a sales tax.

QUESTIONS AND ANSWERS

1. List the factors which may account for the traditions of progressivism and independence in Minnesota's political life. You will find a discussion of this in the Esbjornson reference given below, pp. 119–25, 131–34.
2. How would you explain the thumping victory which Stassen won in the election of 1938?
3. Stassen's Labor Relations Act of 1939 has been referred to as a "forerunner of the Taft-Hartley Act." One of its key provisions was a ten-day "cooling-off period." Explain this provision. The bill was also called "Stassen's Slave Law"; yet CIO-AFL officials supported Stassen for reelection in 1942. Explain.
4. Both Stassen and Youngdahl used the radio freely during legislative sessions, sometimes going over the heads of legislators in an appeal to the people. Did this technique prove to be effective? How did legislators react to this practice?
5. Stassen's attitudes on internationalism helped dispel the view that Minnesotans were isolationists. How far was he ready for the United Nations Charter to go with reference to the veto and the surrender of sovereignty?

6. Characterize Youngdahl's methods in his reform crusades. In what fields were his reform drives most successful? Explain the reaction of the legislature to his tactics.
7. Youngdahl's acceptance of the federal judgeship surprised many in Minnesota. The political ramifications of this appointment departed from the normal in several particulars and "jolted" some of the political leaders. Explain.
8. A "write-in" vote in the Minnesota primary election of 1952 attracted much national attention. Why?
9. The successes won by the Democratic-Farmer-Labor party in the decade 1948–58 might be explained in several ways. Consult the article by Karl Rolvaag cited below for an analysis by one of the leaders of the party.
10. The intense factional fight within the Democratic-Farmer-Labor party which led to the schism of 1948 is excellently treated by Theodore G. Mitau in the *Minnesota History* reference cited below.
11. The careers of several leading Minnesota politicians are worthy of special study and report: Walter H. Judd, Hubert H. Humphrey, Harold E. Stassen, Luther W. Youngdahl.

REFERENCES

ADRIAN, CHARLES R., "Some General Characteristics of Non-Partisan Elections," *American Political Science Review*, 46:766–76 (Sept., 1952). Minnesota adopted the nonpartisan system of electing her state legislators in 1913.

ALEXANDER, JACK, "Governor Stassen: the Republican Party's Minnesota Hopeful Plans to Get Re-elected and Then Join the Navy," *Life*, 13:122–33 (Oct. 19, 1942). Some account of Stassen's background and record as governor for two years.

AMRINE, MICHAEL, *This Is Humphrey: The Story of a Senator* (1960). Published during the 1960 presidential campaign, and should, therefore, be read with care.

BAKER, RUSSELL, "Humphrey: Thunder! . . . Lightning?" *New York Times Magazine*, 12:34–42 (Jan. 11, 1959). A personality portrayal and a picture of Humphrey's political career at a time when presidential prospects were in view.

* BRINGS, LAWRENCE M., ed., *Minnesota Heritage:* Val Bjornson, "Mighty Men in Minnesota," pp. 329–31. A very general estimate of the Republican party's role in the state's history. Karl F. Rolvaag, "The Democratic Farmer-Labor Party in Minnesota's History," pp. 332–36. A good treatment, especially on the rise of the Farmer-Labor party and its merger in 1944 with the Democratic party. Brief.

CATER, DOUGLAS, "What Makes Humphrey Run?" *Reporter*, 20:15–20

(March 5, 1959). A sketch of the man and an analysis of presidential possibilities for 1960.

Current Biography, 1956, pp. 192–93. Orville L. Freeman.

Current Biography, 1949, pp. 282–84. Hubert H. Humphrey.

Current Biography, 1949, pp. 308–9. Walter H. Judd.

Current Biography, 1948, pp. 597–600. Harold E. Stassen.

Current Biography, 1951, pp. 623–25. Edward J. Thye.

Current Biography, 1948, pp. 701–3. Luther W. Youngdahl.

DRUMMOND, ROSCOE, "The Case for Stassen: He Could Swing the Independent Liberal Vote That the Republicans Will Need to Win the Presidency," *Life*, 24:38–39, 45–46, 48, 50, 52 (March 1, 1948). Stassen's background and prospects for the presidential election of 1948.

———"Stassen of Minnesota," *American Mercury*, 64:268–77 (March, 1947).

"Education of a Senator," *Time*, 53:13–16 (Jan. 17, 1949). Humphrey's background and record up to the time he became a United States senator.

ESBJORNSON, ROBERT, *A Christian in Politics: Luther Youngdahl*. Pp. 119–38, Minnesota protest politics, the Stassen regime, campaign of 1946; pp. 139–53, anti-gambling law and law enforcement; pp. 155–68, role as labor conciliator; pp. 169–96, youth conservation, mental health, and other welfare legislation; pp. 215–30, Youngdahl and the 1951 legislature; pp. 230–69, federal judge and the Owen Lattimore case.

GILBERT, BRIAN, "Judge Youngdahl Wins His Fight," *New Republic*, 133:5–6 (July 11, 1955). An interpretation of the settlement of the Lattimore case.

———"New Light on the Lattimore Case," *New Republic*, 131:7–12 (Dec. 27, 1954).

GUNTHER, JOHN, "Stassen: Young Man Going Somewhere," *Harper's Magazine*, 192:10–19 (Jan., 1946).

HARRIS, A. I., "Tories Take Minnesota," *New Republic*, 103:439–41 (Sept. 30, 1940). Highly critical of Stassen's first term as governor.

JARMAN, RUFUS, "The Governor and the Gamblers," *Saturday Evening Post*, 220:22–23 (Dec. 13, 1947). Youngdahl's crusade for law enforcement.

McDERMOTT, WILLIAM F., "Minnesota Miracle," *Reader's Digest*, 37:75–79 (July, 1940). Background for Harold Stassen's political career, his election as governor, and achievements of his first term as governor.

"The Minnesota Explosion," *Time*, 59:19–20 (March 31, 1952). The write-in vote for Eisenhower in the primary election of 1952.

"Minnesota Spells It Out," *Life*, 32:31–33 (March 31, 1952). The astounding write-in vote for Eisenhower in the Minnesota primaries of 1952.

* MITAU, G. THEODORE, "The Democratic-Farmer-Labor Party Schism of 1948," *Minnesota History*, 34:187–94 (Spring, 1955). Rivalry within the ranks between a right wing and a left wing, the left wing accused of being communist inspired. Victory for the right wing.

*———— *Politics in Minnesota*, pp. 18–33. Excellent portrayal of political trends from 1939 to 1960 — Republican resurgence followed by dominance of the Democratic-Farmer-Labor party.

MOOS, MALCOLM, and E. W. KENWORTHY, "Dr. Shipstead Comes to Judgment," *Harper's Magazine*, 193:21–27 (July, 1946). Political aspects of Shipstead's career as United States senator and a suggestion of defeat in the election of 1946.

MORISON, B. L., "Amazing Mr. Humphrey," *Nation*, 167:489–91 (Oct. 30, 1948). Humphrey's victory over Senator Ball.

———— "His Honor at Thirty-Seven," *Survey Graphic*, 37:293–96 (June, 1948). Praise for Humphrey's work as mayor of Minneapolis.

MOTTER, ALTON M., "Crusading Governor," *Christian Century*, 65:204–6 (Feb. 18, 1948). Youngdahl and gambling in Minnesota.

Recommendations of the Minnesota Efficiency in Government Commission (Little Hoover Commission), *How to Achieve Greater Efficiency and Economy in Minnesota's Government* (1950). Note especially pp. 3–16. Introductory and summary.

* *Report of the Governor's Minnesota Tax Study Committee, 1956.* Pp. 76–116, an excellent legislative history of Minnesota's tax structure. Pp. 117–35, the committee's views on Minnesota's tax structure and industrial location. Pp. 136–555, a detailed analysis of the state's several taxes and possible new taxes. Technical, but valuable.

"Senator Humphrey, the Man in the News: A Talk with Khrushchev, A Boost for 1960," *United States News and World Report*, 45:60–63 (Dec. 19, 1958).

SHORT, LLOYD M., CLARA PENNIMAN, and FLOYD O. FLOM, *The Minnesota Department of Taxation: An Administrative History.* An account of efforts at tax reform and of the state's administration of taxation. Emphasis is on the twentieth century.

SHORT, LLOYD M., and CARL W. TILLER, *The Minnesota Commission of Administration and Finance, 1925–39: An Administrative History*, pp. 1–49 (1942). Efforts of the state legislature to carry through reform in state administration. Covers the period from 1899 to 1939.

STASSEN, HAROLD E., *Where I Stand* (1947). A statement of political beliefs.

"Stassen at Work," *Newsweek*, 31:27–30 (April 19, 1948).

"Stassen's Farewell," *Time*, 41:22 (May 3, 1943). Stassen's resignation after the 1943 legislative session to enter the United States Navy.

"Stassen's Parliament," *Time*, 41:23 (Jan. 18, 1943). A report of a speech in which Stassen recommended immediate planning for a world organization to take the place of the League of Nations.

Torkelson, W., "Youngdahl Move Jolts Minnesota," *Christian Century*, 68:968 (Aug. 22, 1951). Youngdahl's resignation as governor to accept a federal judgeship and its political implications.

Williams, Howard Y., "Harold Stassen, Fake Liberal," *New Republic*, 110:756–59 (June 5, 1944). An attack upon Stassen's record as governor.